INSPIRE / PLAN / DISCOVER / EXPERIENCE

NEW YORK CITY

DK EYEWITNESS

NEW YORK CITY

CONTENTS

DISCOVER 6

EXPERIENCE 62

NEED TO KNOW 304

Left: A bustling street in Manhattan's Times Square
Previous page: The East River at dusk
Front cover: Sunset over Manhattan

DISCOVER

Sunrise over the Brooklyn Bridge

WELCOME TO NEW YORK CITY

Stately museums and soaring skyscrapers. Blissful parks and bustling stores. Sultry bars and sublime cocktails. Whatever your dream trip to NYC entails, this DK Eyewitness Guide is the perfect companion.

1 A bartender preparing a cocktail

2 Lofty interior of the Metropolitan Museum of Art

3 Greenery and skyscrapers converge at 230 Fifth's rooftop bar

Dynamic and diverse, New York offers everything in abundance; it's no wonder that, as the song goes, it's a city so nice, they named it twice. The gateway to America, you can follow in the footsteps of millions at Ellis Island and get a sense of 19th-century life at the Lower East Side Tenement Museum, or remember modern history at the National September 11 Memorial. Art is everywhere in New York: goggle at the bounty of Old Masters in the Met and check out street art in Harlem. As for food and drink, you're spoiled for choice. New York has a plethora of superlative bars and restaurants, not forgetting a wealth of cuisines in neighborhoods like Nolita and Chinatown. Bucks burning a hole in your pocket? Go window-shopping along Fifth Avenue, run amok in Bloomingdale's, and find vintage gems at Brooklyn Flea.

You'll love New York's outer boroughs, each with its own distinct personality, too. Catch a Yankees game in The Bronx, board the Staten Island Ferry for unmissable views, try assorted craft beers in Queens, and snap that perfect photo on Brooklyn Bridge after exploring trendy Williamsburg.

From Lower Manhattan to the Bronx, and everything in between, we break New York City down into easily navigable chapters full of expert knowledge. If you're not sure where to begin, we include detailed itineraries and comprehensive maps to help plan the perfect adventure. Add insider tips, and a Need To Know guide that lists all the essentials to be aware of before and during your trip, and you've got an indispensable guidebook. Enjoy the book, and enjoy New York City.

REASONS TO
LOVE NEW YORK

It's undeniably spectacular. It's a world in a city. It never sleeps. Ask any New Yorker and you'll hear a different reason why they love their city. Here, we pick some of our favorites.

1 SHAKESPEARE IN THE PARK

In warm summer twilight, actors entertain audiences at Central Park's Delacorte Theater with free performances of the Bard's greatest plays.

STATUE OF LIBERTY 2

Looming over the harbor, Lady Liberty holds her beacon to light the world – the greatest symbol of the American dream. Climb to her crown for spine-tingling views of Manhattan.

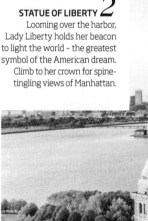

3 JEWISH FOOD IN THE LOWER EAST SIDE

Mountains of pastrami, chewy bagels, freshly baked challah breads: Jewish life in the Lower East Side lives on in its delis, bakeries, and cafés.

HIGH LINE 4

Gliding through Chelsea's rooftop gardens, this stunning transformation of an elevated railroad into a tranquil, tree-lined walkway offers tantalizing perspectives of the city below.

CATCHING A GAME AT YANKEE STADIUM 5

Watching America's most famous baseball team battle with archrivals the Boston Red Sox – or cross-town adversaries the Mets – is electric.

BROOKLYN FLEA AND SMORGASBURG 6

Artsy crafts, antiques stalls, and artisanal food sellers have made these weekend markets across the East River New York institutions.

LIVE JAZZ 7

Live jazz is flourishing in NYC. The legacy of legends lives on at the iconic Village Vanguard, Blue Note, and Birdland clubs, while smaller, intimate venues in Harlem host new talent.

THE METROPOLITAN 8 MUSEUM OF ART

Simply one of the greatest caches of art in the world, with over two million artifacts spanning 5,000 years housed beneath its grand ceilings.

9 EMPIRE STATE BUILDING

King Kong clung to it. Tom Hanks and Meg Ryan kissed on top of it. Still the most elegant skyscraper of them all, the Empire State has been a symbol of New York City since 1931.

10 OPERA AND BALLET AT THE LINCOLN CENTER

Casts of sopranos, tenors, and baritones; achingly beautiful ballet dancers; extravagant sets and costumes. Welcome to the Lincoln Center.

HARLEM GOSPEL AND SOUL FOOD 11

Join the flock and belt out hymns at Harlem's Abyssinian Baptist Church on Sundays. Afterwards schlep to Sylvia's and sample the justly celebrated BBQ ribs and candied yams.

BAR-HOPPING IN WILLIAMSBURG 12

After exploring ever-so-trendy Brooklyn head for once-shabby, now-chic Williamsburg – or Billyburg to locals. Meander from bar to bar, sipping on craft cocktails and bitters.

EXPLORE
NEW YORK CITY

This guide divides New York City into 15 color-coded sightseeing areas, as shown on the map below. Find out more about each area on the following pages. Away from the city, Beyond the Center *(p286)* covers Upper Manhattan, the Bronx, Queens, and Staten Island.

UNION CITY

Hudson River

WEEHAWKEN

NEW JERSEY

THE HEIGHTS

HOBOKEN

NEWPORT

PAULUS
HOOK

World Trade
Center

City Hall

Ellis
Island

Battery
Park

Statue of
Liberty

**LOWER
MANHATTAN**
p64

Governors
Island

RED HOOK

BOERUM
HILL

**MIDTOWN WEST AND
THE THEATER DISTRICT**
p172

MoMa

Rockefeller Center

St. Patrick's
Cathedral

**CHELSEA AND THE
GARMENT DISTRICT**
p160

Grand Central
Terminal

Empire State
Building

**LOWER
MIDTOWN**
p184

**GRAMERCY AND THE
FLATIRON DISTRICT**
p150

**GREENWICH
VILLAGE**
p124

**SOHO AND
TRIBECA**
p114

**CHINATOWN,
LITTLE ITALY,
AND NOLITA**
p102

EAST VILLAGE
p138

East River

**LOWER EAST
SIDE**
p90

Williamsburg
Bridge

Brooklyn
Bridge

Manhattan
Bridge

East

**BROOKLYN
HEIGHTS**

WILLIAMSBURG

BROOKLYN
p268

PROSPECT
HEIGHTS

Riverside
Park

**HARLEM AND
MORNINGSIDE HEIGHTS**
p250

BRONX

Cathedral of
St. John the Divine

**CENTRAL PARK
AND THE
UPPER WEST SIDE**
p234

Marcus
Garvey
Park

Central
Park

American Museum
of Natural History

Solomon R.
Guggenheim
Museum

Harlem River

Randalls
Island

East River

Rikers
Island

Central
Park

Metropolitan
Museum of Art

UPPER EAST SIDE
p214

ASTORIA

**UPPER
MIDTOWN**
p198

Roosevelt
Island

QUEENSBRIDGE

QUEENS

JACKSON
HEIGHTS

LONG
ISLAND
CITY

GREENPOINT

SUNNYSIDE

0 km   1
0 miles   1

N

NORTH AMERICA

CANADA

● Seattle

● Chicago   ● Boston

● San Francisco   U S A

Washington, DC ●   **NEW YORK CITY**

*Pacific
Ocean*   ● Los Angeles

Memphis ●

● Atlanta   *Atlantic
Ocean*

Houston ●

MEXICO   *Gulf of
Mexico*   ● Miami

GETTING TO KNOW
NEW YORK CITY

Global capital of finance and culture, New York is a vast city of over 8 million people. For many, the island of Manhattan *is* New York, with its permanent purr of traffic and bounty of diverse restaurants, not to mention its dizzying assemblage of signature sights and characterful neighborhoods.

PAGE 64

LOWER MANHATTAN

Lower Manhattan's regeneration since 9/11 has been remarkable, and the island's southern tip continues to pulse with industrious energy. It remains the financial center of the world and, as the oldest part of the city, has plenty of historic appeal, with Ellis and Liberty islands looming large in the harbor.

Best for
History and skyscrapers

Home to
Statue of Liberty, Ellis Island, National September 11 Memorial and Museum

Experience
A scenic cruise around New York harbor

PAGE 90

LOWER EAST SIDE

Once the most impoverished of New York's immigrant neighborhoods, the Lower East Side is now known for its hip bars and varied restaurants. Delis are a legacy of its Jewish heritage, while Latino and Chinese eateries have added to its culinary appeal. Prepare for an assault on the senses when walking these clamorous streets.

Best for
Bars and cocktails, Jewish food

Home to
Lower East Side Tenement Museum, Katz's Deli

Experience
Jewish history on a guided tour of the neighborhood

PAGE 102

CHINATOWN, LITTLE ITALY, AND NOLITA

These vibrant enclaves are among the city's most colorful. Swarms of shoppers hungry for a bargain comb Chinatown's stores and sidewalk markets, which overflow with exotic fruits, potent herbs, and Asian antiques. Little Italy has dwindled to a few blocks, but the tempting scents from its old-fashioned bakeries, Sicilian cafés, and red-sauce joints linger. Nolita offers a wholly different ambience, with chic boutiques and cafés along its gentrified streets attracting well-heeled fashionistas.

Best for
Cheap Chinese and Italian restaurants, Chinese culture

Home to
Museum of Chinese in America, New Museum

Experience
Chinatown by trawling its dumpling and noodle shops for cheap eats

PAGE 114

SOHO AND TRIBECA

SoHo's charming village vibe is welcome relief from the relentless jostle of Lower Manhattan. The neighborhood is known primarily for one thing: shopping. Its attractive, cobblestoned streets are crammed with designer-clothing and home-furnishing boutiques, making use of the stunningly ornate cast-iron architecture that dominates the area. The adjoining neighborhood of Tribeca, meanwhile, shelters homes for wealthy New Yorkers and some of the city's finest restaurants.

Best for
Cast-iron architecture, shopping, fine dining

Home to
New York Earth Room, Children's Museum of the Arts

Experience
Pretty Greene St and admire SoHo's most intricate cast-iron architecture

→

PAGE 124

GREENWICH VILLAGE

Referred to simply as "the Village" by New Yorkers, Greenwich Village has been the artistic heart of the city since the 1920s, and it remains one of the more progressive neighborhoods, with a notable LGBT+ and New York University student presence. Visitors flock to the Village to admire its famously handsome brownstones and meander around its quaint side streets that are chock-full of cafés, restaurants, and nightclubs. This is the perfect area for people-watching – you might even spot a celebrity or two.

Best for
Bars and restaurants, reliable nightlife, gorgeous residential streets

Home to
Whitney Museum of American Art

Experience
Historic Washington Square Park while indulging in cupcakes from Magnolia Bakery

PAGE 138

EAST VILLAGE

The East Village, one of New York's most fashionable neighborhoods, is home to a cache of unmissable bars, restaurants, and independent theaters. More alternative and edgier than Greenwich Village, like its neighbor, it has been transformed in recent years, with an influx of New York University students and new condo developments. This is the haunt of effortlessly cool New Yorkers, thanks to its smattering of independent boutiques, thrift stores, record stores, and artsy performance spaces.

Best for
New York's historic counterculture, dive bars, cheap international restaurants

Home to
St. Mark's Church-in-the-Bowery, Stomp, Little Tokyo, Russian and Turkish Baths

Experience
Lively St. Mark's Place, grabbing snacks to enjoy in Tompkins Square Park

GRAMERCY AND THE FLATIRON DISTRICT

These once-quiet neighborhoods are on the rise. New York's biggest farmers' market fills Union Square with a riot of colorful produce, and is attracting stores and restaurants galore. Development has extended to the Flatiron District, where Madison Square is home to the hottest restaurants and the holy grail of food markets, Eataly. Gramercy remains affluent and residential, known for its London-style private park.

Best for
Escaping the bustle, shopping and food markets, award-winning restaurants

Home to
Flatiron Building, Eataly NYC Flatiron, Union Square Greenmarket

Experience
Madison Square Park while munching on a Shack Burger and slurping chocolate frozen custard

CHELSEA AND THE GARMENT DISTRICT

Chelsea is an important center for avant-garde culture and a dynamic hub for gay New Yorkers. Art lovers head for the modish galleries in converted warehouses around the High Line, where the high-rise park has sparked an flurry of new buildings. The Garment District attracts shoppers, with Herald Square and Macy's at the heart of the city's busiest shopping area. Soaring over it all, the Empire State Building marks the start of Midtown.

Best for
Contemporary art galleries, designer flagships, LGBT+ scene

Home to
High Line, Empire State Building, Macy's

Experience
An early morning stroll along the High Line, taking in the local art galleries

→

PAGE 172

MIDTOWN WEST AND THE THEATER DISTRICT

Midtown West offers the New York cityscape of popular imagination, best known for the theaters of Broadway. Times Square anchors the neighborhood, a spectacular showcase of garish neon, where impersonators and street musicians vie with hordes of tourists and the roar of traffic. Scattered throughout are famous restaurants and cocktail bars – perfect for unwinding in after negotiating the ruckus.

Best for
Modern New York, classic skyscrapers, live theater, old-school bars

Home to
Rockefeller Center, New York Public Library

Experience
The Today Show live at Rockefeller Center, before taking the NBC Studio Tour

PAGE 184

LOWER MIDTOWN

Primarily a business district, Lower Midtown contains some of the city's most venerable architecture from New York's golden age. From the iconic spire of the Chrysler Building, to the palatial expanse of Grand Central, and the Modernism of the United Nations, it's all here. Midtown's streets are crowded with office workers during the day, though there is less to do at night, and the blocks near the UN are residential districts for rich New Yorkers and diplomats.

Best for
Modern architecture, classic skyscrapers, New York at work

Home to
United Nations, Grand Central Terminal, Morgan Library, Chrysler Building

Experience
Irresistible Scandinavian delicacies at Great Northern Food Hall

PAGE 198

UPPER MIDTOWN

Upper Midtown is New York City's richest business and shopping district. Primarily the realm of banks, offices, posh hotels, and expensive condos, this is where Trump Tower rose in the 1980s. Fifth Avenue is lined with super-exclusive boutiques and iconic names such as Saks, Barney's, Cartier, and Tiffany's. Most visitors come here to take in the classic skyscrapers and Instagram-friendly street scenes, but also to pay homage to MoMA, one of the world's greatest modern art galleries.

Best for
Famous bars and department stores, luxury shopping, insight into business in New York City

Home to
MoMA, St. Patrick's Cathedral, Bloomingdale's, Tiffany's, Roosevelt Island

Experience
Some retail therapy at Bloomingdale's and grab an iconic "brown bag"

PAGE 214

UPPER EAST SIDE

This area has long been associated with New York's upper crust, and the likes of Fifth Avenue, Madison Avenue, and Park Avenue remain bastions of old-school wealth. The Beaux Arts mansions flanking Fifth Avenue are occupied by embassies and museums, while Madison Avenue's posh boutiques vie with Fifth Avenue for exclusivity. Further east are remnants of the area's German, Hungarian, and Czech heritage, while a sprinkling of hip gastropubs and cocktail bars, frequented by moneyed New Yorkers, has helped to shed the Upper East Side's stuffy image.

Best for
Beaux Arts architecture, fine art, historic churches

Home to
The Met, Guggenheim, Frick Collection

Experience
Klimt's stunning Woman in Gold at the Neue Galerie

→

PAGE 234

CENTRAL PARK AND THE UPPER WEST SIDE

Central Park is the city's greatest green space and offers respite from Manhattan's thronging sidewalks and blaring sirens. In summer, its lawns are packed with families, joggers, soccer players, and cyclists, while in winter it's often shrouded in a magical blanket of snow. Next door, the Upper West Side remains a popular residential neighborhood, home to the fabulous American Museum of Natural History and dynamic Lincoln Center.

Best for
Escaping the hustle and bustle of the city, boating and cycling

Home to
American Museum of Natural History

Experience
Cycling in Central Park before refueling with smoked fish and bagels at Barney Greengrass

PAGE 250

HARLEM AND MORNINGSIDE HEIGHTS

This neighborhood, synonymous with the country's most famous African-American community, is thrumming with life. Visitors are greeted by some of the city's prettiest streets and a vibrant culinary landscape; the mouthwatering aromas of soul food, Caribbean, and West African cuisine drift from bustling restaurants, while a burgeoning bar scene and local jazz clubs keep things buzzing at night.

Best for
African-American culture, street art, soul food, live jazz, Sunday gospel

Home to
Schomburg Center, Hamilton Grange, National Jazz Museum in Harlem

Experience
The uplifting and electrifying Sunday gospel choir at the Abyssinian Baptist Church

PAGE 268

BROOKLYN

Across the East River, Brooklyn is a vast city-within-a-city; a patchwork of neighborhoods anchored by a booming downtown, now with its own mushrooming condo skyscrapers. Between the gorgeous brownstones of Fort Greene and Park Slope, and the hip bars of Williamsburg and Bushwick – where the chatter of bar-hoppers drifts along the weathered streets – you'll find the art galleries of Dumbo, vintage treasures at the Brooklyn Flea, and the nostalgic, seaside delights of Coney Island.

Best for
Flea markets, pizza, brownstone rowhouses, farm-to-table restaurants

Home to
Brooklyn Museum, Smorgasburg, Dumbo, Brooklyn Navy Yard, Coney Island

Experience
The hubbub of vintage treasure-trove Brooklyn Flea, before hitting food market Smorgasburg for snacks

PAGE 286

BEYOND THE CENTER

There's more to New York than Manhattan and Brooklyn; there are, after all, five boroughs that make up the city. Queens is the most multicultural area of the city, with a dynamic culinary scene, while the Bronx boasts beautiful parks, a world-class botanic garden, and the iconic Yankee Stadium. Even Staten Island, the "forgotten borough" and most suburban part of New York, features a fascinating colonial village and a captivating Tibetan gallery, and more history can be found in Upper Manhattan. Turn to p286 for more about Beyond the Center.

Best for
Immigrant New York, authentic cuisines, contemporary and medieval art, baseball

Home to
The Cloisters, New York Botanical Garden, Noguchi Museum, Yankee Stadium

Experience
Life as a real New Yorker, outside of Manhattan

←

1 Pedestrians outside the Stock Exchange

2 A ferry passes the Statue of Liberty in New York City's harbor

3 Enjoying the view from Battery Park

4 A performance of Broadway musical *Wicked*

New York City is bursting at the seams with unmissable sights, diverse cuisines, and truly unique experiences. These itineraries will help you make the most of your visit to the magnificent metropolis.

24 HOURS

Morning

Both historic and symbolic, Liberty and Ellis islands are the best introduction to any visit to New York City. Rise early and head down to Battery Park (p84) to book the 8:30am ferry to the Statue of Liberty (p68), the city's enduring symbol of freedom. On arrival, purchase a "pedestal access" ticket, which gives entry to the museum and viewing deck at the base of the statue (skip the walk up to the crown – it's not worth the extra time, and there's much more to do today). Continue on to Ellis Island (p70), where more than 100 million Americans can trace their roots. The Ellis Island Café is fine for a quick, basic lunch but, if you can hold out, we recommend returning to Battery Park on the ferry and heading for Pier A Harbor House (p81). Next to the ferry dock, this place has fabulous views from the outdoor deck and serves excellent oysters and refreshing craft beers.

Afternoon

From Battery Park it's a relatively short walk up Broadway to historic Trinity Church (p79). Be sure to pay your respects at the tomb of Alexander Hamilton in the cemetery outside. Wall Street (p88) runs east toward the East River from the church and is lined with jaw-dropping, limestone skyscrapers the whole way. Check out the exterior of the world-famous New York Stock Exchange and the statue of George Washington in front of Federal Hall (p78) before jumping on the #6 subway train and heading uptown. Get off at 33rd Street and stroll over to the city's most iconic skyscraper, the Empire State Building (p164). Provided the weather isn't especially bad, the views from the observation deck on the 86th floor are worth the wait. From here, continue on to the 34 St-Herald Square station and proceed to Times Square (p180). Soak up the frenetic scene here before grabbing a pre-theater dinner at Sardi's (www.sardis.com) or Junior's (www.juniorscheesecake.com).

Evening

Enjoy a classic Broadway musical (if you booked tickets in advance), or catch a play in one of the buzzing theaters around Times Square. After the show, jump in a cab or take the #1 subway train down to Christopher St station for dessert and late-night drinks in Greenwich Village.

$\rightarrow$

1 Morning in Central Park

2 Artisan cheese sold at
Eataly NYC Downtown

3 The reflective pools of the National
September 11 Memorial, overlooked
by One World Trade Center

4 Walkers enjoying the elevated
High Line at dusk

2 DAYS

Day 1

Morning Start your day with a take-away bagel and coffee in Central Park *(p238)*. Try to arrive at the Met *(p220)* by opening time at 10am (from the southern end of the park, on 59th St, it takes around 40 minutes to walk to the museum). You could spend days marveling at the wonders inside the Met, but focus on the highlights over 2–3 hours; we suggest the European paintings section, plus the Temple of Dendur.

Afternoon Grab a cab or bus on Madison Avenue down to Grand Central *(p188)* for a quick seafood lunch at the Oyster Bar. From here walk (or take a bus) down to the Empire State Building *(p164)*, to soak up the Art Deco splendor and those magnificent views. If you still have energy left, it's a 15-minute ride on bus #M34 to Hudson Yards and the northern end of the High Line *(p166)*, which makes for a lovely stroll in the late afternoon or early evening light.

Evening Have dinner in the Meatpacking District *(p131)*, at the southern end of the High Line.

Day 2

Morning Grab your camera and jump on a narrated cruise from the Seaport District's Pier 16 *(p86)* around Liberty and Ellis islands. Afterward, walk or take a cab across to the National September 11 Memorial *(p72)*, taking in the waterfalls and tranquil groves of oak.

Afternoon Have lunch at Eataly NYC Downtown, over in 4 World Trade Center, before walking down Broadway to Wall Street and the Stock Exchange *(p88)*. From Pier 11, where Wall Street meets the East River, take the ferry across to the Fulton Ferry District *(p278)* in Brooklyn. Grab an ice cream and enjoy wandering the streets of this historic district before strolling back across the Brooklyn Bridge for unmissable views of Manhattan *(p272)*.

Evening From the bridge it's a short walk to Chinatown *(p109)*, where tasty dinners await at Joe's Shanghai. Night owls should continue on to SoHo for evening drinks in one of the neighborhood's fashionable bars *(p118)*.

←

1 The spectacular interior of the Oculus

2 The Guggenheim

3 Breakfast in SoHo

4 Drinkers unwind in Willamsburg, looking over Manhattan

5 DAYS

Day 1

Morning Reserve the first ferry to the Statue of Liberty (p68); once you've admired the iconic statue up close, head back to Battery Park and spend some time at the National September 11 Memorial and Museum (p72).

Afternoon Buy lunch at Le District food hall before strolling through the Oculus (p75) to St. Paul's Chapel (p80). Visit Trinity Church (p79) and Wall Street, continuing to Seaport District NYC (p86) for some retail therapy.

Evening Stay in Seaport District NYC for aperitifs and then grab dinner in nearby Chinatown (p109).

Day 2

Morning Have breakfast in the Meatpacking District before walking the High Line (p166). At 34th St take a cab or bus across to the Empire State Building (p164), where you can grab a snack on the observation deck.

Afternoon Keep most of the afternoon free for modern art haven MoMA (p202) – it's worth reserving tickets to the museum ahead of time to beat the lines.

Evening Aim to hit Times Square (p180) as it's getting dark, and the neon lights are particularly spectacular, before ending the day with a Broadway show.

Day 3

Morning Get to the Met (p220) right on opening time and focus on just one or two sections, as there's so much to see here. Have lunch at one of the museum's enticing cafés.

Afternoon Wander up to the striking Guggenheim Museum (p218) for another hour or so, before heading into Central Park (p238) for some fresh air. Grab a snack at the Loeb Boathouse, pay your respects to John Lennon at Strawberry Fields, and stroll toward the Sheep Meadow, where New Yorkers relax on the grass.

Evening Catch an opera, musical performance, or ballet at the Lincoln Center (p244). The excellent restaurants here are perfect for dinner, but try to reserve ahead.

Day 4

Morning Breakfast in SoHo, before walking up to Greenwich Village (follow the route on p136). Take a break and soak up the scene in Washington Square Park (p134).

Afternoon For lunch, head down to Little Italy or Nolita (p110) before joining a tour at the historic Lower East Side Tenement Museum (p94). The Museum at Eldridge Street (p96) is also worth a look if you have the time (and energy).

Evening Stay in the Lower East Side for dinner and drinks at Ivan Ramen or Mission Chinese Food (p100).

Day 5

Morning Begin the day with a stroll across the Brooklyn Bridge (p272). Stop at the Fulton Ferry District (p278) for refreshments before exploring Brooklyn Bridge Park (p280), along the waterfront.

Afternoon Have lunch at Fornino At Pier 6 (www.fornino.com). From here it's an easy hike up to Brooklyn Heights, where you can follow our walking tour (p284). Continue on to trendy Dumbo (p278) for the art galleries or a performance at St. Ann's Warehouse.

Evening To end the perfect day in Brooklyn, grab a taxi up to Williamsburg (p279) and sample its justly celebrated nightlife.

The New York Deli

A city institution, the deli was traditionally a Jewish affair. Find smoked fish and bagels at Zabar's *(p247)* and Russ & Daughters (179 East Houston St). Katz's Deli is famed for its giant pastrami sandwiches (205 East Houston St). Alleva Dairy (188 Grand St) is a classic Italian deli, while Brooklyn's Sahadi's (187 Atlantic Av) is a Middle Eastern specialist.

←

Salami and pickles galore at Katz's Deli in the Lower East Side

NEW YORK CITY FOR
FOODIES

Foodies are in for a treat in New York. Just about every type of cuisine is showcased here, from Colombian and Armenian to Korean and Senegalese, with prices ranging from $1 pizza slices to some of the world's most expensive and prestigious French gourmet and farm-to-table restaurants.

BRUNCH IN NYC

Sunday brunch is a big deal in New York. Special brunch menus (which sometimes include booze) attract long lines at the most popular spots; traditionally in Greenwich Village, Soho, and the Lower East Side, but now just as prevalent in Brooklyn. Carroll Gardens, Cobble Hill, and Williamsburg are especially busy. Reserve a table in advance to avoid disappointment.

America's Fine Dining Capital

Looking to splash out? Thomas Keller's Per Se *(p245)* is always top of a long list of award-winning restaurants, while Eric Ripert's Le Bernardin *(p183)* has three Michelin stars. Chef's Table at Brooklyn Fare (431 West 37th St) and Eleven Madison Park *(p157)* are part of a newer wave of fine dining options.

→

Irresistible desserts at Le Bernardin, Midtown West and the Theater District

↑ Drinkers and diners at Dekalb Market Hall in Brooklyn

The New York Food Hall

With the success of Eataly *(p154)* and Brooklyn food fair Smorgasburg *(p282)*, gourmet food halls are all the rage in New York. Le District *(p80)* has a French theme, while Great Northern Food Hall in Grand Central Terminal is Scandinavian *(p193)*, and Plaza Food Hall (1 West 59th St) is upscale. Dekalb Market Hall (445 Albee Sq West, Brooklyn) offers everything from dumplings and sushi, to pastrami sandwiches and key lime pie.

💬 INSIDER TIP
Food Tours

Food walking tours are a great way to see the city and fuel up in the process. Top tours include NoshWalks (www.noshwalks.com), and Scott's Pizza Tours (www.scottspizza tours.com).

THE FLAVOR OF NEW YORK SINCE 1916

American Icons

Lombardi's *(p110)*, founded in 1905, was America's first pizzeria, but Patsy's *(p263)* sold the first pizza slice in 1933. Polish-Jewish Nathan Handwerker popularized Coney Island's hot dog, now sold at Nathan's Famous (1310 Surf Av), while German émigré Arnold Reuben invented New York-style cheesecake, best sampled at Junior's *(p282)*. New icon on the block, Dominique Ansel's 'cronut' (croissant-donut pastry) is sold at 189 Spring St.

↑ Nathan's Famous and cronuts *(inset)*, old and new American icons

Parks

New York is home to a number of gorgeous green spaces, ideal for whiling away a morning, afternoon, or entire day. The High Line (p166) and Central Park (p238) are both free and two of the best parks in America. There's also Bryant Park (p180), Washington Square Park (p134), Tompkins Square Park (p142), and Prospect Park (p282).

$\rightarrow$

A wealth of stunning green spaces await in Central Park

NEW YORK CITY ON A
SHOESTRING

New York can be a very expensive place to visit but, with a bit of planning, savvy visitors can find plenty of free or less costly experiences, ranging from free museums to free performances, parks, and art galleries.

PICNICS

An affordable way to enjoy the sights and flavors of the city is with a picnic. Grab all the food you need at Zabar's (p247), one of the best delis in the city, and head for the Great Lawn in Central Park (p238). There's also Governors Island, which shouldn't be missed (p76). Bring sandwiches with you, or buy take-out treats from the food stalls on the island. For a seaside picnic, make for Coney Island (p283). Load up with Eastern European snacks at Brighton Bazaar (1007 Brighton Beach Av), or grab hot dogs at Nathan's Famous (p31).

Brooklyn Brewery Tours

New York's premier micro-brewer offers free tours; on the half hour from 1 to 6pm Saturdays and Sundays. Tastings of Brooklyn Lager or Brooklyn East IPA aren't part of the free tour, but tokens can be bought without breaking the bank (p279).

Brooklyn Brewery, offering interesting free tours $\uparrow$

Free Museums

The American Museum of Natural History (p242) is always "pay-what-you-wish," but almost every museum in New York has one day (or evening) where you can do the same. Entirely free museums include African Burial Ground (p87); American Folk Art Museum (p247); the Bronx Museum of the Arts (p299); Hamilton Grange (p258); Museum at the FIT (p170); National Museum of the American Indian (p85); the Schomburg Center (p256); and Theodore Roosevelt Birthplace (p157).

← Taxidermy exhibits at the American Museum of Natural History

TOP 7 WHAT'S FREE AND WHEN?

Monday
Museum at Eldridge Street (all day)

Tuesday
National September 11 Memorial Museum (5-8pm)

Wednesday
Museum of Jewish Heritage (4-8pm)

Thursday
Museum of Arts and Design (6-9pm); Museum of Jewish Heritage (4-8pm)

Friday
Asia Society (6-9pm); MoMA (4-8pm); Historic Richmond Town (1-5pm)

Saturday
Jewish Museum (all day)

Sunday
New York Hall of Science (10-11am); Studio Museum in Harlem (all day)

Chelsea Art Galleries

It costs nothing to wander around the art galleries of Chelsea, home to some of the world's most cutting-edge contemporary art (p171). Consider combining these wonderful galleries with a day on the High Line (p166), which is completely free and a New York must see, for an affordable day in the city. Be aware that Saturdays can prove very busy.

↑ One of Chelsea's art galleries, home to innovative modern art and design

Contemporary NYC

The High Line (p166) has sparked a frenzy of innovative building along its borders: Frank Gehry's IAC Building (2007), the 2015 Whitney Museum by Renzo Piano (p128), and Zaha Hadid's 520 West 28th (2017) to name a few. One World Trade Center topped out as the city's tallest building in 2013 (p74), sparking a new bout of "supertall" skyscrapers.

→

IAC Building
by Frank Gehry,
illuminated at dusk

NEW YORK CITY'S
ARCHITECTURE

Skyscrapers aside, New York is a true architectural showcase – all the significant and influential movements of the last two centuries are represented in the city's magnificent structural landmarks.

The Glory Years

Architects began to design Art Deco sky-scrapers in the 1920s (p87). Some of the city's most impressive structures – such as 1 Wall Street (1931), 70 Pine Street (1930), and the Chrysler Building (1930) – went up just after the 1929 Wall Street Crash. The Rockefeller Center complex (p176), which was worked on throughout the 1930s, is perhaps the zenith of Art Deco style in New York.

↑ The Chrysler Building,
an Art Deco icon in
Lower Midtown

The 1950s and 1960s

The Modernist style (the arrival of European architectural movements such as Bauhaus and Le Corbusier) influenced the glass-curtain-wall buildings of Mies van der Rohe: the 1950 United Nations *(p190)*, 1952 Lever House *(p211)*, and the 1958 Seagram Building *(p210)*, all in Midtown. This style culminated, perhaps most famously, in the now-destroyed Twin Towers of the World Trade Center (1973).

←

The Secretariat Building within the United Nations complex

The attractive and uniquely ↓ shaped Flatiron Building

TOP
6 **NEIGHBOR-HOODS FOR BROWNSTONES**

Greenwich Village
The Village is home to quiet mews, handsome rowhouses, and elegant apartment blocks.

Upper West Side
Classic brownstones with bay windows can be found at Riverside Drive, between 80th and 81st streets.

Harlem
Some of the most beautiful residential architecture in the city is best exemplified by Strivers' Row.

Brooklyn Heights
Features a wide range of styles, from early Federal rowhouses to large Neo-Romanesque and Neo-Gothic villas.

Fort Greene, Brooklyn
Gorgeous and leafy residential streets, especially South Portland Avenue.

Park Slope, Brooklyn
Some of the finest Romanesque and Queen Anne residences in the US (built in the 1880s and 1890s).

From Cast Iron to Beaux Arts

It was the advent of cast-iron constructions in the mid-19th century that really thrust New York City to the forefront of architectural sophistication. The 1902 Flatiron Building *(p156)* is regarded as one of the city's first skyscrapers, while the 1913 Woolworth Building *(p87)*, with its decorative Gothic spires and gargoyles, continued the upward trend. The era's Beaux Arts architecture culminated in the 1902 Metropolitan Museum of Art *(p220)*, 1911 New York Public Library *(p178)*, and 1919 Grand Central Terminal *(p188)*.

→

1

2

MANHATTAN'S SKYLINE

The world's most famous skyline is constantly changing. Since the first skyscrapers went up in the 1890s, buildings have become ever taller, with the latest boom in "supertalls" set to make the biggest transformation of New York City since the 1930s. Manhattan has two key clusters of skyscrapers – in Lower Manhattan (sometimes referred to as the Financial District) and Midtown – and its skyline comprises over 260 buildings that reach higher than 500 ft

(152 m). Though structures began topping the 300-ft (91-m) mark in the 1890s, the first major skyscraper was the Woolworth Building at 792 ft (241 m), completed in 1913 (p87). These first towers were sheer vertical monoliths, with no regard to how neighboring buildings were affected. Authorities later invented "air rights," a concept limiting a building's height before it had to be set back from its base.

MANHATTAN'S SUPERTALLS

Supertalls are a special class of skyscraper and Manhattan's skyline includes some of the world's most famous. As the name implies, supertalls are colossal in size, standing at over 1,000 ft (305 m), and they are naturally expensive to build. You can learn more about supertalls and the city's skyline at the Skyscraper Museum (p81).

One World Trade Center
At 1,776 ft (541 m), this symbolic tower became America's tallest skyscraper on its completion in 2013.

Three World Trade Center
This 1,079 ft (329 m) tower topped out in 2016.

Brookfield Place
This office and shopping complex comprises several buildings, the tallest of which reaches 739 ft (225 m).

3

① Battery Park, overlooked by 17 State Street.

② Rebuilt from 1921 to 1928, 26 Broadway was designed to resemble a giant oil lamp.

③ One World Trade Center, an example of Manhattan's evolving skyline, looms large over the city streets.

GREAT VIEW
Manhattan's Skyline

For the best views of Manhattan's skyline, head to the Top of the Rock *(p176)*, The Hills at Governors Island *(p76)*, the top of the Empire State Building *(p164)*, Roosevelt Island *(p211)*, Brooklyn Bridge Park *(p280)*, or ride the Staten Island Ferry *(p86)*.

↓ Manhattan's southern tip as seen from the Hudson River

Woolworth Building
The handsomely decorated "cathedral of commerce" is 792 ft (241 m) tall.

One Wall Street
An Art-Deco skyscraper completed in 1931 and reaching 927 ft (282 m).

17 State Street
This 541-ft (164-m) building has a distinct curved-glass facade.

26 Broadway
Formerly the Standard Oil Building, 26 Broadway stands at 520 ft (158 m).

One Liberty Plaza
Replacing the former Singer Building, which was the tallest structure ever dismantled, this skyscraper is 743 ft (226 m) tall.

Frick Collection

Henry Clay Frick's personal art collection, displayed in his mansion on the Upper East Side (p224), contains some real gems, not least Holbein's infamous portraits of one-time rivals Thomas More and Thomas Cromwell. Vermeer's *Officer and Laughing Girl*, Bellini's sublime *St Francis in the Desert*, and Rembrandt's enigmatic *Polish Rider* are also on display here.

←

The stunning Garden Court, in the center of the Frick Collection building

NEW YORK CITY FOR
ART LOVERS

New York remains at the center of the global art market, with hundreds of dealers and galleries, illustrious auction houses like Christie's and Sotheby's, and high-profile art colleges attracting some of the best talent in the world. Perhaps best of all is the city's dynamic public art programme.

TOP 5 NEW YORK ARTISTS

Jean-Michel Basquiat (1960-88)
Street artist whose work can sell for $110 million.

Keith Haring (1958-90)
Graffiti mural artist.

Jeff Koons (1955-)
Pop artist known for his steel balloon animals.

Florine Stettheimer (1871-1944)
Ground-breaking painter and art patron.

Andy Warhol (1928-87)
Iconic Pop artist.

The Guggenheim

Though Frank Lloyd Wright's seminal building often overshadows the changing exhibitions inside, the Guggenheim contains an exceptional Kandinsky collection, as well as paintings by Picasso, Van Gogh, Monet, and Cézanne (p218).

The striking tiered exterior of the Guggenheim
↓

GUGGENHEIM M

MOMA

Some of the world's most iconic artwork is preserved here at the Museum of Modern Art, or MoMA for short *(p202)*. From Dalí's *The Persistence of Memory* and Van Gogh's *The Starry Night*, to *Dance* by Matisse and *Les Demoiselles d'Avignon* by Picasso, this modern art giant is a must see.

💬 INSIDER TIP
Street Art Tours

Pioneer graffiti artists started "tagging" in the late 1960s. Graff Tours (www.grafftours.com) and Brooklyn Unplugged (www.brooklynunpluggedtours.com) offer highly rated street art tours.

↑ *The Starry Night* (1889), by Vincent van Gogh, on display at MoMA

The Whitney

At the foot of the High Line, this is New York's premier showcase for modern and contemporary American art *(p128)*. The permanent collection is especially rich in works by Alexander Calder, Jasper Johns, Reginald Marsh, Georgia O'Keeffe, Claes Oldenburg, and Cindy Sherman.

←

The Whitney Museum of American Art, designed by Renzo Piano

The Met

New York's *grande dame* of art holds massive collections spanning over 5,000 years of world history *(p220)*. Everything from Duccio's priceless *Madonna and Child,* to a ton of French Impressionism and modern work by Clyfford Still, Andy Warhol, and Chuck Close.

→ *Water Lilies* (1916–19), by Claude Monet in The Met

◁ Museum of the Moving Image
The Museum of the Moving Image in Queens *(p301)* has a popular permanent exhibit on all things Muppet-related. More than 300 artifacts are on view, including 47 actual Muppets. Older kids will enjoy the exhibits on film-making, television, and the latest in digital art.

▷ Children's Museums
New York is well served by interactive museums dedicated to children. The Children's Museum of Manhattan *(p246)* is packed with toys and games, while the Children's Museum of the Arts *(p118)* encourages kids to get creative with hands-on exhibits. Brooklyn Children's Museum *(p280)* features a fun "block lab," sensory room, and special play areas for kids under 6 years.

NEW YORK CITY FOR
FAMILIES

New York is a wonderland for children. From colorful Broadway musicals and thrilling ferry rides, to cavernous stores and expansive green spaces – the Big Apple has something for kids of all ages.

◁ American Museum of Natural History
This is the city's most popular family destination *(p242)*. Giant dinosaur skeletons, a butterfly conservatory, a simulated African rainforest, 3D IMAX theaters, and a massive planetarium await, along with special exhibitions. Head to nearby Central Park *(p238)* after to let off steam.

◁ Carousels
Little ones especially will enjoy New York's old-time carousels. The vintage Central Park Carousel features 57 hand-carved horses, while the fish-themed SeaGlass Carousel in Battery Park *(p84)* is designed to resemble an undersea garden. A third option is Jane's Carousel in Brooklyn Bridge Park *(p280)*, easily combined with the walk across Brooklyn Bridge.

◁ Madison Square Park and Shake Shack
There's always something happening in Madison Square Park in the summer, from outdoor yoga classes to huge installations of public art. It's also well known as the home of the original Shake Shack burger hut. Grab some Shackburgers, cheese fries, and chocolate frozen custards, and enjoy them in the park.

△ Cycling, Skating, or Boating in Central Park
Central Park is fun to tour by bike – pick up some wheels at Bike and Roll *(p240)*. In summer, the Lasker Pool is a great place to swim, while rowboats are available from the Loeb Boathouse *(p241)*. In winter, the Wollman Rink and Lasker Rink both offer ice-skating (and skate rentals).

EAT

Big Daddy's
Brightly colored diner.
🔟 E7 🏠 239 Park Av S
🆆 bigdaddysnyc.com

$⑤$$

Bubby's
Great for big breakfasts.
🔟 C8 🏠 73 Gansevoort St 🆆 bubbys.com

$⑤$$

Ellen's Stardust Diner
Singing waitstaff.
🔟 D3 🏠 1650 Broadway 🆆 ellensstardustdiner. com

$⑤$$

Markets

The weekend Brooklyn Flea *(p279)* has become the doyen of New York markets, packed with hundreds of furniture, vintage clothing, art, and antique stalls. In Manhattan, Chelsea Flea Market *(p168)* has up to 135 vendors, with Hell's Kitchen Flea Market and Green Flea Market even bigger. Union Square *(p157)* has the largest farmers' market. Seasonal markets also appear.

←

Fresh produce and flowers at Greenmarket in Union Square

NEW YORK CITY FOR
SHOPPERS

Shops are one of New York's killer attractions, and the city is the undisputed commercial capital of America. Here you'll find flagship stores for every major brand, local boutiques, street markets, and vintage stores, plus the country's most famous department stores – Bloomingdale's and Macy's.

SHOPPING IN SOHO

SoHo is Manhattan's prime clothes-shopping neighborhood, centering on Broadway and Spring St. Popular and affordable brands, including Uniqlo, Forever 21, H&M, Nike, Victoria's Secret, and Topshop, all have giant emporiums here. High-end designers including Marc Jacobs, Balenciaga, Stella McCartney, Paul Smith, Louis Vuitton, and Christian Dior also have boutiques on the side streets here. Aim to shop in SoHo on a weekday if possible, as it gets unbearably crowded on weekends.

Department Stores

Bloomingdale's is perhaps New York's most famous department store, though Macy's *(p169)* is certainly larger (and cheaper). Barneys, Bergdorf Goodman, and Saks Fifth Avenue are all upscale department stores, famed for their designer fashions and lavish window displays *(p208)*.

Luxury brands

Audrey Hepburn's favorite in *Breakfast at Tiffany's*, Tiffany & Co *(p208)* is still a palace of diamond jewelry. New York designers with flagship stores include Alexander Wang (103 Grand St), Marc Jacobs (113 Prince St), and Vera Wang (991 Madison Av). Prada's lavish store at 575 Broadway is a trend-setter in SoHo, while TV series *Sex and the City* sparked the demand for luxury shoe designers Louboutin (967 Madison Av) and Manolo Blahnik (31 West 54th St).

→

Manolo Blahnik, a New York City landmark for fashionistas

Books and Comics

The Strand Bookstore *(p147)* is the place for cheap books. In Brooklyn, try indie WORD (126 Franklin St) and in Manhattan, Housing Works (126 Crosby St) for second-hand books. Look to St. Mark's Comics *(p147)* for comics and Bluestockings (172 Allen St) for LGBT+.

←

Browsing the array of books outside the Strand Bookstore

Vintage and Thrift Stores

In Brooklyn, head to Beacon's Closet *(p279)*, Amarcord (223 Bedford Av), or Domsey Express (431 Broadway). Across in Manhattan, try Edith Machinist (104 Rivington St), Michael's Consignment (1041 Madison Av), or Resurrection (45 Great Jones St).

→

Vintage treasure trove Beacon's Closet, in Greenpoint, Brooklyn

▷ Cheer on the Knicks at Madison Square Garden

The New York Knicks remain a fanatically supported basketball team (with the likes of Spike Lee, Alec Baldwin, and Howard Stern in regular attendance), despite a comically long run of poor form. Games at Madison Square Garden (p169) are quite the spectacle, with plenty of music, pageantry, and tasty snacks on offer.

◁ Play Ping Pong

Susan Sarandon is a co-owner (and often appears at) SPiN (48 East 23rd St), a sprawling table tennis club with 19 tables and a restaurant. Open till 2am on weekends, this is more like a lounge bar than a sports club, with high-quality cocktails and snacks.

NEW YORK CITY FOR
SPORTS

New York is one of America's great sports cities, home to iconic teams like the Knicks (basketball) and the Yankees and the Mets (baseball). You can get moving yourself; many of the city's activities are free or surprisingly cheap.

◁ Catch a Baseball Game at Yankee Stadium

Cheering for America's most successful baseball team is a summer tradition, best enjoyed with hot dogs and cold beers. Established in 1913, the Yankees have won 27 World Series championships; watch the team yourself (p299).

▷ Cycle in the Park

New York has become a lot more bike-friendly lately. Bike lanes run almost the whole length of Manhattan along the Hudson River, and crisscross Central Park; both places offer cool breezes and gorgeous views in summer. Check out our list of bike rentals for Central Park (p240), or utilize the Citi Bike bike-share scheme (www.citibikenyc.com).

◁ Go Kayaking on the Hudson River

Kayaking on the Hudson River is a popular and surprisingly tranquil activity, especially in summer, and gives a totally new perspective of New York's famous skyline. Kayaking at the Downtown Boathouse, at Pier 26, is free mid-May to mid-October. The Manhattan Kayak Company at Pier 84, meanwhile, offers lessons and stand-up paddleboarding.

💬 INSIDER TIP
Game Tickets

The easiest tickets to get are summer games at Yankee Stadium (from $9 for bleachers); buy online or on the day. For basketball, it's easiest to see the Brooklyn Nets at the Barclays Center.

▷ Don a Pair of Ice Skates

From November to March, the city opens its outdoor ice rinks. It's hard to beat the magical views from the Lasker and Wollman rinks in Central Park (p241), or the beatiful rink at Rockefeller Center (p176). Seasonal rinks also pop up at the Standard High Line hotel, and at Bryant Park (which is free).

◁ The Cloisters Museum

It's worth trekking up to the northern end of Manhattan to view the Met's collection of medieval tapestries, paintings, and sculpture. Perched high above the Hudson, with portions of five (real) medieval cloisters incorporated into the structure, it's easy to believe you've left North America altogether (p290).

▷ Hispanic Society, Washington Heights

With its dimly lit main gallery shimmering with the rosy hues of an Andalucían palace, the society owns one of the largest collections of Hispanic art outside Spain. Highlights include Goya's imperious portrait of the Duchess of Alba, and the monumental mural cycle *Vision of Spain*, by Joaquín Sorolla y Bastida (p292).

OFF THE
BEATEN PATH

With so many world-famous sights in New York, it can be easy to overlook the city's lesser-visited gems. If here for a longer stay, or visiting for the second or third time, seek out these off-the-beaten track highlights.

◁ Green-Wood Cemetery, Brooklyn

In the 19th-century, Green-Wood Cemetery was the place New York's movers and shakers chose to be buried. Today, the beautifully landscaped site can be toured individually or with guides, taking in the tombs of newspaper editor Horace Greeley, famed preacher Henry Ward Beecher, glass-maker Louis Comfort Tiffany, and composer Leonard Bernstein (p283).

◁ The Rockaways, Queens

Surfing in New York? It's possible in the Rockaways, with a long stretch of lovely sand easily accessible by subway. The beach at Jacob Riis Park is generally tranquil and pristine, though things get lively during the summertime at Riis Park Beach Bazaar, which features live bands and a food market (www.riisparkbeachbazaar.com).

◁ The Jacques Marchais Museum of Tibetan Art, Staten Island

This museum is the most unlikely treasure in New York, clinging to the Staten Island hills like an ancient Tibetan monastery. Founded in the 1940s by Jacques Marchais, a successful art dealer, the complex is full of rare Tibetan artwork, including delicate, colorful prayer flags. This unique museum, which holds the largest collection of Tibetan art outside of China, is well worth the excursion (p302).

MICRO-BREWERIES

Some of the city's most highly prized craft beers come from the outer boroughs, where most of the small-batch producers have tap rooms for sampling brews. Visit the Bronx Brewery (856 East 136th St, Port Morris), or Finback Brewery (7801 77th Av, Ridgewood) and SingleCut Beersmiths (19-33 37th St, Astoria) in Queens. In Brooklyn, Other Half Brewing (195 Centre St, Carroll Gardens) and Threes Brewing (333 Douglass St, Gowanus) compete with Brooklyn Brewery (p279).

△ Greenpoint, Brooklyn

New York's biggest Polish community retains plenty of character. *Kielbasa*- and *pierogi*-sellers like Polka Dot (726 Manhattan Av) are clustered along the main drag, Manhattan Avenue. Hip Danish brewpub Torst (615 Manhattan Av) and cozy Café Grumpy at 193 Meserole Av (which featured in TV show *Girls*), symbolize the new artsy side of the neighborhood (p279).

On the Trail of George Washington

George Washington (1732–99) was a Virginian, but he spent many crucial years in New York during the Revolutionary War. The General requisitioned Morris-Jumel Mansion *(p292)* in 1776 as army headquarters, returning to the city and Fraunces Tavern *(p85)* in 1783 to bid farewell to his troops. The Washington Statue outside Federal Hall *(p78)* commemorates the president's inauguration here in 1789, while his pew is preserved, shrine-like, at St. Paul's Chapel *(p80)*.

→
George Washington's statue standing outside Federal Hall

NEW YORK CITY FOR
HISTORY BUFFS

New York was officially founded by the Dutch (as "New Amsterdam") in 1625, and numerous reminders of the city's relatively short history remain, from old synagogues and churches, to crumbling forts, fine mansions, and a host of specialist museums.

TOP 5 BEST HISTORY MUSEUMS

Museum of the City of New York
The city's history *(p231)*.

New York Historical Society
Changing exhibits on New York themes *(p246)*.

National Museum of the American Indian
A million artifacts are housed here *(p85)*.

Museum of Chinese in America
The Chinese experience since the 1700s *(p108)*.

Italian American Museum
Focuses on the history of Little Italy *(p111)*.

Jewish History

Jewish culture is a key component of New York's identity. The restored synagogue at the Museum at Eldridge Street *(p96)* is a good introduction to Jewish life in the Lower East Side, where food tours and synagogue tours can enhance the experience. For a fuller understanding of Jewish history, visit the Museum of Jewish Heritage *(p81)* and the Jewish Museum *(p225)*. The still active Temple Emanu-El *(p226)* is one of the largest synagogues in the world.

The stunning interior ↑ of the Museum at Eldridge Street

African-American History

Colonial New York City was largely built by African-American slaves, remembered at the African Burial Ground in Lower Manhattan (p87). Harlem remains the most famous black community in America, and its legacy is preserved at the likes of the Schomburg Center (p256), Apollo Theater (p264), Studio Museum in Harlem (p262), and Langston Hughes House (p259). Across in Queens, the Louis Armstrong House Museum (p300) commemorates the legendary jazzman and trumpeter, who lived here with his wife for almost three decades.

← The monument at the African Burial Ground, in Lower Manhattan

FOLLOW IN THE FOOTSTEPS OF NEW YORK CITY'S FOUNDING FATHER

Alexander Hamilton (c. 1755–1804) was born on the island of Nevis, in the British West Indies, but spent most of his adult life in New York. His role as first Secretary of the Treasury is commemorated at the Museum of American Finance (p78). His last home, Hamilton Grange (p258), is preserved north of Harlem, while his tomb lies in Trinity Church cemetery (p79). The 2015 smash-hit musical *Hamilton*, written by Lin-Manuel Miranda, shows at the Richard Rodgers Theatre. Tickets are pricey and competitive; try www.hamilton musical.com/lottery.

Immigrant History

Immigrants have always played a crucial role in the history of New York. The enlightening museum on Ellis Island (p70), which served as an inspection station from 1892 until 1954, provides the best introduction. The story continues at the Lower East Side Tenement Museum (p94), where a restored tenement shows how newly arrived immigrants lived and worked.

↑ Photograph showing a slum on East Broadway, c. 1900, where immigrants lived in close quarters

→ Led Zeppelin tribute concert at prestigious Carnegie Hall

NEW YORK CITY
LIVE!

Although the glittering lights of Broadway are mesmerizing, New York offers countless forms of live entertainment across the city – from music and comedy, to live TV recordings. Better still, there's something to suit every budget, from lavish concerts at Carnegie Hall to free jazz nights.

Comedy Clubs

New York's comedy clubs often feature stand-up artists you'll recognize, with shows every night. Carolines on Broadway (1626 Broadway) is one of the most famous, while Comic Strip Live (1568 Second Av) has been around since 1975, and Dangerfield's (1118 First Av) was founded in 1969. The Gotham Comedy Club (208 W 23rd St) has starred in many shows and movies.

Sydnee Washington performs stand-up at Caroline's on Broadway ↑

Music

You're spoiled for choice when it comes to live music in the Big Apple. Arlene's Grocery (95 Stanton St) offers grungy rock and punk at its Lower East Side venue, which hosted bands such as The Strokes, Lady Gaga, and Arcade Fire in their early years. Prestigious Carnegie Hall *(p181)*, meanwhile, is New York's *grande dame* of concert venues, and primarily hosts classical music (and some pop concerts). New York is one of the cradles of jazz. Major venues include the iconic Blue Note (131 West 3rd St) and Village Vanguard (178 Seventh Av) in Greenwich Village, and Birdland (315 West 44th St) in Midtown, and Nuyorican Poets Café *(p143)*, in the East Village, is a Latino-oriented venue hosting live hip-hop, performance art, live poetry readings, and other theater performances.

← Live jazz performance at iconic Birdland in Midtown

TOP
5 NEW YORK JAZZ LEGENDS

Louis Armstrong (1901–71)
The legendary trumpet player settled in Queens in 1943 and lived here for almost 30 years.

Duke Ellington (1899–1974)
Based in New York City from the mid-1920s, he had a famed residency at the Cotton Club.

Billie Holiday (1915–1959)
"Lady Day" began singing in Harlem jazz clubs in 1929.

Wynton Marsalis (1961–)
Trumpeter and current artistic director of Jazz at Lincoln Center.

Sonny Rollins (1930–)
The saxophonist grew up in Harlem and recorded live at Village Vanguard in 1957.

> 💬 INSIDER TIP
> **Free Live Music**
>
> Arlene's Grocery has free punk karaoke with a live band on Mondays. Sidewalk Café, Saint Vitus, Warsaw, and Otto's Shrunken Head are free indie venues. Marjorie Eliot's has free jazz 3.30–6pm Sundays.

Live Late-Night TV Show Tapings

To experience American TV up close, apply online for free tickets to be part of the "live audience" at shows taped in New York. Comedy Central's *Daily Show with Trevor Noah* is recorded at 733 11th Av, while *The Late Show with Stephen Colbert* tapes at 1697 Broadway. NBC rival *The Tonight Show with Jimmy Fallon* shows at 30 Rockefeller Plaza. *Late Night with Seth Meyers* is also taped here.

↑ Bryan Cranston with host Stephen Colbert on *The Late Show with Stephen Colbert*

Old-School Cocktails

Vintage cocktails can be enjoyed at Dead Rabbit (30 Water St), while the venerable 21 Club is the place for the "perfect Manhattan" *(p209)*. Maxfield Parrish murals adorn the King Cole Bar *(p210)*, the birthplace of the Bloody Mary, and Ludwig Bemelmans' drawings trim Bemelmans Bar *(p225)*. Black-and-white Bar Pléiades is a stylish homage to Chanel *(p225)*.

→

A bartender mixes a cocktail in The St. Regis Hotel's King Cole Bar

NEW YORK CITY FOR
COCKTAILS

New York is cocktail heaven. This is where the Bloody Mary and the Manhattan were invented, and the Cosmopolitan and Martini were perfected. You'll find "mixologists" everywhere, plus a range of ritzy and romanic hangouts; the 21 Club is where Humphrey Bogart took Lauren Bacall on their first date.

Cocktails for Fashionistas

The Fashion Week crowd hang out at Paul's Casablanca *(p118)* and chic Paul's Cocktail Lounge in the Tribeca Grand Hotel (2 Sixth Av). The Standard High Line's (848 Washington St) Boom Boom Room and Top of the Standard are also feted. Apotheke (9 Doyers St) in Chinatown feels like an underground club, while Pegu Club *(p118)* perfected the "Gin-Gin Mule."

A tempting cocktail, prepared with a theatrical flourish ↑

The Japanese Connection

Japanese owned or themed cocktail bars, in the likes of Chinatown and the Lower East Side, often feature sleek, minimalist decor and sake-based cocktails. A fine example is relative newcomer Bar Goto (245 Eldridge St), while hard-to-find Angel's Share (8 Stuyvesant St) has been a candlelit and atmospheric haven since 1993 (tip: look for the unmarked door in Village Yokocho restaurant). Aside from sake, Decibel (240 East 9th St) also serves lychee martinis and "kamikaze" cocktails.

← Chinatown and the Lower East Side both offer creative and exotic cocktails

TOP 5 COCKTAILS WITH A VIEW

Loopy Doopy Rooftop Bar
Conrad New York, 102 North End Av; www.conradnyhotel.com

The Ides
Wythe Hotel, 80 Wythe Av, Williamsburg; www.wythehotel.com/the-ides

230 Fifth
230 Fifth Av; www.230-fifth.com

Roof Garden Café
The Met, 1000 Fifth Av; www.metmuseum.org/visit/dining

Press Lounge
Ink48 Hotel, 653 11th Av; www.thepresslounge.com

The Speakeasy

The city that tried to ignore Prohibition has revived the "speakeasy," often with concealed entrances. Death & Co (p143) has bartenders in bow ties and braces, while a black door marks 124 Old Rabbit Club (124 Macdougal St). The Back Room (102 Norfolk St) serves drinks in teacups.

↑ The Night in Tunisia cocktail at 1920s-themed bar Death & Co, in the East Village

A YEAR IN
NEW YORK CITY

JANUARY

△ **New York Jewish Film Festival** *(mid–late Jan)*
Showcase of international films at the Lincoln
Center exploring the Jewish experience.

FEBRUARY

△ **Westminster Kennel Club Dog Show** *(mid-Feb)*
Some 2,500 canines compete for rosettes and
trophies, watched by puppy-dog-eyed fans, at
Madison Square Garden.

MAY

△ **Sakura Matsuri** *(early May)* This festival entails
events and performances celebrating traditional
and contemporary Japanese culture beneath the
blooming cherry trees of Brooklyn Botanic Garden.

JUNE

National Puerto Rican Day Parade *(second Sun)*
Some two million spectators gather to watch
merrymakers parade along Fifth Av in celebration
of all things Puerto Rican.

△ **Pride Week** *(mid-Jun)* New York's annual
celebration of LGBT+ culture includes New York
City Pride March along Fifth Av (from 37th St and
ending at Greenwich St).

Mermaid Parade *(mid-Jun)* Participants dress like
mermaids and sea creatures on Coney Island.

SEPTEMBER

△ **West Indian-American Day Parade and
Carnival** *(first Mon)* With steel-drum bands
providing an irresistible soundtrack, Brooklyn's
largest parade takes place on Labor Day in
Crown Heights.

Brooklyn Book Festival *(early Sep)* New York's
City's largest free literary event can be found at
Brooklyn Borough Hall.

Feast of San Gennaro *(ten days in mid-Sep)* The
patron saint of Naples is honored with cannoli-
eating contests, games, food markets, and a
boisterous parade in Little Italy.

New York Film Festival *(late Sep–mid-Oct)*
American films and international art films are
screened at the Lincoln Center.

OCTOBER

New York Comic Con *(early Oct)* Fans of comics,
graphic novels, anime, and manga converge in
costume at Jacob K. Javits Convention Center.

Columbus Day Parade *(second Mon in Oct)*
Along Fifth Av, this celebrates Italian-American
heritage and Columbus's first sighting of America.

△ **Village Halloween Parade** *(Oct 31)*
America's largest Halloween celebration, featuring
spectacular costumes and giant puppets, takes place
along Sixth Av (from Spring St to West 23rd St).

MARCH

△ **St. Patrick's Day Parade** *(Mar 17)*
Revelers continue to parade along Fifth Av
ever since Irish militiamen first marched
on St. Paddy's Day in 1762.

Easter Parade *(Mar/Apr)*
Hundreds of New Yorkers promenade up
Fifth Av (from 49th St to 57th St) in
elaborate, flower-bedecked Easter
bonnets on Easter Sunday.

APRIL

△ **Tribeca Film Festival** *(late Apr)*
Established by New Yorker Robert De
Niro, this ten-day event screens more
than 100 films from around the world at
Tribeca Film Center and local cinemas.

JULY

△ **Independence Day** *(Jul 4)* Massive firework
display above either the East River or Hudson
River – head to the waterfront for the best view.

AUGUST

△ **US Open** *(last Mon in Aug/first Mon
in Sep)* The world's best tennis players
compete at Flushing Meadows–Corona
Park, Queens.

NOVEMBER

△ **New York City Marathon** *(first Sun in Nov)*
Around 50,000 runners start on Staten Island
and run through all five boroughs.

Macy's Thanksgiving Day Parade *(fourth Thu)*
This famous parade sees colossal balloon characters, spectacular floats, marching bands, and an
appearance from Santa – head for Central Park
West, from West 77th St to Columbus Circle, and
along Broadway down to Herald Square.

Rockefeller Center Christmas Tree Lighting
(late Nov) The lighting of the Christmas tree that
overlooks the ice rink at the Rockefeller Center
officially begins the city's holiday season.

DECEMBER

△ **New Year's Eve in Times Square**
(Dec 31) Party-goers drink, dance, and
make merry before counting down the
annual ball drop in Times Square.

A BRIEF
HISTORY

The gateway to America for millions of immigrants, New York has always been a cosmopolitan port city where the only constant is change. Beginning with Dutch fur traders, it has morphed into a financial capital, home to iconic skyscrapers and an arts scene that produced Beat poets, jazz, and hip-hop.

The Dutch and the British

New York was a forested wilderness populated by the Lenape people when the Dutch West India Company established a fur-trading post on Governors Island, in 1624. The following year the Dutch named their subsequent Manhattan outpost New Amsterdam; it had previously been called *Manna-Hata*, the Lenape word for "Island of the Hills." Peter Stuyvesant arrived in 1647 to bring order to the unruly Dutch colony, but in 1664 the Dutch let it fall to the British. They renamed it New York, in honor of Charles II's brother, the Duke of York.

1 New Amsterdam as it appeared in 1660.

2 The Battle of Long Island, in Brooklyn, 1776.

3 Statue of George Washington outside the city's Federal Hall.

4 Manhattan's Times Square, photographed in 1917.

Timeline of events

1624
Dutch colony established on Governors Island.

1653
A wall is built for protection from possible invasions; the adjacent street is named Wall Street.

1664
Dutch surrender to the British, who rename the colony New York.

1776
Revolutionary war breaks out; fire destroys much of the city.

The Revolution

New York did not play a large role in the War of Independence. Citizens fled at the prospect of approaching war and, when battle began in the autumn of 1776, a quarter of troops lost their lives in a matter of days. Though George Washington was in command, the campaign was a disaster, ending with the occupation of the city by the British until 1783, at the conclusion of the war. Soon after, New York became the nation's capital. The seat of the federal government was transferred to Philadelphia a year later.

New York in the 19th Century

In 1825, the completion of the Erie Canal (running from the Hudson River to the Great Lakes) opened up internal trade and created a boom in New York. The first waves of immigrants began to arrive in the mid-19th century; some found prosperity, others crowded into slums in Lower Manhattan. When the Civil War broke out in 1861, New York sided with the Union (North) against the Confederates (South). In 1863, a conscription law provoked the draft riots, with impoverished New Yorkers burning buildings, looting shops, and lynching African-Americans.

ALEXANDER HAMILTON (C. 1755-1804)

Hamilton came to New York in 1772 and served under Washington in the Revolution. Later, as first Secretary of the Treasury, he set up the First Bank of the United States and the US Mint. He was killed in a duel. The musical *Hamilton* is based on his life (*p49*).

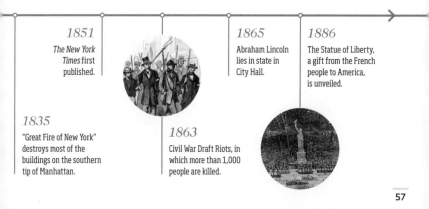

1851
The New York Times first published.

1835
"Great Fire of New York" destroys most of the buildings on the southern tip of Manhattan.

1863
Civil War Draft Riots, in which more than 1,000 people are killed.

1865
Abraham Lincoln lies in state in City Hall.

1886
The Statue of Liberty, a gift from the French people to America, is unveiled.

The Gilded Age

New York's merchant princes grew ever wealthier after the Union won the Civil War, in 1865, and the city entered "The Gilded Age." Cornelius Vanderbilt controlled a vast shipping and railroad empire from here. J.P. Morgan, the banking mastermind, was instrumental in organizing giant financial mergers, and created the country's first major corporations. In 1898, New York City – formerly just Manhattan – assumed its current size by officially intergrating Brooklyn, Staten Island, Queens, and the Bronx.

Between the Wars

In the 1920s, the city entered the Jazz Age in spite of Prohibition, which was a constitutional ban on alcohol. The Harlem Renaissance was propelled by African-American writers like Langston Hughes and Zora Neale Hurston, and music from Duke Ellington, Cab Calloway, and Billie Holiday. The good times ended with the 1929 stock market crash and, as a result of this, the Great Depression. By 1932, one-quarter of New Yorkers were unemployed. With Mayor Fiorello La Guardia's 1933 election, New York began to recover and thrive.

SHIRLEY CHISHOLM (1924–2005)

In 1968, Brooklynite Chisholm became the first African-American woman to be elected to Congress. Barack Obama awarded her the Presidential Medal of Freedom in 2015. A monument to Chisholm will be erected in Prospect Park by 2020.

Timeline of events

1929
Wall Street Crash.

1964
Race riots in Harlem and Brooklyn.

1977
The city lights go out for 25 hours; city suffers looting and civil unrest.

1989
David Dinkins becomes first black mayor of New York City.

2001
Terrorists attack the World Trade Center, causing the Twin Towers to collapse.

Post-War New York City

New York became America's cultural capital in the 1950s, with cutting-edge movements in art and poetry, while the 1960s saw the Stonewall Riots and birth of the Gay Rights Movement. A decade later, punk music developed in the East Village, and hip-hop emerged in the Bronx. In 1975, New York almost went bankrupt, and the tough times continued with the recession of 1989. New York elected Rudolph Giuliani in 1993 – the city's first Republican mayor in 28 years. Giuliani's finest hour came during America's darkest; on September 11, 2001, two hijacked planes were flown into the World Trade Center's Twin Towers.

New York City Today

The city's recovery after 9/11 has been impressive. New skyscrapers grace the skyline, crime figures continue to fall, and tourist numbers are at their highest. This in spite of the financial crisis of 2008 and the flood waters of Hurricane Sandy in 2012. In 2013, Bill de Blasio became the first Democratic mayor in 20 years, and he won a landslide re-election in 2017. Despite the growing economy, De Blasio faces an aging transportation infrastructure, unaffordable housing, and a homeless problem.

[1] Jazz musician Duke Ellington, a key player in the Harlem Renaissance. ↑

[2] The Twin Towers of the World Trade Center after being hit by two hijacked airliners, September 11, 2001.

[3] An aid center set up in response to Hurricane Sandy, 2012.

[4] New York City Mayor Bill de Blasio being sworn into office by former U.S. President Bill Clinton, January 1, 2014.

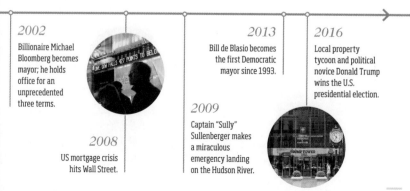

2002
Billionaire Michael Bloomberg becomes mayor; he holds office for an unprecedented three terms.

2013
Bill de Blasio becomes the first Democratic mayor since 1993.

2016
Local property tycoon and political novice Donald Trump wins the U.S. presidential election.

2009
Captain "Sully" Sullenberger makes a miraculous emergency landing on the Hudson River.

2008
US mortgage crisis hits Wall Street.

←
Harold Ramis, Dan Aykroyd,
Ernie Hudson, and Bill Murray
in *Ghostbusters*

A BRIEF HISTORY
ON SCREEN

Parts of New York can feel surprisingly familiar, even for first-time visitors. The city has served a backdrop for thousands of popular movies and TV shows since the 1930s, and it continues to play a starring role on screen.

From Marilyn Monroe's flying skirt in *The Seven Year Itch* and Macaulay Culkin's friendship with Central Park's Pigeon Lady in *Home Alone 2*, to the exterior of Monica's apartment in *Friends* and the Magical Congress building in *Fantastic Beasts and Where to Find Them*, New York City has been a living and breathing movie set since the birth of cinema. Why not pay homage to the city's most iconic scenes, both historic and new, and visit some of its filming locations? We've created a map marking just a few of New York's most famous locations to get you started.

↑ Melanie Griffith on the Staten Island Ferry in *Working Girl*

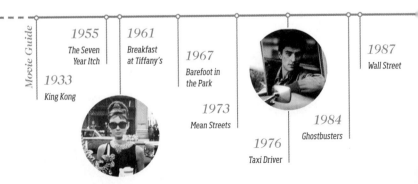

Movie Guide

1933
King Kong

1955
The Seven
Year Itch

1961
Breakfast
at Tiffany's

1967
Barefoot in
the Park

1973
Mean Streets

1976
Taxi Driver

1984
Ghostbusters

1987
Wall Street

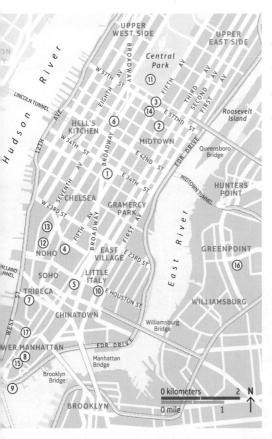

FILMING LOCATIONS

① *King Kong*, Empire State Building

② *The Seven Year Itch*, Lexington Av & E 52nd St

③ *Breakfast at Tiffany's*, Tiffany & Co.

④ *Barefoot in the Park*, Washington Sq Park

⑤ *Mean Streets*, St. Patrick's Old Cathedral

⑥ *Taxi Driver*, Times Sq

⑦ *Ghostbusters*, Hook and Ladder Company No. 8

⑧ *Wall Street*, 21 W 52nd St

⑨ *Working Girl*, Staten Island Ferry

⑩ *When Harry Met Sally*, Katz's Deli

⑪ *Home Alone 2*, Central Park

⑫ *Friends*, 90 Bedford St

⑬ *Sex and the City*, 66 Perry St

⑭ *The Devil Wears Prada*, the King Cole Bar

⑮ *Inside Man*, 20 Exchange Pl

⑯ *Girls*, Café Grumpy

⑰ *Fantastic Beasts and Where to Find Them*, Woolworth Building

SEX AND THE CITY

Cult TV series *Sex and the City* was filmed entirely in New York. Guided tours of the gang's favorite hangouts take in "Carrie's Stoop" (66 Perry St), Steve's bar (Onieals, 174 Grand St), Charlotte's gallery (141 Prince St), and Samantha's pad (300 Gansevoort St). Visit www.onlocationtours.com to book.

1988
Working Girl

1989
When Harry Met Sally

1992
Home Alone 2

1994–2004
Friends

1998–2004
Sex and the City

2006
The Devil Wears Prada; Inside Man

2012–17
Girls

2016
Fantastic Beasts and Where to Find Them

EXPERIENCE

Neon lights illuminating 42nd Street

The Statue of Liberty, backed by Manhattan's skyline

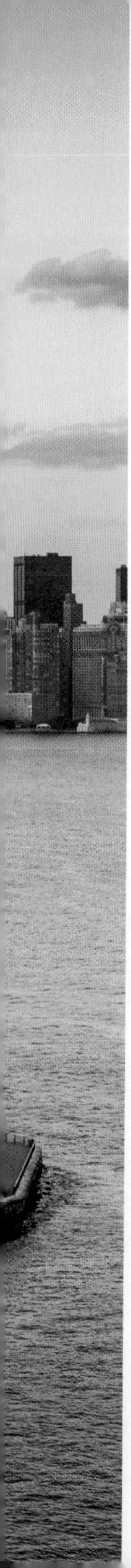

LOWER MANHATTAN

The old and the new converge in Lower Manhattan, where Colonial churches and early American monuments stand in the shadow of skyscrapers. New York was born here in the 1620s and, with the emergence of Wall Street, it has remained at the heart of the world's financial markets. Since the September 11 attacks, there has been startling regeneration: the new One World Trade Center soars 1,776 ft (541 m) above the city, with a spate of modern office towers, hotels, and transportation hubs dotting the area, including the skeletal Oculus. To the north, the federal goverment's courthouses signal the area's civic role, while nearby Seaport District NYC is a restored dock area of stores, restaurants, and old ships.

SOHO AND TRIBECA
p114

C   **D**   **E**

HUDSON ST

BROADWAY

FRANKLIN ST
S Franklin St 1

CHURCH ST

BROADWAY

LOWER MANHATTAN

WEST BROADWAY

PACE PLAZA

African Burial Ground **26**

Rockefeller Park

CHAMBERS ST

WARREN ST

CHAMBERS ST 1.2.3 **S**

CHAMBERS ST A.C **S**

WARREN ST

CHAMBERS

City Hall **24**

MURRAY ST

Park Place 2.3 **S**

PARK PLACE

City Hall R **S**

BROADWAY

City Hall Park

RIVER TERRACE

NORTH END AV

MURRAY ST

WESTSIDE

GREENWICH ST

BARCLAY ST

VESEY ST

Battery Park City and Irish Hunger Memorial **12**

World Trade Center **4**

Woolworth Building **27**

ST PETER'S ST

World Trade Center E **S**

St. Paul's Chapel **10**

PARK ROW

Paulus Hook ←

Brookfield Place **4**

FULTON ST

i

ANN

Fulton St A.C.4.5 **S**

13

Brookfield Place / Battery Park City 🚢

Cortlandt St R **2**

DEY ST **S**

Fulton St **6** J.Z

North Cove Yacht Harbor

National September 11 Memorial and Museum **3**

GREENWICH ST

CHURCH ST

CORTLANDT ST **5**

JOHN ST

Warren St Pier ←

3

Federal Reserve Bank **6**

Battery Park City

LIBERTY ST

LIBERTY ST

Zuccotti Park

CEDAR ST

NASSAU ST

ALBANY ST

THAMES ST

Federal Hall **7**

SOUTH END AV

ALBANY STREET

WASHINGTON ST

CARLISLE ST

Trinity Church **9**

Wall St 4.5 **S**

H u d s o n   R i v e r

9A (WEST ST)

RECTOR PLACE

RECTOR ST 1.R **S**

TRINITY PL

Broad St J.Z **S**

EXCHANGE PL

W THAMES ST

9/11 Tribute Museum **11**

BROADWAY

NEW ST

BROAD ST

14

THIRD PLACE

Cunard Building

BEAVER ST

i

South Cove

SECOND PLACE

Charging Bull **18**

Bowling Green 1 **S**

Bowling Green **19**

FIRST PLACE

13

National Museum of the American Indian **20**

Whitehall R **S**

STATE ST

PEARL STREET

Museum of Jewish Heritage

Skyscraper Museum **14**

Battery Park **17**

WHITEHALL

Pier A Harbor House **15**

Castle Clinton National Monument

SeaGlass Carousel

South Ferry 1 **S**

🚢 Battery Park

US Coast Guard

BROOKLYN - BATTERY TUNNEL

NEW JERSEY

Hudson River

LOWER MANHATTAN

East River

Battery Park 🚢 🚢 BMB

Area of main map

Liberty State Park

Ellis Island **2** 🚢

GOVERNORS ISLAND **5**

Governors Island

Upper Bay

Statue of Liberty **1** 🚢

15

| 0 km | 1 |
| 0 miles | 1 |

↓ *Liberty Island, Ellis Island*

C   **D**   **E**

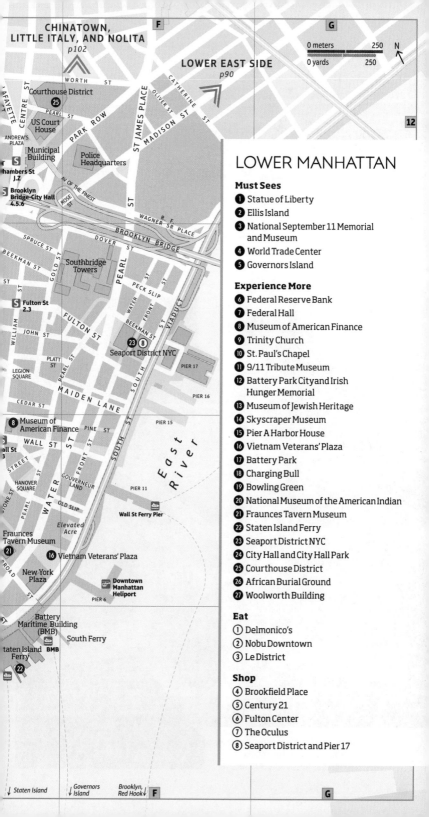

LOWER EAST SIDE
p90

WORTH ST

Courthouse District ㉕

PEARL ST

US Court House

ANDREWS PLAZA

Municipal Building

Police Headquarters

Chambers St J.Z S

Brooklyn Bridge-City Hall 4.5.6 S

ROSE ST

WAGNER SR PLACE

R. F. PLACE

BROOKLYN BRIDGE

DOVER ST

SPRUCE ST

Southbridge Towers

BEEKMAN ST

GOLD ST

PEARL ST

PECK SLIP

Fulton St 2.3 S

WATER ST

FRONT ST

BEEKMAN ST

VIADUCT

FULTON ST

WILLIAM ST

JOHN ST

PLATT ST

PEARL ST

SOUTH ST

Seaport District NYC ㉓ ⑧

PIER 17

LEGION SQUARE

MAIDEN LANE

CEDAR ST

SOUTH ST

PIER 16

Museum of ⑧ American Finance

PINE ST

PIER 15

WALL ST

Wall St S 3

STREET

WATER ST

FRONT ST

HANOVER SQUARE

GOUVERNEUR LAND

OLD SLIP

East River

PIER 11

STONE ST

PEARL ST

Wall St Ferry Pier

Fraunces Tavern Museum ㉑

Elevated Acre

Vietnam Veterans' Plaza ⑯

New York Plaza

BROAD ST

Downtown Manhattan Heliport

PIER 6

Battery Maritime Building (BMB)

South Ferry

Staten Island Ferry

BMB

㉒

↓ Staten Island   ↓ Governors Island   Brooklyn, Red Hook ↓

LOWER MANHATTAN

Must Sees

❶ Statue of Liberty
❷ Ellis Island
❸ National September 11 Memorial and Museum
❹ World Trade Center
❺ Governors Island

Experience More

❻ Federal Reserve Bank
❼ Federal Hall
❽ Museum of American Finance
❾ Trinity Church
❿ St. Paul's Chapel
⓫ 9/11 Tribute Museum
⓬ Battery Park City and Irish Hunger Memorial
⓭ Museum of Jewish Heritage
⓮ Skyscraper Museum
⓯ Pier A Harbor House
⓰ Vietnam Veterans' Plaza
⓱ Battery Park
⓲ Charging Bull
⓳ Bowling Green
⓴ National Museum of the American Indian
㉑ Fraunces Tavern Museum
㉒ Staten Island Ferry
㉓ Seaport District NYC
㉔ City Hall and City Hall Park
㉕ Courthouse District
㉖ African Burial Ground
㉗ Woolworth Building

Eat

① Delmonico's
② Nobu Downtown
③ Le District

Shop

④ Brookfield Place
⑤ Century 21
⑥ Fulton Center
⑦ The Oculus
⑧ Seaport District and Pier 17

0 meters 250
0 yards 250
N

With a height of 305 ft (93 m) from ground to torch, the Statue of Liberty dominates the New York harbor

❶ 🖉 🖵 🛍

STATUE
OF LIBERTY

📍C15 🛆Liberty Island 🚇South Ferry (1), Bowling Green (4, 5), Whitehall (R, W) 🚌M15, M20, M55 to South Ferry 🕐9:45am–4:45pm; hours vary during hols 🌐nps.gov/stli

A gift from the French to the American people, the Statue of Liberty has become an enduring symbol of freedom throughout the world.

The Statue

In Emma Lazarus's poem, engraved on the statue's base, Lady Liberty says: "Give me your tired, your poor, Your huddled masses yearning to breathe free." The brainchild of French sculptor Frédéric-Auguste Bartholdi, and the first sight of immigrants upon arrival in New York, the statue was intended as a monument to the freedom Bartholdi found lacking in his own country. Liberty remains an icon today, and visitors can even climb up to her crown (advance booking essential).

The Ferry

Essential to the Statue of Liberty experience is riding the Statue Cruises Ferry across the harbor. The ferry crosses from Battery Park to Liberty Island every 20–30 minutes, 9:30am–3:30pm; the fare includes entry to Ellis and Liberty islands.

FRÉDÉRIC-AUGUSTE BARTHOLDI

Bartholdi devoted 21 years to making the Statue of Liberty a reality, even traveling to America in 1871 to talk President Ulysses S. Grant into funding it and installing it in New York's harbor. A series of graduated scale models enabled Bartholdi to build this, the largest metal statue ever constructed, with 300 copper sheets riveted together to make Lady Liberty. The statue's frame was designed by Gustave Eiffel.

←

Staten Island Ferry passing the Statue of Liberty in the city harbor

Construction Timeline

1874
▲ Bartholdi starts construction in Paris, beginning with a terracotta model.

1884
▼ Statue is completed and shipped from Paris to New York in 350 individual pieces.

1886
Lady Liberty is unveiled by President Grover Cleveland.

1916
Public access to the balcony surrounding Liberty's outstretched torch is barred for safety reasons.

1986
▲ In celebration of her 100th birthday, Lady Liberty undergoes a $100-million restoration.

2 🔑 🏍 🍴 🖥 🛍

ELLIS ISLAND

📍 C15 🚇 Ellis Island 🚊 Bowling Green (4, 5), South Ferry (1), Whitehall (R, W), then Statue Cruises Ferry from Battery Park 🕐 9:30am–5:15pm daily (extended hours during Federal hols) 🌐 libertyellisfoundation.org

Around 40 per cent of the country's population can trace their roots to historic Ellis Island, the country's immigration depot from 1892 until 1954. The gateway to America is now a remarkable museum paying homage to the greatest wave of migration the world has ever known.

Ellis Island Immigration Museum

During its tenure, nearly 12 million people passed through Ellis Island's gates and dispersed across the country. Centered on the Great Hall, or Registry Room, the site today houses the three-story Ellis Island Immigration Museum. Its history is told with photographs and the voices of actual immigrants, and an electronic database traces ancestors. Outside, the American Immigrant Wall of Honor is the largest wall of names in the world, with more than 12,000 inscriptions. No other place explains so well the "melting pot" that formed the character of the nation.

Visit early to avoid the crowds. Entry to the museum is included in the ferry fare. The ferry generally departs every 20–30 mins but do check online in advance.

↑ The Medical Examining Rooms, where immigrants with contagious diseases could be refused entry

→ Ellis Island, New York City's immigration depot (1892–1954)

The architects were inspired by the French Beaux Arts style.

The ferry office sold tickets to New Jersey.

← Some of the immigrants' meager possessions, held in the Baggage Room

GREAT HALL

Newly arrived immigrants were made to wait for "processing" in the huge, vaulted Great Hall on the second floor. Some days, over 5,000 people would wait to be inspected and registered; if required, medical and legal examinations also took place here. Once the scene of so much trepidation, today the room has been left imposingly bare, with just a couple of inspectors' desks, and original wooden benches.

The railroad office sold onward tickets.

The vast ceiling and large arched windows accentuate the enormity of the complex.

Dormitories were separate for men and women.

Great Hall

The metal-and-glass awning is a re-creation of the original.

Main entrance

Baggage Room

Migrants arrived in America via Ellis Island.

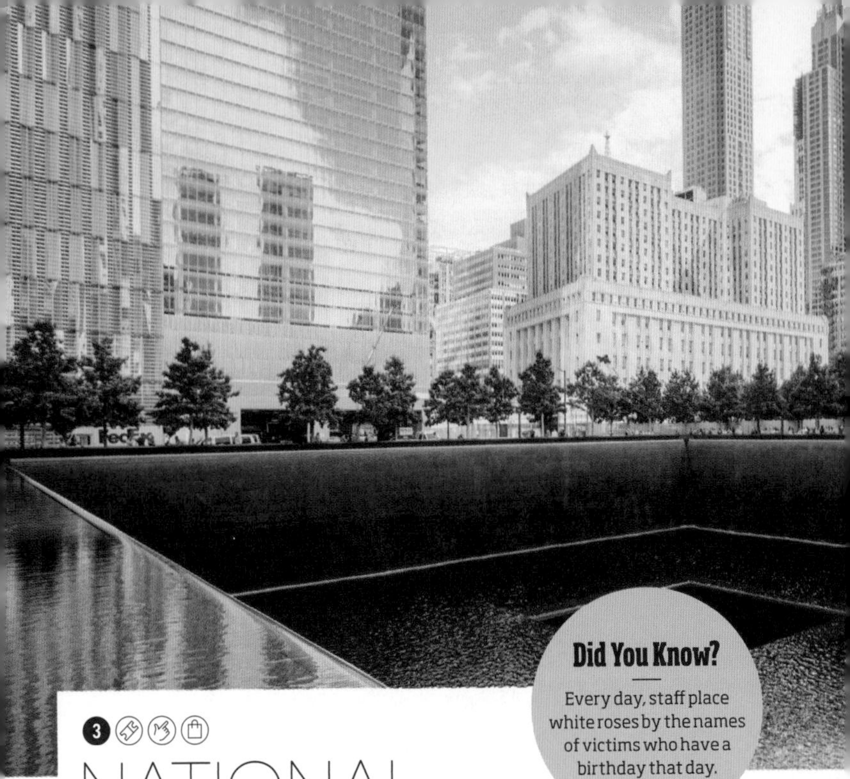

Did You Know?

Every day, staff place white roses by the names of victims who have a birthday that day.

3

NATIONAL SEPTEMBER 11 MEMORIAL & MUSEUM

D13 180 Greenwich St Rector St (R, W), World Trade Center (E) Memorial: 7:30am-9pm daily; Museum: 9am-8pm Sun-Thu, 9am-9pm Fri & Sat 911memorial.org

The events of 9/11 took a heavy toll on New York City. Poignant and dignified, the National September 11 Memorial and Museum together ensure that the thousands of victims who lost their lives in the worst attack on American soil will never be forgotten.

NATIONAL SEPTEMBER 11 MEMORIAL

Designed by Israeli architect Michael Arad, this moving memorial commemorates the terrorist attacks of September 11, 2001. Two vast memorial pools represent the footprints of the original Twin Towers, with 30-ft (9-m-) waterfalls tumbling down their sides. The bronze parapets that encircle the pools display the names of the 9/11 victims, while the surrounding plaza is studded with 400 white oak trees. Also here is a lone Callery pear tree, or "the Survivor Tree," which miraculously survived the attacks. The tree was planted in the 1970s, and suffered grave damage during 9/11. It was replanted in the Bronx, where it slowly recovered, before it was returned to its original spot in 2010.

INSIDER TIP
Museum Tickets

To skip the line and ensure admission into the National September 11 Museum, reserve a timed-entry ticket on the website ahead of time (this can be purchased six months in advance). The National September 11 Memorial itself is free with open access.

←
Reflective waterfalls of the National September 11 Memorial, where the names of 9/11 victims have been immortalized *(inset)*

NATIONAL SEPTEMBER 11 MEMORIAL MUSEUM

The underground 9/11 Memorial Museum at the heart of the complex chronicles the horrific events of September 11. The museum comprises poignant exhibits, personal accounts, voice recordings, and videos. There is also a crushed FDNY fire truck, and the iconic final piece of steel to be removed from Ground Zero, referred to as the Last Column. Unlike the memorial, there is an admission charge.

↑ The crushed FDNY fire truck and Last Column, both of which were removed from Ground Zero, are now displayed in the National September 11 Memorial Museum

SEPTEMBER 11, 2001

On September 11, 2001, two hijacked planes flew into the Twin Towers of the World Trade Center. Millions watched in horror, both on the ground and live on TV, as the towers collapsed. In all, 2,977 people perished at the World Trade Center and in a simultaneous attack on the Pentagon. Osama bin Laden's terrorist network, al-Qaeda, claimed responsibility for the attacks. The 1,368-ft (417-m) tall Twin Towers, designed by Minoru Yamasaki, had been a striking and iconic presence on the New York skyline since 1973.

④ 🍴 🖥

WORLD
TRADE CENTER

📍D13 🚇World Trade Center 🚆Rector St (R, W), World Trade Center (E) 🕐One World Trade Center Observatory: Sep-Apr: 9am-9pm daily; May-Aug 8am-9pm daily 🌐oneworldobservatory.com

A new World Trade Center has risen from the ashes of 9/11 with America's tallest skyscraper, One World Trade Center, at its heart. The new complex features truly innovative architecture, such as the visionary Oculus terminal, and skyscrapers continue to grow into the skies above the city.

One World Trade Center

The centerpiece of the new World Trade Center, and the tallest skyscraper in the United States, One World Trade Center stands at the symbolic height of 1,776 ft (541 m), reflecting America's declaration of independence in 1776. The soaring tower of glass and steel is a modified version of the "Tower of Freedom" designed by Polish-born architect Daniel Libeskind. Supervised by David Childs, the center finally topped out in 2012. Five high-speed elevators, known as Sky Pods, transport visitors to One World Observatory at the top of the building in just 60 seconds. From here, there are mesmerizing views of the harbor, Staten Island, and Manhattan's rooftops.

Entry to One World Observatory includes access to the upscale One Dine restaurant on the 101st floor, featuring seasonally inspired, contemporary American cuisine (reservations are recommended) and the more casual One Mix bar, along with a number of exhibits.

↓ One World Trade Center looms high over the city skyline

1,362 ft

The height of the observation deck; the same height as the Twin Towers (415 m).

←

The Oculus, designed by Santiago Calatrava, opened in 2016. Its two spiky steel ribs resemble a dinosaur skeleton, and its futuristic interior *(inset)* contains a subway station and a Westfield shopping mall.

GREAT VIEW
World Trade Center

For some of the best views of the whole World Trade Center site, head across to the other side of West Street and stand at the entrance of Brookfield Place. For pictures of One World Trade Center itself, walk north along West Street.

⑤ Ⓜ 🍴 🖵 🛍

GOVERNORS ISLAND

📍D15 🏛Governors Island ⛴From Battery Maritime Building, 10 South St 🕐May-Oct: 10am-6pm Mon-Fri, 10am-7pm Sat & Sun 🌐govisland.com

Nowhere in New York is quite like Governors Island. A blend of tranquil green spaces and historic buildings cast in the heart of the harbor – this urban park offers a welcome break from the busy pace of city life.

Reminiscent of a college campus, this 172-acre (70-ha) island has been developed into a public space since 2003. There is a wealth of green spaces in which to lounge in the sun, as well as a breezy 2.2-mile (3.5-km) promenade – you can stroll or cycle right down to the southern tip, dubbed Picnic Point, via The Hills, man-made humps rising 80 ft (24 m) above the harbor. En route, Hammock Grove is an enticing space studded with red hammocks. Many of the island's buildings continue to be restored for the public to enjoy. Near the dock, Fort Jay was the island's original late-18th-century fortification, used to deter the British. Completed on the northwest corner of the island in 1811, Castle Williams is a circular brick and sandstone fort that is nearly identical to Castle Clinton in Battery Park. Up to 1,000 Confederate soldiers were held in its cramped cells during the Civil War, and it served as a prison until 1966.

💬 INSIDER TIP
Getting There and Around

The ferry from the Battery Maritime Building, in Manhattan, arrives at Soissons Landing, where you'll find the visitor center. Ferries also run to the island from Brooklyn Bridge Park's Pier 6, Red Hook, and other locations along the East River. The island can be explored on foot or by bike, and two food courts provide a range of eating options.

1699
▽ Under British rule the island is reserved for the "benefit and accommodation of His Majesty's Governors."

1912
Landfill from the New York subway doubles the size of the island.

2003
▽ Ownership is shared between the City and State of New York, and the National Park Service.

1800
△ New York transfers the island to the US government for military use.

1878
Becomes a major army headquarters and garrison.

↑ Entrance point of green and leafy Governors Island, in New York City's harbor

NOLAN PARK

Nolan Park is home to some beautifully preserved Neo-Classical and Federal-style mansions (once army officers' homes), including Governor's House and Admiral's House (the site of the Reagan–Gorbachev Summit in 1988). Many of these continue to be converted into seasonal art galleries, and studios such as Holocenter House, which specializes in light-based installations.

EXPERIENCE MORE

6 Federal Reserve Bank

📍E13 🏠33 Liberty St
🚇Fulton St (A, C, 2, 4) 🕐1pm
& 2pm Mon–Fri 🚫Federal
hols 🌐newyorkfed.org

Occupying a full city block, this Italian Renaissance-style building is the largest of America's 12 Federal Reserve banks, implementing US monetary policy, regulating financial institutions and maintaining US payment systems. Secured 80 ft (24 m) below street level is 10 per cent of the world's gold reserves – a whopping 7,700 tons of it.

Gold Tours are free and last 45 minutes to an hour. Be sure to make an online reservation at least a week in advance. Arrive at 44 Maiden Lane 30 minutes early with your e-ticket and photo ID (a passport is best). Note that taking pictures and videos is forbidden.

↑ The dome of the Federal Hall's Rotunda, recalling the Pantheon in Rome

7 Federal Hall

📍E14 🏠26 Wall St 🚇Wall St (2, 3, 4, 5) 🕐9am–5pm Mon–Fri 🚫Federal hols 🌐nps.gov/feha

A bronze statue of George Washington on the steps of Federal Hall marks the site where the nation's first president took his oath of office in 1789. Thousands of New

Yorkers jammed Wall and Broad streets for the occasion, roaring their approval when the Chancellor of the State of New York shouted, "Long live George Washington, President of the United States." The present structure, built between 1834 and 1842 as the US Customs House, is one of the city's finest Greek Revival designs. Display rooms off the Rotunda include the Bill of Rights Room and illustrate the Washington connection. Tours take place at 10am, and 1, 2, and 3pm.

8 Museum of American Finance

📍E14 🏠48 Wall St 🚇Wall St (2, 3, 4, 5) 🔄Moving to a new location 🌐moaf.org

In 2018, the Museum of American Finance at 48 Wall Street was devastated by a flood – it is expected to

---

THE NEW YORK STOCK EXCHANGE

Haphazard trading in stocks and shares had become common in New York and so, in 1792, a group of 22 stockbrokers and merchants gathered beneath a buttonwood tree on Wall Street to sign the "Buttonwood Agreement." This formed the trading group that would be called the New York Stock Exchange (NYSE) in 1817.

The NYSE has since weathered a succession of slumps ("bear markets") and booms ("bull markets"), growing from a local marketplace into the world's financial heart. The stock exchange's public viewing galleries were closed indefinitely after 9/11, so it can only be admired from its exterior at 18 Broad Street.

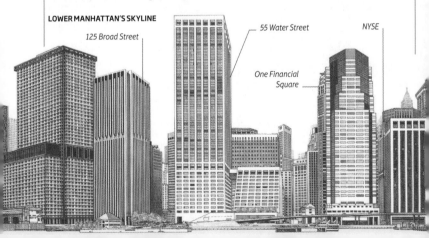

LOWER MANHATTAN'S SKYLINE

125 Broad Street

55 Water Street

NYSE

One Financial Square

↑ Warm hues and historic lines of Trinity
Church amid modern architecture

eventually reopen elsewhere in Lower Manhattan so check the website for the latest in advance to your visit.

The museum unmasks the workings and history of New York's financial district. It covers and explains all aspects of stocks, bonds, and futures trading, with multi-media displays and exhibits explaining all there is to know about the city's financial trading rooms. It owns some rare artifacts, including a bond signed by George Washington in 1792, a gold ingot from the 1850s, and tickertape from the opening moments of the Great Crash in 1929. It also pays homage to Alexander Hamilton – the first Secretary of the Treasury (c. 1755–1804). Hamilton was a financial pioneer in his time, and the museum has a whole section dedicated to his legacy.

9 🚇 🖥️ 🛍️

Trinity Church

📍E14 🏛️79 Broadway at Wall St Ⓢ Wall St (4, 5), Rector St (R, W) 🕐7am–6pm daily 🌐trinitywall street.org

This square-towered Episcopal church incongruously situated at the head of Wall Street is reminiscent of an English parish church, thanks to its English architect Richard Upjohn. Designed in 1846, it was among the grandest churches of its day, heralding America's best period of Gothic Revival architecture. Richard Morris Hunt's sculpted brass doors were inspired by Lorenzo Ghiberti's *Gates of Paradise* at the Baptistery in Florence.

Restoration has uncovered the original rosy sandstone, long buried beneath layers of city grime. The 280-ft (85-m) steeple, the tallest structure in New York until 1890, still commands respect despite its modern, towering neighbors.

Many prominent early New Yorkers are buried in the graveyard, including statesman and Founding Father Alexander Hamilton, steamboat inventor Robert Fulton, and William Bradford, founder of New York's first newspaper in 1725.

← Historic St. Paul's Chapel, survivor of 9/11, surrounded by modern architecture

10

St. Paul's Chapel

📍E13 🏠209-211 Broadway
📞(212) 602-0800 🚇Fulton St (A, C, 2, 3) 🕐10am-6pm Mon-Sat, 7am-6pm Sun
🚫Most Federal hols

A Georgian Classical-Revival gem dating back to 1766, St. Paul's is Manhattan's only extant church pre-dating the Revolutionary War. The church was miraculously untouched when the World Trade Center towers collapsed in 2001, and the chapel acted as a sanctuary for rescue workers at Ground Zero for eight months after the tragic event. Visitors can view touching momentos of this period in the Chapel of Remembrance, at the back of the church. The wonderful piece of art that appears in the center of the windows is the "Glory" altarpiece, designed by architect Pierre L'Enfant (more famously known as the planner of Washington, D.C.).

11

9/11 Tribute Museum

📍E14 🏠92 Greenwich St
🚇Cortlandt St (R, W), World Trade Center (E), Rector St (1) 🕐10am-6pm Mon-Sat, 10am-5pm Sun
🌐911tributemuseum.org

The 9/11 Tribute Museum was established by the September 11th Families' Association, an organization set up by the victims' families, and gives a personal perspective on the attacks. Opened in 2006, while the nearby National September 11 Memorial was under development, the museum stands separately and houses five small galleries.

Exhibits include a model of the Twin Towers and a section on the day of the attacks, with videos and recorded accounts of the survivors. Daily walking tours led by family members, rescue workers, survivors, civilian volunteers, and local residents take in the National September 11 Memorial.

12

Battery Park City and Irish Hunger Memorial

📍 D13 🏠 7 Battery Park City 🚇 Rector St (1)

Construction of the former World Trade Center, in the 1970s, created a million cubic yards of landfill. This was poured into the Hudson to form a neighborhood of restaurants, apartments, sculptures, and gardens. The 1.2-mile (2-km) Battery Park City esplanade offers amazing views of the Statue of Liberty.

Overlooking the Hudson at the end of Vesey Street, the Irish Hunger Memorial is a monument to the Irish who starved to death during the Great Famine of 1845–52. The centerpiece is an abandoned stone cottage and stone walls containing rocks from each of Ireland's 32 counties.

13

Museum of Jewish Heritage

📍 D14 🏠 36 Battery Pl
🚇 Bowling Green (4, 5)
🚌 M5, M15, M20 🕐 10am–
6pm Sun-Tue, 10am–8pm
Wed & Thu, 10am–5pm Fri
(Nov-Mar: to 3pm) 🔒 Jewish
holidays, Thanksgiving
🌐 mjhnyc.org

This museum stands as a memorial to the victims of the Holocaust. The core exhibition, covering three floors, occupies a remarkable six-sided building symbolizing the six million Jews who died under the Nazis and the six points of the Star of

David. The collection begins with the rituals of everyday Eastern European Jewish life pre-1930, moves on to the Holocaust, and ends with the 1948 establishment of the state of Israel and subsequent achievements. Audio tours and lectures are offered – check the website.

14

Skyscraper Museum

📍 D14 🏠 39 Battery Pl
🚇 Bowling Green (4, 5)
🕐 Noon-6pm Wed-Sun
🌐 skyscraper.org

This museum celebrates New York's architectural heritage and examines the historical forces and individuals that shaped its iconic skyline. Exhibits include a digital reconstruction of the ways in which the city has changed and a collection of hand-carved models of Manhattan. Temporary exhibitions analyze various definitions of tall

buildings: as objects of design, products of technology, construction sites, real-estate investments, and places of work and residence.

15

Pier A Harbor House

📍 D15 🏠 22 Battery Pl
🚇 Bowling Green (4, 5)
🕐 11am–midnight daily
(to 2am Thu-Sat)
🌐 piera.com

Facing the harbor on the western side of Battery Park, Pier A Harbor House is an ornate pier dating from 1886, and was originally the headquarters of the New York Harbor Police. After extensive renovation, the structure now contains bars and restaurants. The Long Hall and the Oyster Bar incorporate the original searchlight and restored gauges, while outdoor tables allow guests to admire those fine harbor views over a plate of oysters or a craft beer.

STONE STREET

Tucked away between Hanover Square and Coenties Alley is narrow, cobblestoned Stone Street. Many of its atmospheric Greek Revival-style houses were built in the wake of the Great Fire of 1835, which destroyed much of the area. Today, this is a great place to eat and drink. On summer nights it's a vast open-air beer garden, with bars like Ulysses and restaurants such as Adrienne's Pizzabar covering the street with picnic tables.

Skyscrapers rising high on the southern tip of Manhattan

16

Vietnam Veterans' Plaza

📍E14 🚇Between Water St and South St Ⓢ Whitehall (R, W), South Ferry (1)

This multilevel brick plaza features, in its center, an enormous wall of translucent green glass. The glass is engraved with excerpts from speeches, news stories, and moving letters to families from servicemen and women who died in the Vietnam War, between 1959 and 1975.

17

Battery Park

📍E14 🚇Battery Pl Ⓢ Whitehall St (R, W), South Ferry (1), Bowling Green (4, 5) 🌐nps.gov/cacl

This is one of the best places in the city for views of the harbor. Named for the British cannons that once protected New York, it has more than 20 statues and monuments, such as the Netherlands Monument and memorials to the Korean War, World War II, immigrants, and the Coast Guard. Newer attractions include the SeaGlass Carousel, an aquatic-themed merry-go-round.

Castle Clinton was built just offshore in 1811 as an artillery defense post, but landfill gradually linked it to the mainland. In 1824 it reopened as Castle Garden, containing a theater, beer garden, and an opera house, where Phineas T. Barnum introduced "Swedish nightingale" Jenny Lind in 1850. In 1855 it preceded Ellis Island as the immigration point, and, by 1890, had processed over 8 million newcomers. There's a small exhibit and a section of the original "Battery Wall." Tickets to Ellis and Liberty islands are also available.

18

Charging Bull

📍E14 🚇Broadway at Bowling Green Ⓢ Bowling Green (4, 5) 🌐charging bull.com

At 1am on December 15, 1989, Italian sculptor Arturo Di

↑ Views from Battery Park's wonderful waterfront

Modica (b. 1941) and 30 friends unloaded his 7,000-lb (3,200-kg) *Charging Bull* bronze statue in front of the New York Stock Exchange. The group had eight minutes between police patrols, but managed it in just five. The bull was removed for obstructing traffic and lacking a permit, but public outcry ensued. The Parks Department gave it a "temporary" permit on Broadway, where it remains to this day as the unofficial Wall Street mascot.

Di Modica created the sculpture after the 1987 stock-market crash, to symbolize the "strength, power, and hope of the American people for the future." It took two years, and cost him $350,000.

FEARLESS GIRL AND THE BULL

In 2017, Wall Street's famous *Charging Bull* was challenged by another bronze sculpture dubbed the *Fearless Girl*. Designed by Kristen Visbal, the image of a small girl defiantly staring down the beast quickly became a feminist icon, despite being commissioned as part of a marketing campaign for a gender-diverse index fund. Mayor De Blasio agreed that *Fearless Girl* could stay for 11 months; in 2019, she was moved to a more accessible location in front of the New York Stock Exchange as the crowds milling around the statues on Broadway posed a traffic hazard.

KRISTEN VISBAL'S FEARLESS GIRL

19

Bowling Green

📍E14 Ⓢ Bowling Green (4, 5)

This triangular plot north of Battery Park was originally the city's earliest park, originally a cattle market and later used as a bowling ground. A statue of

Did You Know?

Battery Park is an annual stopover for thousands of migrating birds and monarch butterflies.

King George III stood here until the signing of the Declaration of Independence, when, as a symbol of British rule, it was hacked to pieces and smelted for ammunition. The governor of Connecticut's wife is said to have melted down enough pieces to mold 42,000 bullets.

Beyond the green is the start of Broadway, which runs the length of Manhattan and, under its formal name of Route 9, north to the state capital in Albany.

20

National Museum of the American Indian

📍 E14　🏠 1 Bowling Green
🚇 Bowling Green (4, 5)
🕙 10am–5pm daily
(to 8pm Thu)　🌐 american indian.si.edu

Cass Gilbert's stately US Custom House now houses the Smithsonian National Museum of the American Indian. The outstanding collection of about a million artifacts, along with an archive of many thousands of photographs, spans the breadth of the native cultures of North, Central, and South America. Exhibitions include works by contemporary

Native American artists as well as changing displays drawn from the museum's permanent collection.

Completed in 1907, and in use until 1973, the Beaux Arts Custom House is also a part of the attraction. The impressive facade, with elaborate statues by Daniel Chester French, depicts the major continents, and some of the world's great commercial centers. Inside, the magnificent marble Great Hall and rotunda are beautifully decorated. The 16 murals covering the 135-ft (41-m) dome were painted by Reginald Marsh in 1937, and show the progress of ships sailing into the harbor.

21

Fraunces Tavern Museum

📍 E14　🏠 54 Pearl St
🚇 Wall St (2, 3), Broad St
(J, Z), Bowling Green (4, 5)
🕙 Noon–5pm Mon–Fri,
11am–5pm Sat & Sun
🚫 Federal hols　🌐 fraunces tavern museum.org

New York's only remaining block of 18th-century commercial buildings contains an exact replica of the 1719 Fraunces Tavern where George Washington said a tearful

farewell to his officers in 1783. An upstairs museum displays changing exhibits interpreting the history and culture of early America. George Washington's famous farewell speech took place in the Long Room, which has been re-created in the manner of the time. The adjacent Federal-style Clinton Room is an atmospheric dining room, decorated in rare French wallpaper from 1838. There are galleries of art pertaining to the Revolution, such as the Sons of the Revolution gallery, which gives details about much of the society's history. The restaurant has wood-burning fires and great charm.

The tavern had been an early casualty of the Revolution: the British ship *Asia* shot a cannonball through its roof in August 1775. The building was bought in 1904 by the Sons of the Revolution and its restoration in 1907 was one of the first efforts to preserve the nation's heritage.

Visitors can join an hour-long tour of the museum at 2pm on Thursday, and at 1 or 2pm Friday through Sunday.

22
Staten Island Ferry

9 E15 **A** Whitehall St
S South Ferry (1) **O** 24 hrs
w siferry.com

With unforgettable views of the harbor and city skyline, this remains the city's best ride – and it's free. The ferry was the first business venture of Cornelius Vanderbilt, in 1810, who later became a railroad magnate. It's popular with tourists and commuters alike.

23
Seaport District NYC

9 F13 **A** Fulton St **S** Fulton St (A, C, 2, 3, 4, 5) **O** Museum: 11am–5pm Wed–Sun
w seaportdistrict.nyc

Part of New York's original dockyards, the Seaport District has been gradually restored

> **INSIDER TIP**
> **TKTS Box Office**
>
> The Seaport District's TKTS box office, at 190 Front Street, sells same-day, half-price tickets to Broadway shows – like its counterpart in Times Square, but with a fraction of the lines.

since 1966, with a multitude of restaurants and stores replacing its historic warehouses and fish markets. The former Fulton Market Building now contains several posh boutiques and a branch of luxury movie theater chain iPic Theaters, while Pier 17 has stores, restaurants, and a concert venue. Next door, the refurbished 1904 Tin Building will eventually host a Jean-Georges Vongerichten food market. To enjoy the best views of the Brooklyn Bridge, go to the Heineken Riverdeck on the north side of Pier 17.

The South Street Seaport Museum has a large collection of maritime art and artifacts, plus several historic ships docked nearby. The main galleries, which are based in Federal-style warehouses dating back to 1812, include the permanent "Street of Ships: The Port and its People." This charts the history of the area and the restoration of the *Wavertree*, a British tall ship built in 1885. Museum admission includes guided tours of the *Wavertree* and the *Ambrose*, a lightship from 1908. The museum also owns the 1893 fishing schooner

↑ The *Ambrose* light-ship in Manhattan's Seaport District

Lettie G. Howard and the 1885 cargo schooner *Pioneer*, offering harbor cruises in the summer. Also run by the museum are two historic stores and workshops on Water Street: Bowne Printers at No. 209 and Bowne & Co Stationers at No. 211.

24
City Hall and City Hall Park

9 E12 **A** City Hall Park
S Brooklyn Bridge-City Hall (4, 5, 6), Park Pl (2, 3)
O Tour times vary, check website **w** nyc.gov

A gleaming marble palace, New York's Federal-style City Hall is the oldest in the US to retain its original government function. The interior features a spectacular coffered dome, ringed by ten Corinthian columns and a floating marble staircase that spirals up to the second floor, where the city council

> **To enjoy the best views of the Brooklyn Bridge, go to the Heineken Riverdeck on the north side of Pier 17.**

still meets once a month. Also here is the French Regency-style Governor's Room, with a portrait gallery of early New York leaders. In 1865, Abraham Lincoln's body lay in state here.

Tours of City Hall are free, and generally take place on Wednesday (noon) and Thursday (10 am). Both require advance booking – check the website for all details.

Once a 17th-century communal pasture, City Hall Park has been the seat of New York's government since 1812. An almshouse for the poor stood on this site between 1736 and 1797 and, during the Revolutionary War (1775–83), the British used the nearby debtors' prison to hold and hang 250 prisoners.

25
Courthouse District

🅠E12 🅐Center and Chambers streets 🅢Brooklyn Bridge-City Hall (4, 5, 6)

Grand Neo-Classical buildings dominate New York's courthouse district, the inspiration for many movie settings. The pyramid-topped Thurgood Marshall US Courthouse, designed by Cass Gilbert in 1936, soars at 590 ft (180 m), and continues to serve as a federal courthouse today. The adjacent New York County Courthouse (1927) is a state supreme court, and its elaborate rotunda has Tiffany lighting fixtures and murals by Attilio Pusterla.

Surrogate's Court (1907), on Chambers Street, has an ornate columned facade and figures by Henry K. Bush-Brown, representing life's different stages, from childhood through old age. The ceiling mosaic high above the stunning central hall, meanwhile, was designed by William de Leftwich Dodge, and features the 12 signs of the zodiac.

↑ The Woolworth Building, a stunning monument to an inspired retail giant

26
African Burial Ground

🅠E12 🅐Duane St 🅢Chambers St (A, C), City Hall (R, W) 🅓Visitor Center: 9am-4pm Tue-Sat 🅦nps.gov/afbg

An elegant, black granite monument occupies part of a cemetery that previously lay outside the city. Once the only place African slaves could be buried, the site was discovered by chance in 1991, followed by the exhumation of 419 skeletons. After being examined, the remains were reinterred here in 2003. The nearby visitor center houses an exhibition on the history of slavery in New York.

27
Woolworth Building

🅠E13 🅐233 Broadway 🅢City Hall (R, W), Park Pl (2, 3) 🅓Daily for tours 🅦woolworthtours.com

In 1879, sales clerk Frank W. Woolworth opened a new kind of store, where shoppers could see and touch the goods, and everything cost 5 cents. The chain of stores that followed made him a fortune and changed retailing forever.

His 1913 headquarters set the standard for the great skyscrapers; it was New York's tallest building until 1929. Architect Cass Gilbert's two-tiered design is adorned with gargoyles of wildlife, a pyramid roof, pinnacles, and towers. The interior is rich with sculpted reliefs and a glass-tile mosaic ceiling. Gilbert's sense of humor shows in the bas-reliefs of the founder counting out his fortune in nickels and dimes. Paid for with $13.5 million in cash, the building has never been mortgaged.

Woolworth's went out of business in 1997 but the building is open daily for tours. Book ahead.

ART DECO SKYSCRAPERS

Lower Manhattan boasts some of New York's most iconic Art Deco skyscrapers. The 1931 Bank of New York at 1 Wall Street (654 ft/200 m) has a mosaic lobby. The 1912 Bankers Trust Building at 14 Wall Street (539 ft/164 m) is best known for its step-pyramid top, modeled on the Greek Mausoleum at Halicarnassus. The Bank of Manhattan Trust Building *(right)* at 40 Wall Street was the world's tallest (at 927 ft/283 m) in 1930. Today, it's known as the Trump Building. Stupendous Art Deco wonder 70 Pine Street (952 ft/290 m), completed in 1932 for the precursor of CITGO, is one of New York's most graceful and iconic Art Deco towers.

A SHORT WALK
WALL STREET

Distance 0.6 mile (1 km) **Nearest subway** Wall St
Time 15 minutes

No intersection has been of greater importance to the city's early evolution than the one at Wall and Broad streets. Federal Hall marks the place where, in 1789, George Washington was sworn in as president. The New York Stock Exchange, founded in 1817, is to this day a financial nerve center whose ups and downs cause tremors globally. Its sights of historical importance aside, this is one of the city's greatest business centers and the very heart of New York's famous financial district. The sense of industry is palpable, with bankers pounding the streets on weekdays.

The Equitable Building (1915) deprived its neighbors of light, prompting a new law: skyscrapers had to be set back from the street.

An early 20th-century Gothic skyscraper, Trinity Building was designed to complement nearby Trinity Church.

Built in 1846 in Gothic style, Trinity Church is the third church on this site. Once the city's tallest structure, the bell tower is now dwarfed by skyscrapers (p79).

Wall St subway (lines 4, 5)

Built in 1932, 1 Wall Street has an outer wall patterned to look like fabric, and an Art Deco lobby.

This, 26 Broadway, was the home of the Standard Oil Trust and was designed to look like an oil lamp.

FINISH

START

BROADWAY

EXCHANGE PLACE

NEW STREET

BROAD STREET

NA...

| 0 meters | 100 |
| 0 yards | 100 |

N ↑

The hub of the world's financial markets, the New York Stock Exchange is housed in a 17-story building dating from 1903 (p78).

← The grand exterior of 26 Broadway, once the headquarters of Standard Oil

The Marine Midland Building rises straight up 55 stories. This dark glass tower occupies only 40 per cent of its site. The other 60 per cent is a plaza in which a large red sculpture by Isamu Noguchi, Cube, balances on one of its points.

The Chamber of Commerce is a fine Beaux Arts building of 1901.

The Liberty Tower is clad in white terra-cotta and is in the Gothic style. Built in 1910, it was later turned into apartments.

28 Liberty has the famous Jean Dubuffet sculpture Four Trees located in the plaza.

In the style of a Renaissance palace, the Federal Reserve Bank is a bank for banks. US currency is issued here (p78).

Louise Nevelson Plaza is a park containing Nevelson's sculpture Shadows and Flags.

Locator Map
For more detail see p66

LOWER MANHATTAN

MAIDEN LANE

LIBERTY STREET

CEDAR STREET

WALL STREET

WILLIAM STREET

Wall Street is named for the wall that kept enemies and hostile Native Americans out of Manhattan – the street is now the heart of the city's business center.

Federal Hall was built as the US Custom House in 1842. The Classical building houses a fascinating exhibit about George Washington (p78).

↑ The Federal Reserve Bank looming over the snowy streets of Manhattan

Lower East Side institution, Katz's Delicatessen

LOWER EAST SIDE

Nowhere does the strong ethnic flavor of New York come through more tangibly than in the Lower East Side, where the city's first tenement buildings were raised and immigrants began to settle in the mid-19th century. Here Italians, Germans, Chinese, Jews, Irish, and, more recently, Dominicans established distinct neighborhoods, preserving their languages, customs, foods, and religions. It wasn't until the 1990s that retro clubs, chic bars, creative restaurants, and boutiques revived the Lower East Side, and today it's this melding of cultures that provides most of area's appeal. The Lower East Side Tenement Museum and Museum on Eldridge Street are the key historic attractions, both paying homage to the area's gritty, immigrant past.

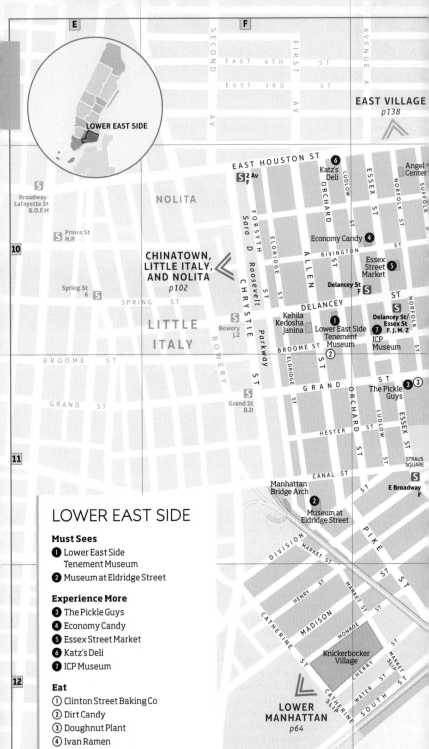

E

F

SECOND AV

FIRST ST

AVENUE A

EAST 4TH ST

EAST 3RD ST

EAST VILLAGE
p138

SECOND AV

EAST HOUSTON ST

S 2 Av
F

Katz's Deli 6

Angel Center

ORCHARD

LUDLOW

ESSEX

NORFOLK

SUFFOLK

S Broadway-Lafayette St B.D.F.M

NOLITA

Sara D Roosevelt

FORSYTH ST

ELDRIDGE ST

ALLEN ST

RIVINGTON ST

Economy Candy 4

Essex Street Market 5

S Prince St N.R

CHINATOWN, LITTLE ITALY, AND NOLITA
p102

10

Delancey St F S

ST

S Spring St 6

SPRING ST

CHRYSTIE ST

Parkway

DELANCEY

Delancey St/ Essex St F. J. M. Z S

NORFOLK ST

LITTLE ITALY

Kehila Kedosha Janina

Lower East Side Tenement Museum 1

ICP Museum 7

S Bowery J.Z

BOWERY

BROOME ST 2

BROOME ST

ELDRIDGE ST

ST

GRAND

ORCHARD ST

The Pickle Guys 3 3

GRAND ST

S Grand St B.D

HESTER ST

LUDLOW ST

ESSEX ST

11

CANAL ST

STRAUS SQUARE

Manhattan Bridge Arch

Museum at Eldridge Street 2

S E Broadway F

DIVISION ST

MARKET ST

PIKE ST

LOWER EAST SIDE

HENRY ST

Must Sees
1 Lower East Side Tenement Museum
2 Museum at Eldridge Street

CATHERINE ST

MADISON ST

MONROE ST

CHERRY ST

MARKET SLIP

Experience More
3 The Pickle Guys
4 Economy Candy
5 Essex Street Market
6 Katz's Deli
7 ICP Museum

Knickerbocker Village

WATER ST

SOUTH ST

CATHERINE SLIP

Eat
① Clinton Street Baking Co
② Dirt Candy
③ Doughnut Plant
④ Ivan Ramen
⑤ Mission Chinese Food

12

LOWER MANHATTAN
p64

E

F

LOWER EAST SIDE TENEMENT MUSEUM

📍F10 🏠97 Orchard St (Visitor Center: 103 Orchard St) 🚇Grand St (B, D), Delancey St (F), Essex St (J, M, Z) 🕐10am-6:30pm Fri-Wed, 10am-8:30pm Thu 🌐tenement.org

New York has long been a gateway for immigrants, and this illuminating museum brings the immigrant experience to life. Here, visitors can explore the interior of a 19th-century tenement home in what was once the city's most overcrowded neighborhood.

The Immigrant Experience

Abandoned in 1935, this tenement building was restored by the museum founders in the 1990s. Crumbling and claustrophobic, the tenements lacked any electricity, plumbing, or heating. There were also no indoor toilets – two external toilets would instead have been shared among four families. Apartments were re-created with period furnishings and artifacts found on site, humanizing the lives of those who once lived between these four walls.

15,000

immigrants from over 20 countries lived at No. 97 from the 19th to 21st centuries.

Tours of the Tenements

Aided by documents, photographs, and the apartments themselves, guided tours (which are compulsory) provide an insight into the carefully researched lives of several families who once lived here. Tickets are available at the nearby visitor center, where a couple of introductory videos (lasting around 20 minutes) offer context. There is also a great bookstore and art gallery.

These tenements on Orchard Street now house the museum ↓

TOP 5 LOWER EAST SIDE TENEMENT MUSEUM TOURS

Under One Roof
See the post-World War II homes of Jewish, Puerto Rican, and Chinese immigrants.

Shop Life
Stop by the 1870s German saloon, owned by John and Caroline Schneider.

Sweatshop Workers
Visit the Levine family's garment workshop, and the Rogarshevsky family's Sabbath table.

Hard Times
Learn about the lives of the German-Jewish Gumpertz family, and the Italian-Catholic Baldizzi family.

Irish Outsiders
Meet the Irish Moore family in 1869.

① Worn parlor of the Rogarshevsky family.

② Actors play the Schneiders at work in their store.

③ Historical photographs of life in the Lower East Side's tenements are shown to a group.

TENEMENTS IN THE LOWER EAST SIDE

New York City's first tenement buildings were constructed in the Lower East Side in 1833, with the development of Little Germany. By 1860, Irish immigrants had started to dominate the neighborhood, but between 1880 and 1920 more than 25 million immigrants, including over 2.5 million Jews, came to the United States. Arrivals in the Lower East Side found low standards of hygiene, abysmal housing, and diseases rife. Reformers like Jacob Riis and Stephen Crane recorded the plight of the city's immigrants in the 1890s, which eventually led to much-needed reform in the 20th century.

❷

MUSEUM AT ELDRIDGE STREET

⦿ F11 🏠 12 Eldridge St **Ⓢ** East Broadway (F), Grand St (B, D) 🕐 10am–5pm Sun–Thu, 10am–3pm Fri **ⓦ** eldridgestreet.org

The Museum at Eldridge Street showcases the Lower East Side's rich Jewish history in one of the city's most beautiful synagogues. The house of worship is still used by New Yorkers, but visitors are welcome to admire its stunning interiors as part of a guided tour.

Jewish History on the Lower East Side

Constructed in 1887, the Eldridge Street synagogue was the country's first to be built by Eastern European Orthodox Jews. It became part-museum in 2007 after a massive restoration project, but remains a functioning house of worship. The facade is an ornate hybrid of Romanesque, Moorish, and Gothic influences in terra-cotta and brick, but the real attraction is the main sanctuary inside. This features stained-glass windows, a spectacular chandelier, richly carved woodwork, and a beautifully painted ceiling. The rose window, an incredible Star of David roundel, looks stunning on the western wall. There are also displays showing the building's state of dilapidation in the 1970s, and tour guides offer entertaining stories about life in the Lower East Side and the synagogue's role in the local community.

←
The ornate exterior of the synagogue, a National Historic Landmark

> 💬 INSIDER TIP
> **Museum Tours**
>
> Note that the main sanctuary of the synagogue can only be visited with a tour guide. Tours of the Museum at Eldridge Street are "pay-what-you-wish" on Mondays, but it's best to arrive as early as possible on the day, as the tours can be over-subscribed. Museum tours begin on the hour throughout the week, starting on the lower level, where the Bes Medrash (House of Study) serves as the current synagogue.

Timeline

1887
▼ Synagogue opened by the Kahal Adath Jeshurun, descended from America's first congregation of Russian Jews.

1918
Famed Talmudist Rabbi Aharon Yudelovitch is hired to serve as the first full-time pulpit rabbi.

2014
▼ Seven years after restoration is completed, the visitor center and permanent exhibit are opened.

1940s
After worshiper numbers dwindle, remaining congregation relocates to the lower level; the main sanctuary is closed.

1986
▲ Eldridge Street Project established to preserve and restore the virtually derelict synagogue.

Did You Know?

The synagogue took ten months to build and 20 years to restore.

↑ A congregation worshipping in the spectacular Lower East Side synagogue

Sunrise over a street in the Lower East Side

EXPERIENCE MORE

EXPERIENCE Lower East Side

EAT

Clinton Street Baking Co

Buzzy brunch spot, known for its blueberry pancakes. Walk-in only.

🅚 G10 🅐 4 Clinton St
🆆 clintonstreetbaking.com

$$$ⓈⓈⓈ

Dirt Candy

Stylish vegetarian food; dinner features two set menu choices only.

🅚 F10 🅐 86 Allen St
🆆 dirtcandynyc.com

ⓈⓈⓈ

Doughnut Plant

Doughnuts with seasonal flavors, from pumpkin to chestnut.

🅚 G11 🅐 379 Grand St
🅓 D Sun 🆆 doughnutplant.com

ⓈⓈⓈ

Ivan Ramen

Sesame noodles, red chili ramen and steamed pork buns.

🅚 G10 🅐 25 Clinton St
🆆 ivanramen.com

ⓈⓈⓈ

Mission Chinese Food

Danny Bowien's creative take on Sichuan food.

🅚 G11 🅐 171 East Broadway 🆆 missionchinesefood.com

ⓈⓈⓈ

3

The Pickle Guys

🅚 G11 🅐 357 Grand St
🆂 Grand St (B, D) 🕒 9am–6pm Sat–Thu, 9am–4pm Fri
🆆 pickleguys.com

The scent of pickles permeates this little section of Grand Street, just as it did in the early 1900s, when Jewish pickle stores filled the area. True to the traditional Eastern European recipe, The Pickle Guys store their pickles in barrels filled with brine, garlic, and spices; this mixture preserves the pickles for months on end. Pickle varieties include full sour, three-quarters sour, half-sour, new, and hot. No chemicals or preservatives are added, and the store operates to strict Kosher rules.

The store also sells pickled tomatoes, pickled celery, olives, mushrooms, hot peppers, sun-dried tomatoes, sweet kraut, sauerkraut, and herring. It is run like a family business, with a friendly, chatty atmosphere, which perpetuates the neighborhood's traditions.

4

Economy Candy

🅚 G10 🅐 108 Rivington St 🆂 2 Av (F) 🕒 10am–6pm Mon & Sat, 9am–6pm Tue–Fri & Sun
🆆 economycandy.com

A Lower East Side landmark since 1937, this family-owned candy store stocks hundreds of varieties of candy, nuts, and dried fruit. Lined with floor-to-ceiling shelves packed with old-fashioned dispensers, the store is one of the few businesses on the Lower East Side that has remained almost unchanged in name and specialty throughout the neighborhood's fluctuating fortunes over 50 or so years.

This is due in no small part to Jerry Cohen's enterprise in transforming his father's "Nosher's Paradise" from a penny candy store to a national company. The store carries treats from all over the world, as well as gum, no less than 47 types of licorice, all manner of chocolates (including fruit and pretzels covered in the stuff), and even sugar-free candy.

→ Customers lining up for traditional pickles in the Lower East Side

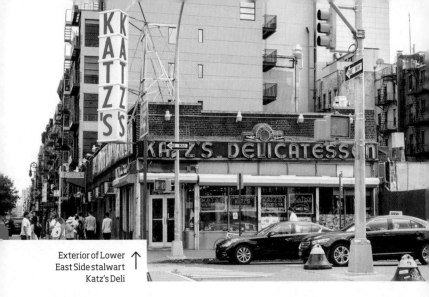

Exterior of Lower East Side stalwart Katz's Deli ↑

 5

Essex Street Market

📍 G10 🏠 88 Essex St
Ⓢ Essex St, Delancey St (F, J, M, Z) 🕒 8am-7pm Mon-Sat, 10am-6pm Sun
🌐 essex streetmarket.com

The original indoor market was created in 1939 by Mayor Fiorello H. La Guardia to bring pushcart vendors together and away from traffic. In 2018, the Essex Street Market moved to the Essex Crossing complex, taking Formaggio Essex, Shopsin's iconic diner, and its other tenants to a shiny building that reflects the upwardly mobile character of the neighborhood. The move added more vendors and two full-service dining options.

 6

Katz's Deli

📍 F10 🏠 205 E Houston St
Ⓢ Delancey St (F), 2 Av (F)
🌐 katzsdelicatessen.com

Perhaps most famous for its starring role in *When Harry Met Sally*, Katz's Deli is a city icon. This Jewish deli opened in 1888.

 7

ICP Museum

📍 G10 🏠 242 Broome St
Ⓢ Essex St, Delancey St (F, J, M, Z) 🕒 10am-6pm Tue-Sun (to 9pm Thu) 🌐 icp.org

All things photography and photojournalism are celebrated at this sleek, dynamic museum, which moved into new digs at Essex Crossing in 2019. Founded by Cornell Capa in 1974, the ICP aims to conserve the work of photojournalists. The collection consists of 12,500 original prints, plus temporary exhibits.

💬 **INSIDER TIP**
Deli Delights

The Lower East Side is famed for its Jewish delis, which are great for affordable, filling food: on East Houston, head to Katz's Deli for pastrami sandwiches, Yonah Schimmel for potato-and-meat *knishes*, and Russ & Daughters for bagels.

LOWER EAST SIDE SYNAGOGUES

Jewish heritage is kept alive in the Lower East Side, in part by its historic synagogues. One of the best is the Museum at Eldridge Street *(p96)*, but the Bialystoker (7-11 Willett Street) is another gem. The Kehila Kedosha Janina Synagogue (280 Broome Street) has served the area's Romaniote Jews since 1927, while the section of East Broadway between Clinton and Montgomery streets is known as Shtiebel Row, home to dozens of storefront *shtieblach* (small Jewish congregations).

The buzzing streets of Little Italy

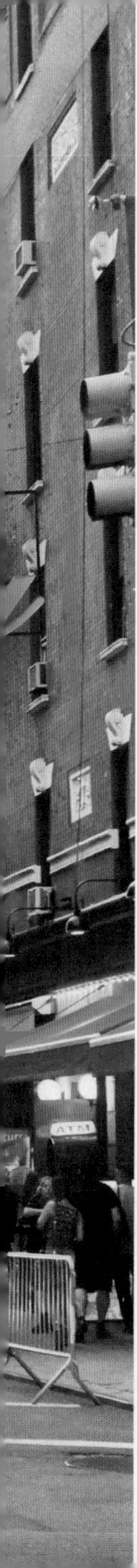

CHINATOWN, LITTLE ITALY, AND NOLITA

Representing multicultural New York City, these communities have lived here for generations, with Chinese immigrants first arriving in the 1850s. Since the 1980s, Chinatown – Manhattan's most densely populated ethnic neighborhood, and the oldest and largest Chinatown in the Western hemisphere – has pushed into Little Italy, now just a narrow strip along Mulberry Street. Both are colorful neighborhoods with numerous places to eat. To the north is Nolita, home to chic boutiques, restaurants, and bars.

GREENWICH VILLAGE
p124

WEST HOUSTON ST

New York
Earth Room

CHINATOWN,
LITTLE ITALY,
AND NOLITA

PRINCE ST

Singer
Building

10

VARICK ST

AVENUE OF THE

SULLIVAN ST

BROADWAY

Spring St S
C.E

SPRING ST

St. Nicholas
Hotel

HUDSON ST

SPRING

AMERICAS (SIXTH AV)

New York City
Fire Museum

SOHO

ST

WEST

BROOME ST

WATTS ST

GRAND ST

GREENE ST

Canal St S
A.C.E

ST. JOHN'S LANE

CANAL ST

CHINATOWN, LITTLE ITALY, AND NOLITA

TRIBECA

WALKER ST

Must Sees

❶ New Museum

❷ Museum of Chinese in America

Experience More

❸ Chinatown

❹ Mahayana Buddhist Temple

❺ Little Italy and Nolita

❻ Basilica of St. Patrick's Old Cathedral

❼ Italian American Museum

❽ Church of the Transfiguration

ST

FRANKLIN ST

S Franklin St
1

CHURCH ST

Eat

① Chinatown Ice Cream Factory

② Chinese Tuxedo

③ Joe's Shanghai

④ Nom Wah Tea Parlor

⑤ Xi'an Famous Foods

⑥ Emilio's Ballato

⑦ Ferrara Café

⑧ Lombardi's

⑨ Pasquale Jones

⑩ Rubirosa

BROADWAY

WORTH ST

BROADWAY

12

DUANE ST

WEST

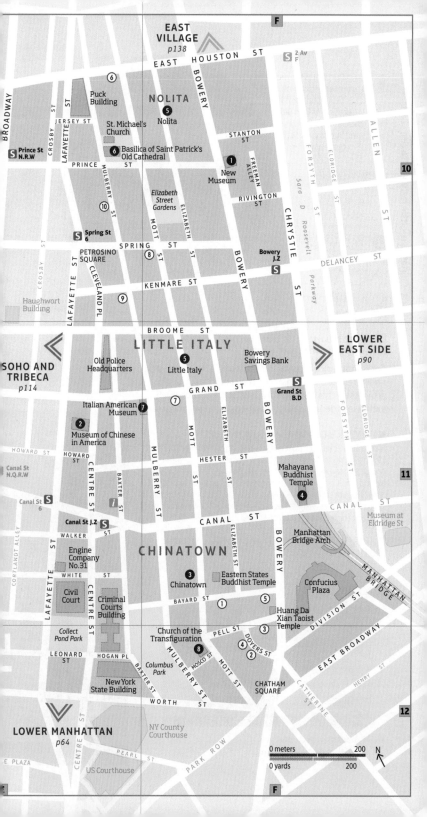

→

Don't miss the museum's rooftop terrace, offering rare panoramas of the Lower East Side. It's open on Saturdays and Sundays during museum hours.

❶ ⊘ ⓜ 🖥 🛍

NEW MUSEUM

📍 F10 🏛 235 Bowery 🕐 11am–6pm Tue–Sun (to 9pm Thu) Ⓢ 2 Av (F) 🌐 newmuseum.org

Contemporary art continues to boom in New York, and nowhere more so than at the New Museum. A work of art in itself, this fittingly futuristic space houses quality exhibitions dedicated to cutting-edge art in all mediums.

New York's Contemporary Art Hub

Marcia Tucker left her post as a curator at the Whitney (p128) in 1977 to found the cutting-edge New Museum of Contemporary Art, or the New Museum for short. Her aim was to exhibit the work she felt was missing from more traditional museums. The New Museum comprises 60,000 sq ft (5,574 sq m) of exhibition space and the rotating collection features a wide range of art, from photographs of 1960s America to abstract installations. The museum showcases both emerging and established artists, including heavyweights Mark Rothko and Roy Lichtenstein.

↑ Visitors stopping to study one of the museum's rotating art displays

INSIDER TIP
Money-Saving Tips

Thursday evening (7–9pm) is "pay-what-you-wish," with a suggested minimum of $2. You can also take advantage of the free 45-minute museum tours (12:30pm Tue–Sun; 3pm Thu, Sat & Sun).

↑ The spectacular seven-story New Museum building, designed by Japanese architects Sejima & Nishizawa and completed in 2007

2 ⬡ ⬡ ⬡

MUSEUM OF CHINESE IN AMERICA

⊙ E11 **⌂** 215 Centre St **S** Canal St (J, N, Q, R, W, Z, 6)
⊙ 11am–6pm Tue–Sun (to 9pm Thu) **W** mocanyc.org

Fascinating displays bring past generations back to life at this compelling museum, which honors the legacy of one of New York City's largest immigrant communities, who first settled here in the 19th century.

💬 INSIDER TIP
Money-Saving Advice

Admission to the Museum of Chinese in America is free on the first Thursday of every month, except for major public and Federal holidays. There are also some concessions. The museum doesn't have a café, but it's not far from Chinatown, which has lots of options for an affordable bite to eat.

New York City's Tribute to Chinese-Americans

Visitors can learn about the Chinese-American experience, from the 19th century to the present day, at the engaging Museum of Chinese in America. Issues explored include the Chinese Exclusion Act of 1882, which forbade Chinese workers entry for ten years, and the immigration quotas imposed in the early 20th century, such as the 1924 National Origins Provision (N.O.P.), which restricted entry even further. Via artifacts and multimedia displays, the museum flags various historical and cultural phases in the Chinese-American narrative – from the emergence of "Chop suey" restaurants and so-called "Yellowface" movies in the 1930s, to the evolution of identity for second-generation Chinese-Americans in the 1960s. The museum itself was designed by Maya Lin, who is best known for her creation of the Vietnam Memorial in Washington, D.C. The museum was born from a community-based organization that sought to develop a better understanding of the city's Chinese-American community.

↑ Early-risers awaiting entry into the Museum of Chinese in America

200,000

Chinese immigrants arrived in 1965 after the N.O.P. was abolished.

← Cabinets of artifacts inside the Museum of Chinese in America

EXPERIENCE MORE

❸

Chinatown

❾ F11 **⌂ Streets around Mott St** **Ⓢ Canal St (N, Q, R, W, 6)** **ⓦ explore chinatown.com**

More than 100,000 Chinese-Americans live in this vibrant neighborhood, one of the biggest and oldest Chinese districts in the West. Since the 1850s, Chinese immigrants have been settling in this part of New York, which today attracts visitors looking to sample the neighborhood's cuisine, visit its galleries, trawl the countless curio stores, and partake in the neighborhood's colorful festivals.

The neighborhood is divided by the east–west Canal Street, with Mott Street cutting north–south. The streets around, which include Pell, Bayard, Doyers, and the Bowery, are lined by fresh fish and fruit stands, dim sum restaurants, souvenir and antiques shops, and tea-and-rice stores.

On the corner of Pell Street and the Bowery lies Huang Da Xian Temple, one of the few remaining Taoist temples, with a converted storefront. Farther along Pell Street, No. 16 is the headquarters of the Hip Sing Tong, once a secret society. During an attack in 1924, 70 people were killed when On Leong Tong, a rival criminal fraternity, attacked the building. Halfway along Pell is tiny, crooked Doyers Street, once known as the "Bloody Angle" for its role as a battleground during the Tong Wars in the early 1900s.

To glimpse another side of Chinatown, step into the incense-scented Eastern States Buddhist Temple at 64 Mott Street, where offerings are piled up before tiny golden Buddhas. The temple is open daily.

EAT

Chinatown Ice Cream Factory
Asian flavors, from black sesame and taro, to green tea and lychee.

❾ F11 **⌂ 65 Bayard St** **ⓦ chinatownicecream factory.com**

$⑤$⑤

Chinese Tuxedo
Hip and contemporary Cantonese restaurant with inventive cocktails.

❾ F12 **⌂ 5 Doyers St** **⌚ Lunch** **ⓦ chinese tuxedo.com**

$$⑤

Joe's Shanghai
Shrine to American-Chinese cuisine (think deep-fried chicken) and "soup dumplings."

❾ F12 **⌂ 9 Pell St** **ⓦ joeshanghai restaurants.com**

$$⑤

Nom Wah Tea Parlor
Elegant and old-fashioned dim sum spot dating back to 1920.

❾ F12 **⌂ 13 Doyers St** **ⓦ nomwah.com**

$$⑤

Xi'an Famous Foods
Spicy specialties from northwest China, such as noodles with cumin-spiked lamb.

❾ F11 **⌂ 45 Bayard St** **ⓦ xianfoods.com**

$⑤⑤

4

Mahayana Buddhist Temple

📍 F11 🏛 133 Canal St
Ⓢ Canal St (N, Q, R, W, 6)
🕐 8:30am–6pm daily
🌐 mahayana.us

Larger than its counterpart on Mott Street, this opulent Buddhist temple, at the foot of the Manhattan Bridge, was built by the Ying family, who are from the city of Ningbo, in China. Constructed in 1997, the temple boasts classic Chinese designs, and the main altar contains a massive gold idol of the Buddha. Bathed in blue neon lighting, and surrounded by candles, the statue is 16 ft (5 m) tall. The 32 plaques along the walls tell the story of Buddha's life. A small shrine to Guanyin, the Chinese Goddess of Mercy, stands in the entrance hall. There is a small store upstairs that sells statues, books, and other knickknacks.

On the other side of the Bowery, the former Citizens Savings Bank is a local landmark, with a Neo-Byzantine bronze dome that was completed in 1924. The building now functions as a branch of HSBC.

TEN REN'S TEA

Founded in Taiwan back in 1953, Ten Ren's Tea remains Manhattan's premier tea merchant. The branch at 75 Mott Street opened in 1984 and quickly developed a cult following. Sample the huge array of teas while you shop, from expensive oolongs and pu'erh teas to simple green varieties. The highly prized Dongfang, or "Oriental Beauty," tea is a heavily fermented oolong with a sweet hint of honey.

↑ The impressive, golden Buddha at the Mahayana Buddhist Temple

5

Little Italy and Nolita

📍 F10 & F11 🏛 Streets around Mulberry St
Ⓢ Canal St (N, Q, R, W, 6)
🌐 littleitalynyc.com

The most exciting time to visit these neighborhoods is during the 11-day Festa di San Gennaro, in mid-September. Italians from around the city meet at Mulberry Street for a wild celebration in honor of the patron saint of Naples. The street is full of stands and Italian snack vendors, and there is plenty of lively music and dancing.

Many of Little Italy's restaurants offer simple, rustic food served in friendly surroundings at reasonable prices. Some original cafés and *salumerias* (specialty food stores) still survive, such as Ferrara's at 195 Grand Street. Nolita, meanwhile, is home to stylish boutiques and vintage stores frequented by well-heeled New Yorkers.

Originally inhabited by the Irish, Little Italy and Nolita (or NoLita, shortened from "north of Little Italy") saw an influx of Italian immigrants in the 19th century. Natives of Campania and Naples settled on Mulberry Street, while the Sicilians stayed on Elizabeth Street. Mott Street was divided between people

EAT

Emilio's Ballato

Old-school Italian, with a low-key, clubby atmosphere. Popular with celebrities.

📍 E10 🏛 55 East Houston St 📞 (212) 274-8881 🕐 L Sat, L Sun

$$$⑤

Ferrara Café

Traditional Italian café, around since 1892, serving cheesecake, cannoli, and gelato.

📍 F11 🏛 195 Grand St
🌐 ferraranyc.com.

⑤$$

Lombardi's

America's oldest pizzeria (1905) offers classic margherita and clam pizzas.

📍 F10 🏛 32 Spring St
🌐 firstpizza.com

$$⑤

Pasquale Jones

Modern diner known for wood-burning ovens, pasta, and pizzas.

📍 E10 🏛 187 Mulberry St 🕐 L Mon–Thu
🌐 pasqualejones.com

$$⑤

Rubirosa

A contemporary take on classic red-sauce and pizza restaurants.

📍 E10 🏛 235 Mulberry St 🌐 rubirosanyc.com.

$$⑤

→

Little Italy's colorful streets, lined with numerous restaurants from Calabria and Puglia. However, after World War II, many Italians relocated to the suburbs and today the district is much smaller – Mulberry Street is the only remaining Italian territory. For more about the history of the area, visit the Italian-American Museum, in the building that formerly housed the Banca Stabile.

⑥ Basilica of St. Patrick's Old Cathedral

♀ E10 🏛 Corner of Mott and Prince sts Ⓢ Prince St (N, R, W) 🕐 8am–12:30pm & 3:30–6pm Thu-Tue ⓦ oldcathedral.org

The first St. Patrick's on this site was consecrated in 1815. It was destroyed by fire in the 1860s, but was rebuilt much as it is today. When the archdiocese transferred the See to the new St. Patrick's Cathedral uptown, Old St. Patrick's became the local parish church, and it has flourished with a constantly changing multicultural congregation.

Below the church are the vaults containing the remains of, among others, one of New York's most famous families of restaurateurs, the Delmonicos. Pierre Toussaint was also buried here, but in 1990 his remains were moved from the graveyard beside the church to a more prestigious burial place in a crypt in St. Patrick's Cathedral. Born a slave in Haiti in 1766, Toussaint was brought to New York, where he lived as a free man and became a prosperous wig-maker. He was later devoted to caring for the poor and tending cholera victims, and used the money he had made to build an orphanage.

⑦ 🔯 🏛 Italian American Museum

♀ E11 🏛 155 Mulberry St at Grand St Ⓢ Canal St (J, N, Q, R, W, Z, 6) 🕐 For renovation until early 2020 ⓦ italianamericanmuseum.org

Housed in the 1885 Banca Stabile premises (still containing the old bank vault), this museum chronicles the history of Little Italy through original artifacts, rare photographs, and documents, including a 1914 extortion note from a "Black Hand" mafia member. One particular display pays tribute to Giuseppe Petrosino, one of the first Italian-American NYPD officers, murdered working on a mafia case in Sicily in 1909.

The museum is currently undergoing renovation and will open again in early 2020 with additional exhibition and performance space.

⑧ Church of the Transfiguration

♀ F12 🏛 29 Mott St Ⓢ Canal St (N, Q, R, W, 6) 🕐 2–5pm Sat ⓦ transfigurationnyc.org

Built as a Lutheran church in 1801, and sold to the Roman Catholic Church of the Transfiguration in 1853, this Georgian-style stone church is typical of the influence of successive influxes of immigrants in New York. The church has changed with the nationalities of the community it serves, first Irish, then Italian (the plaque honoring those killed in World War I lists mainly Italian names), and now Chinese. As the focal point of today's Chinese Roman Catholic community, it offers classes to help newcomers and holds Mass in Cantonese, English, and Mandarin.

A SHORT WALK
LITTLE ITALY AND CHINATOWN

Distance 1.25 mile (2 km) **Nearest subway** Canal St
Time 25 minutes

Manhattan's largest and most colorful neighborhood is Chinatown, which is growing so rapidly that it is running into nearby Little Italy as well as the Lower East Side. Streets here teem with grocery stores, gift shops, and hundreds of Chinese restaurants; even the plainest offering delicious food and tempting aromas. What is left of Little Italy can be found at Mulberry and Grand streets, where old-world flavor abounds.

↑ Vibrant storefronts in New York's lively Chinatown

Canal St subway (lines R, N, Q, W, 6) **START**

The market stalls on Canal Street have a wide range of bargains, including clothes and fresh produce.

Home to a thriving – and still expanding – community of Chinese immigrants, this neighborhood is famous for its restaurants and hectic street life (p109).

Once run-down, Columbus Park now fills with local residents playing mahjong.

Bloody Angle, where Doyers Street turns sharply, was the gruesome site of many gangland ambushes during the 1920s.

Chatham Square has a memorial dedicated to the Chinese-American war dead, and to Lin Zexu, a Qing dynasty official, revered for his crackdown on the opium trade.

FINISH

The dome of the Old Police Headquarters towers over the whole area. In 1973, the police moved out of this Baroque civic building; 10 years later, the building was turned into apartments.

Locator Map
For more detail see p104

CHINATOWN, LITTLE ITALY, AND NOLITA

The tantalizing scents of Italy still waft from the traditional restaurants and bakeries of Little Italy, once home to thousands of immigrants (p110).

Umbertos Clam House, known as the place where Mafia boss Joey Gallo was shot in 1972, once occupied this location on Mulberry Street.

Stanford White designed Bowery Savings Bank in 1894. Today it hosts private functions.

MOTT STREET

STREET

HESTER STREET

The Eastern States Buddhist Temple at 64 Mott Street contains over 100 golden Buddhas.

BOWERY

CHRYSTIE STREET

ELDRIDGE STREET

↑ The Old Police Headquarters, now luxury apartments

0 meters 100
0 yards 100
N ↑

Confucius Plaza is marked by sculptor Liu Shih's monument to the Chinese philosopher.

Built in 1887, the Museum at Eldridge Street was the first synagogue built in the U.S. by European Jews (p96).

Attractive fire escapes line apartments in SoHo

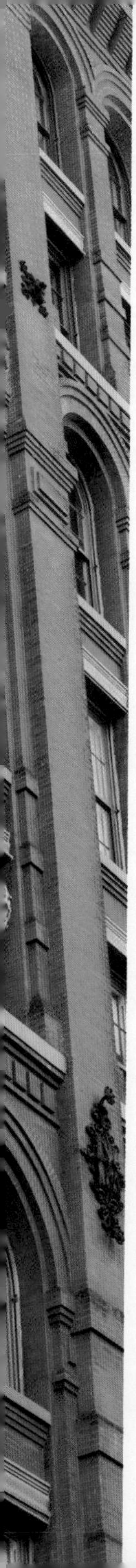

SOHO AND TRIBECA

Stores, eateries, and architecture have transformed these formerly industrial districts. SoHo was threatened with demolition back in the 1960s until preservationists drew attention to its rare and historic cast-iron architecture. The district was saved, and by the 1980s SoHo had developed its own vibrant art scene. It now serves as an enormous outdoor shopping mall, scattered with bars and bistros. Neighboring Tribeca, meanwhile, was once a wholesale food district. When Robert De Niro set up his Tribeca Film Center in 1988, the area became one of the hottest neighborhoods in the city, attracting galleries, boutiques, and restaurants. The Tribeca Film Festival followed in 2002.

SOHO AND TRIBECA

SOHO AND TRIBECA

Experience

❶ Children's Museum of the Arts
❷ New York Earth Room
❸ New York City Fire Museum
❹ 56 Leonard
❺ Hudson River Park
❻ Hook and Ladder Company No. 8
❼ Chocolate Museum and Experience with Jacques Torres
❽ Drawing Center
❾ Leslie-Lohman Museum of Gay and Lesbian Art

Eat

① Balthazar
② Le Coucou
③ The Odeon
④ Grand Banks

Drink

⑤ Paul's Casablanca
⑥ Pegu Club

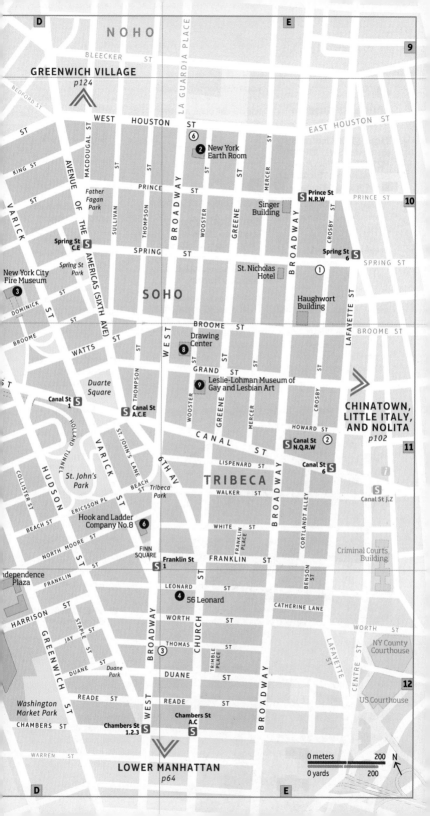

EXPERIENCE

➊
Children's Museum of the Arts

⊙ D10 **⌂** 103 Charlton St **Ⓢ** Houston St (1) **🚌** M20, M21 **◷** Noon–5pm Mon & Fri, noon–6pm Thu, 10am–5pm Sat & Sun **ⓦ** cmany.org

Founded in 1988, this innovative museum aims to make the most of children's artistic potential by providing plenty of hands-on activities, sing-alongs, workshops, and performances. Children under 13 can busy themselves with paint, glue, paper, and other messy materials to create their own drawings and sculptures. For inspiration, displays of work by local artists are exhibited alongside examples of children's art from across the world. Kids can play around in the dressing-up room and the ball pond, and the museum also hosts a varied program of events appealing to children and families.

➋
New York Earth Room

⊙ E10 **⌂** 141 Wooster St **Ⓢ** Prince St (N, R, W) **◷** Noon–3pm & 3:30–6pm Wed–Sun **◷** Mid-Jun–mid-Sep **ⓦ** diaart.org/sites/main/earthroom

Of the three Earth Rooms created by conceptual artist Walter De Maria (1935–2013), this is the only one still in existence. Commissioned by the Dia Art Foundation in 1977, the interior earth

DRINK

Paul's Casablanca
Opened by Paul Sevigny, this cocktail bar and nightclub has a loyal following among celebs and fashion icons. Open from 10pm until 4am, the interior is decked out like a Moroccan palace, with mosaic tiles, lanterns, and leather beanbag chairs. Staff wear kaftans and DJs spin a different genre every night, from rock through to hip hop.

⊙ D10 **⌂** 305 Spring St **◷** Mon, Wed **ⓦ** pauls casablanca.com

Pegu Club
Elegant cocktail lounge, themed around the original Pegu Club in Burma, a British colonial bar built in the 1880s. Like the original, this lounge serves the gin-based "Pegu Club" cocktail as well as perfecting the Gin-Gin Mule, which consists of ginger beer with Tanqueray gin, fresh mint, and lime juice. Open from 5pm until the very early hours.

⊙ E10 **⌂** 77 Houston St **ⓦ** peguclub.com

←

Multi-million dollar penthouses, occupying the uppermost floors of 56 Leonard, tower over Tribeca

Cyclists and walkers enjoying the view along Hudson River Park

Did You Know?

The majority of Hudson River Park's total area is located in the river itself.

sculpture consists of 280,000 lb (127,000 kg) of dirt piled 22 inches (56 cm) deep in a 3,600-sq-ft (334-sq-m) room. *The Broken Kilometer*, another sculpture by De Maria, can be seen at 393 West Broadway. It is composed of 500 solid brass rods arranged in five parallel rows.

3

New York City Fire Museum

📍 D10 🏠 278 Spring St 🚇 Spring St (6) 🕙 10am–5pm daily 🚫 Federal hols 🌐 nycfiremuseum.org

This museum is housed in a Beaux Arts-style 1904 firehouse. New York City's unsurpassed collection of firefighting equipment and memorabilia from the 18th century to 1917 includes scale models, bells, and hydrants. Upstairs, fire trucks are neatly lined up for an 1890 parade. An interactive fire simulation, available for groups, gives an insight into firefighting. The museum's first floor features an exhibition on 9/11, filled with tributes.

4 56 Leonard

📍 E12 🏠 56 Leonard St 🚇 Franklin St (1) 🕙 Closed to the public 🌐 56leonard tribeca.com

Completed in 2016, and a new addition to Manhattan's ever-evolving skyline, 56 Leonard is composed of a jaw-dropping stack of cantilevered glass blocks. Tribeca's tallest building has been dubbed the "Jenga Building" by local media, thanks to the stack of units designed by Swiss architects Herzog & de Meuron. The interior of the 821-ft (250-m) condominium building is private but you can visit the giant, bean-like object at its base. This highly polished pod by British sculptor Anish Kapoor is similar to his "Cloud Gate" in Chicago.

5 Hudson River Park

📍 C10 🚇 Houston, Canal or Franklin sts (1) 🌐 hudsonriverpark.org

Immediately beyond West Side Highway is the Hudson River Park, a landscaped promenade that stretches north toward Chelsea and Midtown. Visitors can walk south to the tip of the island along the shady Battery Park City Esplanade all the way to Battery Park. The once-decaying piers and wharves have been transformed, with fountains, gardens, dog parks, and tennis courts. Pier 25 features Grand Banks, an oyster bar on an old sailing ship, mini-golf, and beach volleyball, plus snack stands.

EAT

Balthazar

This brasserie's buzzy atmosphere is hard to resist. Keith McNally's restaurant features ornate Parisian decor and the classics - moules frites, oysters, and Bordeaux wine.

📍E10 🏠80 Spring St
🌐balthazarny.com

$$$

Le Coucou

Highly acclaimed French restaurant featuring oak tables, contemporary chandeliers and French antiques. Great spot for breakfast - don't miss the pancakes.

📍E11 🏠138 Lafayette St 🌐lecoucou.com

$$$

The Odeon

Famously appearing in Jay McInerney's *Bright Lights, Big City*, this iconic bistro offers all the French and American standards.

📍E12 🏠145 West Broadway 🌐theodeon restaurant.com

$$$

Grand Banks

Indulge on oysters and cocktails aboard the 1942 wooden schooner *Sherman Zwicker*, which is now a docked restaurant. Get there before 5pm - limited online reservations.

📍C12 🏠Pier 25, North Moore St 🕐Mid-Apr-Oct only 🕐L Mon-Tue 🌐grandbanks.org

$$$

↑ Hook and Ladder Company No. 8 firehouse, a popular draw for fans of the *Ghostbusters* movies

⑥ Hook and Ladder Company No. 8

📍D11 🏠14 North Moore St 🚇Franklin St (1) 🕐To the public

This handsome fire station's claim to fame is revealed by the ghost logos painted on the sidewalk outside. The station starred as the base of the iconic *Ghostbusters* films of the 1980s, and was reportedly chosen by writer and actor Dan Aykroyd, who liked the 1903 Beaux Arts building. The building also featured in the 2016 remake, with its all-female cast.

In real life, Hook and Ladder Company No. 8 played a major role in the rescue efforts following the terrorist attack of September 11, 2001. Today it remains a working firehouse of the New York Fire Department, so it can only be viewed from the outside.

⑦ Chocolate Museum and Experience with Jacques Torres

📍D10 🏠350 Hudson St 🚇Houston St (1) 🕐10am-5pm Wed-Sun 🌐mrchoco late.com/pages/museum

New York's first chocolate museum opened in 2017, next to one of Jacques Torres' beloved cafés and chocolate shops. The museum features exhibits tracing the history of chocolate, starting with its Mesoamerican roots, but it's the enticing demonstrations held throughout the day (and plenty of free samples) that make visiting a real treat.

Born in the small Provençal town of Bandol, France, chocolatier Jacques Torres (aka "Mr Chocolate") came to New York in 1988 and opened his first chocolate factory in 2000.

Drawing Center

⊙ E11 ⌂ 35 Wooster St
Ⓢ Canal St (A, C, E, N, Q, R, W)
⊙ Noon–6pm Wed–Sun (to 8pm Thu) Ⓦ drawing center.org

SoHo's legacy of fine art galleries is maintained here at the Drawing Center, with a primary focus on changing exhibitions of historical and contemporary drawings. Founded in 1977, the center has featured masters such as Marcel Duchamp and Richard Tuttle, as well as emerging artists. Each year an artist is invited to create a wall drawing in the gallery's main entryway and stairwell. Inka Essenhigh's *Manhattanhenge* was on display until mid-2019.

———————————

Leslie-Lohman Museum of Gay and Lesbian Art

⊙ E11 ⌂ 26 Wooster St
Ⓢ Canal St (A, C, E, F)
⊙ Noon–6pm Wed–Sun (to 8pm Thu) Ⓦ leslie lohman.org

Founded by J. Frederic "Fritz" Lohman and Charles W. Leslie in 1990, this innovative museum has over 30,000 objects, spanning over three centuries of LGBT+ art. Exhibitions have included a retrospective on the work and impact of artist and filmmaker Barbara Hammer, while the permanent collection contains works by Berenice Abbott, David Hockney, Andy Warhol, Jean Cocteau, Robert Mapplethorpe, and many others.

Did You Know?

———

Though Hook and Ladder No. 8 featured in 1984's *Ghostbusters*, interior filming took place at a firehouse in L.A.

CAST-IRON ARCHITECTURE

SoHo is noted for its striking cast-iron architecture, a style that dominated construction here from 1860 to the turn of the 20th century. Molding components from iron meant cheaper and faster construction than buildings of brick or stone. Heavy iron crossbeams could carry the weight of the floors, allowing greater space for windows and high ceilings. In addition, almost any style or decoration could be cast in iron, painted or plastered, and bolted to the front of a building to resemble marble. Some of the best examples are on Greene Street, where No. 72–76 is known as the "King of Greene Street," and No. 28–30, the "Queen." The Haughwout Building, at 492 Broadway, was erected in 1857 and the Venetian-style palazzo is considered the quintessential cast-iron building. The charmingly ornate Little Singer Building, at 561–563 Broadway, was designed by Ernest Flagg, at the very end of the cast-iron era, in 1904.

A SHORT WALK

SOHO CAST-IRON HISTORIC DISTRICT

Distance 0.16 mile (1 km) **Nearest subway** Canal St, Prince St
Time 15 minutes

The largest concentration of cast-iron architecture in the world survives in the area between West Houston and Canal streets. The heart of the district is Greene Street, where 50 buildings erected between 1869 and 1895 are found on five cobblestoned blocks. Most of their intricately designed cast-iron facades are in the Neo-Classical Revival style. Now they are rare works of industrial art, well suited to the present character of this district, which is largely inhabited by artists, actors, and wealthy New Yorkers. Others visit here for the charming village vibe and cache of excellent bars and restaurants.

↑ Attractive, cobblestoned Greene Street in New York's SoHo

West Broadway, as it passes through SoHo, combines striking architecture with a string of galleries and restaurants.

The Broken Kilometer, at 393 West Broadway, is by Walter De Maria. It plays tricks with perspective (p119).

72–76 Greene Street, the "King of Greene Street," is a splendid Corinthian-columned building, created by Isaac F. Duckworth, a master of cast-iron design.

Performing Garage is a tiny experimental theater that pioneers the work of avant-garde artists.

Of all Greene Street's fine cast-iron buildings, one of the best is 28–30, the "Queen," which was erected by Duckworth in 1872 and has a tall mansard roof.

15–17 Greene Street is a late addition, dating from 1895, in a simple Corinthian style.

START

10–14 Greene Street dates from 1869. The glass circles in the risers of the iron stoop meant daylight could reach the basement.

WEST BROADWAY

WEST BROADWAY

GREENE ST

WEST BROADWAY

WOOSTER STREET

BROOME STREET

GRAND STREET

Richard Haas, the prolific muralist, has transformed a blank wall into a convincing cast-iron frontage.

Did You Know?

SoHo stands for "South of Houston," and Tribeca for "Triangle Below Canal Street."

Locator Map
For more detail see p116

A terra-cotta beauty, the Little Singer Building was built in 1904 for the famous sewing machine company.

Dean & DeLuca is one of the best gourmet food stores in New York. Its range includes a global choice of coffee beans.

FINISH

Prince St subway station (lines N, R, W)

101 Spring Street, with its simple, geometric facade and large windows, is a fine example of the style that led to the skyscraper.

During the Civil War, St. Nicholas Hotel was a luxury hotel, and was used as a headquarters for the Union Army.

Dating back to 1857, the Haughwout Building was built for the E.V. Haughwout china and glassware company and featured the first Otis safety elevator.

PRINCE ST
MERCER STREET
BROADWAY
CROSBY STREET

↑ Shoppers at gourmet food store Dean & DeLuca

Chess-players in Washington Square Park

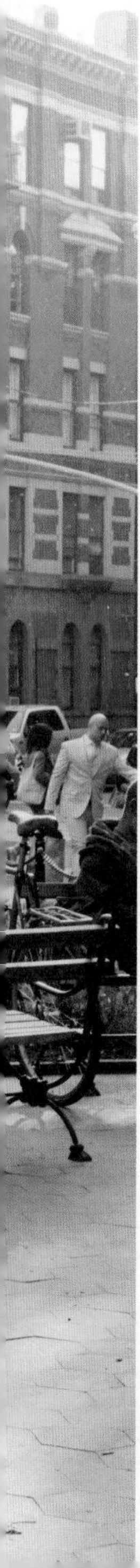

GREENWICH VILLAGE

Since the 1920s, Greenwich Village has been the bohemian heart of New York. Popularly known as the West Village, or just "the Village," the area became a sanctuary for city dwellers during the yellow fever epidemic in 1822. The 1950s saw the emergence of the Beat Movement, while in the 1960s folk singers like Bob Dylan launched their careers here. The Stonewall Riots of 1969, the catalyst for the Gay Rights Movement, began at the Stonewall Inn. With its quaint streets and charming brownstones, today Greenwich Village is one of the city's more artistic, liberal neighborhoods. It has steadily become an expensive part of Manhattan, with large expanses owned by New York University.

GREENWICH VILLAGE

Must See
❶ Whitney Museum of American Art

Experience More
❷ Comedy Cellar
❸ Grove Court
❹ Center for Architecture
❺ Renee & Chaim Gross Foundation
❻ Sheridan Square
❼ Meatpacking District
❽ Washington Square Park
❾ West 4th Street Courts
❿ NYU and Grey Art Gallery
⓫ NY City AIDS Memorial
⓬ Keith Haring's Carmine Street Mural

Eat
① Blue Hill
② Chumley's
③ Caffe Reggio
④ Magnolia Bakery

0 meters 200
0 yards 200

N

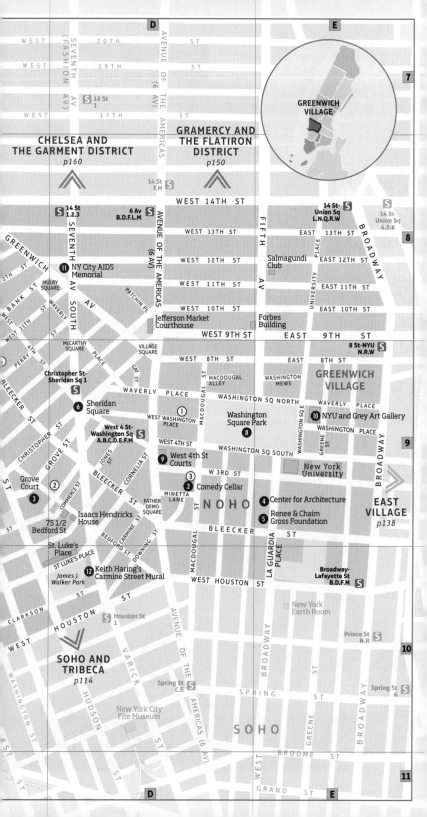

CHELSEA AND
THE GARMENT DISTRICT
p160

GRAMERCY AND
THE FLATIRON
DISTRICT
p150

GREENWICH
VILLAGE

7

WEST 20TH ST

WEST 19TH ST

WEST 18TH ST

WEST 17TH ST

S 18 St
1

WEST 14TH ST

14 St
F.M **S**

14 St
1.2.3 **S**

6 Av
B.D.F.L.M

14 St-
Union Sq
L.N.Q.R.W **S**

14 St-
Union Sq
4.5.6 **S**

8

WEST 13TH ST

EAST 13TH ST

GREENWICH
ST

11 NY City AIDS
Memorial

MULRY
SQUARE

WEST 12TH ST

Salmagundi
Club

EAST 12TH ST

BANK ST

WAVERLY PL

WEST 11TH ST

EAST 11TH ST

WEST 10TH ST

EAST 10TH ST

PERRY ST

McCARTHY
SQUARE

Jefferson Market
Courthouse

Forbes
Building

WEST 9TH ST

EAST 9TH ST

VILLAGE
SQUARE

WEST 8TH ST

EAST 8TH ST

8 St-NYU
N.R.W **S**

Christopher St-
Sheridan Sq 1

6 Sheridan
Square

WAVERLY PLACE

MACDOUGAL
ALLEY

WASHINGTON
MEWS

GREENWICH
VILLAGE

WAVERLY PLACE

West 4 St-
Washington Sq
A.B.C.D.E.F.M **S**

① WEST WASHINGTON
PLACE

WASHINGTON SQ NORTH

Washington
Square Park

8

10 NYU and Grey Art Gallery

WASHINGTON PLACE

9

WEST 4TH ST

WASHINGTON SQ SOUTH

9 West 4th St
Courts

New York
University

9

BLEECKER ST

Grove
Court

②

③

W 3RD ST

③

2 Comedy Cellar

MINETTA
LANE

NOHO

4 Center for Architecture

5 Renee & Chaim
Gross Foundation

EAST
VILLAGE
p138

75 1/2
Bedford St

Isaacs Hendricks
House

FATHER
DEMO
SQUARE

BLEECKER ST

LA GUARDIA
PLACE

St. Luke's
Place

12 Keith Haring's
Carmine Street Mural

ST LUKE'S PLACE

James J.
Walker Park

WEST HOUSTON ST

Broadway-
Lafayette St
B.D.F.M **S**

CLARKSON
ST

HOUSTON ST

S Houston St
1

New York
Earth Room

10

SOHO AND
TRIBECA
p114

New York City
Fire Museum

Spring St
C.E **S**

SPRING ST

Prince St
N.R **S**

Spring St
6 **S**

SOHO

BROOME ST

11

GRAND ST

The cascading levels of the Whitney Museum of American Art, found at the foot of the High Line

❶ 🎨 🚫 🖥 🛍

WHITNEY MUSEUM OF AMERICAN ART

📍 B8 🏛 99 Gansevoort St 🚇 14 St (A, C, E), 8 Av (L) 🕐 10:30am–6pm
Mon, Wed–Sun (to 10pm Fri & Sat); Jul & Aug: 10:30am–6pm daily
🚫 Some Federal hols 🌐 whitney.org

The foremost showcase for American art of the 20th and 21st centuries, the Whitney is housed in a stunning building by architect Renzo Piano.

The Whitney was founded by Gertrude Vanderbilt Whitney after the Met turned down her collection of works by artists such as Bellows and Hopper. The Whitney moved from the Upper East Side to this innovative building in 2015. The sixth and seventh floors showcase pieces from the museum's collection – there isn't a permanent display, rather a constant rotation of works. Temporary exhibits occupy the first, fifth, and eighth floors. The Whitney Biennial, held in even years, is the most significant exhibition of new trends in American art.

↑ *Three Flags* (1958) by Jasper Johns, a key Pop Art influencer

← Tom Wesselman's *Still Life Number 36* (1964), part of the Whitney's art collection

→ Detail of George Bellows' *Dempsey and Firpo* (1924), depicting a famous prizefight

GERTRUDE VANDERBILT WHITNEY

Born into the prosperous Vanderbilt family in 1875, Gertrude married wealthy Harry Payne Whitney in 1896. She became an accomplished sculptor and a patron of the arts, promoting female artists in particular. In 1908, she opened the Whitney Studio Gallery in Greenwich Village and, in 1931, she founded the Whitney Museum.

EXPERIENCE MORE

↑ The stunning gardens and desirable real estate of Grove Court

Comedy Cellar

📍 D9 🚇 117 MacDougal St
🚇 W 4 St (A, B, C, D, E, F, M)
🕐 For shows only
🌐 comedycellar.com

One of the city's most iconic comedy clubs was founded in 1982 by comedian Bill Grundfest, who has since become a TV writer and producer. Shows are held every evening from 7:30pm and normally comprise between five and seven comics performing sets of around 20 minutes each. Regular comics include Todd Barry, Jim Norton, Patrice O'Neal, Michelle Wolf, and Dave Chappelle.

③ Grove Court

📍 C9 🚇 Christopher St-Sheridan Sq (1)

An enterprising grocer named Samuel Cocks built the six town houses here, in an area formed by a bend in the street. (The bends in this part of the Village originally marked divisions between colonial properties.) Cocks reckoned that having residents in the empty passage between 10 and 12 Grove Street would help his

business at No. 18. However, residential courts, which are now highly prized, were not considered respectable in 1854, and the lowbrow residents attracted to the area earned it the nickname "Mixed Ale Alley." O. Henry later chose this block as the setting for his 1902 work *The Last Leaf*.

Center for Architecture

📍 E9 🚇 536 LaGuardia Pl
🚇 W 4 St (A, B, C, D, E, F, M)
🕐 9am-8pm Mon-Fri, 11am-5pm Sat 🌐 centerfor architecture.org

Established by the American Institute of Architects in 2003, this bold and stylish hub for conferences, lectures, and film screenings also hosts temporary exhibitions highlighting every aspect of architectural design. Topics cover everything from Modernism and the 1964 World's Fair to European social housing projects. The center also leads New York City's annual month-long architecture and design festival, Archtober. Check the website for details of tours of the neighborhood.

⑤ Renee & Chaim Gross Foundation

📍 E9 🚇 526 LaGuardia Pl
🚇 W 4 St (A, B, C, D, E, F, M)
🕐 Thu & Fri for tours
🌐 rcgrossfoundation.org

Born in Austrian Galicia (now Ukraine) in 1904, celebrated Jewish sculptor Chaim Gross emigrated to the United States in 1921. He was a pioneer of the direct carving method, and rose to popularity in the 1930s.

EAT

Blue Hill

Dan Barber's celebrated farm-to-table cuisine.

📍 D9 🚇 75 Washington Place 🕐 Lunch
🌐 bluehillfarm.com

$$$

Chumley's

Old speakeasy turned high-end American restaurant.

📍 D9 🚇 86 Bedford St
🕐 Lunch 🌐 chumleys newyork.com

$$⑤

Caffe Reggio

Open since 1927, this Italian coffee house is crammed with antiques.

📍 D9
🚇 119 MacDougal St
📞 (212) 475-9557

$⑤⑤

Magnolia Bakery

Colorful cupcakes, as seen on *Sex and the City*.

📍 C9
🚇 401 Bleecker St
🌐 magnoliabakery.com

$⑤⑤

He lived here from 1963 until his death in 1991, and his 1830s town house is open for tours. His first-floor sculpture studio remains much as he left it (with a permanent installation of Gross's sculpture next door), while his living quarters upstairs feature works from his personal art collection.

One-hour tours take place at 1 and 3pm, Thu and Fri. Online reservations required.

The buzzing Meatpacking District, teaming with shoppers during the day ↓

6
Sheridan Square

D9 **S** Christopher St-Sheridan Sq (1)

This square is the heart of the Village. It was named for the Civil War General Philip Sheridan, who became commander-in-chief of the US Army in 1883. His statue stands in nearby Christopher Park.

The Draft Riots of 1863 took place here and, over a century later, another disturbance rocked the square. The Stonewall Inn, at 53 Christopher Street, was a gay bar (the inn here today is not the original). Such establishments were illegal and it had only stayed in business by paying off the police but on June 28, 1969, patrons rebelled, sparking the Stonewall Riots.

7
Meatpacking District

C8 **S** 14 St (A, C, E), 8 Av (L)

Once the domain of butchers in blood-stained aprons, these days (and particularly nights) the Meatpacking District is very different. Squeezed into an area south of 14th Street and west of Ninth Avenue, the neighborhood is now dotted with trendy clubs, lounges, and boutique hotels that swell with New Yorkers out for a good time.

Hipsters and fashionistas arrived in droves when Soho House, the New York branch of the London private members' club, moved in. This was followed by the classy Hotel Gansevoort, with its enviable rooftop swimming pool. These institutions aside, fashion designers (including Stella McCartney and Marc Jacobs) have outlets here. There's also upscale restaurants, tempting wine bars, cool nightclubs, and exclusive galleries, with more continuing to pop up.

The greatest allures of the Meatpacking District include the Whitney Museum of American Art (*p128*) and the High Line (*p166*), which begins on Gansevoort Street and offers gorgeous views of the neighborhood.

THE STONEWALL RIOTS
The Stonewall Inn dates back to the 1840s, but after becoming a gay bar in 1966 it suffered regular police harassment. During a police raid on June 28, 1969, protestors fought with police for the first time, resulting in several arrests and some injured police officers. The event formally inaugurated the gay-rights movement. In 2016, the "Stonewall National Monument" was dedicated to the LGBT+-rights movement.

Historic brownstones in Manhattan's Greenwich Village

↑ Leafy Washington Square Park, home to the Washington Square Arch *(inset),* a popular place to relax

8

Washington Square Park

📍 D9 🚇 W 4 St (A, B, C, D)

This vibrant open space was once marshland through which the quiet Minetta Brook flowed. By the late 1700s, the area had been turned into a public cemetery – when excavation began for the park, some 10,000 skeletal remains were exhumed. The square was used as a dueling ground for a time, then as a site for public hangings until 1819. The "hanging elm" in the northwest corner remains. In 1826, the marsh was filled in and the brook diverted underground, where it still flows; a small sign on a fountain at the entrance to 2 Fifth Avenue marks its course. The magnificent marble arch

by Stanford White, at the park's northern entrance, was completed in 1892 to mark the centenary of George Washington's inauguration, replacing an earlier wooden arch that spanned lower Fifth Avenue. A stairway is hidden in the right side of the arch. In 1916, a group of artists led by Marcel Duchamp and John Sloan broke in, climbed atop the arch, and declared the "free and independent republic of Washington Square, the state of New Bohemia."

Across the street is "the Row." Now part of NYU, this block was once home to New York's most prominent families. The Delano family, writers Edith Wharton, Henry James, and John Dos Passos,

and artist Edward Hopper all lived here. No. 8 was once the mayor's official home.

Today, families, joggers, street entertainers, skate-boarders, dog-walkers, and chess-players enjoy the park side by side – particularly when the sun shines.

9

West 4th Street Courts

📍 D9 🚇 Sixth Av at West 3rd St 🚇 W 4 St (A, B, C, D, E, F, M)

These public basketball courts are known as "The Cage" for the physical style of pick-up games typically on display here. Open since 1935, the courts still attract ambitious amateur players from all over the city, hoping to get noticed. Former NBA players Stephon Marbury, Anthony Mason, and Smush Parker all played here

Families, joggers, street entertainers, skateboarders, dog-walkers, and chess-players enjoy the park side by side – particularly when the sun shines.

The building was demolished in 1892. The Silver Center now occupies the site and contains NYU's Grey Art Gallery, at 100 Washington Square E. Here, exemplary traveling exhibitions are hosted in a wide range of media, such as photography, experimental video art, paintings, and sculpture. There are also temporary exhibits from the permanent collection: American paintings from the 1940s to the present are particularly well represented.

Did You Know?

Washington Square Park featured in Will Smith's movie *I Am Legend* (2007).

housed the city's first and largest AIDS ward during the 1980s.

⑪
NY City AIDS Memorial

◎ D8 ⌂ West 12th St
Ⓢ 8 Av (L), 14 St (1, 2, 3)
ⓦ nycaidsmemorial.org

Inaugurated in 2016, this poignant memorial pays tribute to all the New Yorkers who have died from AIDS since the 1970s – more than 100,000 in total. Designed by New York-based Studio ai, the memorial comprises a giant 18-ft (5.5-m) steel canopy and acts as a gateway to St. Vincent's Hospital Park. The granite paving stones below were designed by visual artist Jenny Holzer and are engraved with lines from Walt Whitman's poem *Song of Myself*. The park itself is close to the site of the former St. Vincent's Hospital, which

⑫
Keith Haring's Carmine Street Mural

◎ D10 ⌂ 1 Clarkson St at 7th Av Ⓢ W 4 St (A, B, C, D, E, F, M)

Pop artist Keith Haring's magnificent Carmine Street mural overlooks the public swimming pool at the back of the Tony Dapolito Recreation Center. Created in 1987, and measuring 18 ft (5.5 m) high by 170 ft (52 m) long, the mural features Haring's trademark colorful, cartoonish designs. The bold, stylized motifs of fish and children, as well as abstract yellow and blue shapes, almost appear to be dancing. You can get a good look from Clarkson Street – or go in for a swim. Haring (1958–90) painted several murals in the city.

in their early years. The courts regularly host high-quality street tournaments; Kenny Graham's West 4th Street summer league usually runs from May through September. Handball is also played here.

⑩
NYU and Grey Art Gallery

◎ E9 ⌂ Washington Sq
Ⓢ W 4 St (A, C, E, F, M), 8 St (N, R, W) ⓦ nyu.edu
ⓦ greyartgallery.nyu.edu

Originally named the University of the City of New York, New York University (NYU) was founded in 1831 as an alternative to Episcopalian Columbia University. It is now the largest private university in the US and extends for many blocks around Washington Square. The visitor center is on West 4th Street.

Construction of the school's first building sparked the Stonecutters' Guild Riot of 1833, in which contractors protested against the use of prison inmates to cut stone. The National Guard was brought in to restore order.

↑ The impressive NY City AIDS Memorial at St. Vincent's Hospital Park

A SHORT WALK
GREENWICH VILLAGE

Distance 0.80 mile (1.25 km) **Nearest subway** Houston St, Christopher St **Time** 15 minutes

A stroll through historic Greenwich Village is a feast of unexpected small pleasures – charming row houses, hidden alleys, and leafy courtyards. The often quirky architecture suits the bohemian air of the Village. Many famous people, particularly artists and writers, such as playwright Eugene O'Neill and actor Dustin Hoffman, have made their homes in the houses and apartments that line these old-fashioned narrow streets. By night, the Village really comes alive. Late-night coffeehouses and cafés, experimental theaters, and music clubs, including some of the city's best jazz venues, beckon you at every turn.

Christopher St subway (lines 1, 2)

Christopher Street, once the main drag for New York's gay community, is lined with shops, bookstores, and bars.

The Lucille Lortel Theater is at No. 121 Christopher Street; it opened in 1955 with The Threepenny Opera.

Twin Peaks at No. 102 Bedford Street began life in 1830 and was rebuilt in 1926 to house artists, writers, and actors.

The apartment block at 90 Bedford Street was used as the exterior of Monica's apartment in Friends.

Six houses dating from 1853–4 are set in the quiet leafy courtyard of Grove Court (p130).

Built in 1873, No. 75½ Bedford Street is the city's narrowest house. Poet Edna St. Vincent Millay lived here.

The Cherry Lane Theatre was founded in 1924. Originally a brewery, it was one of the first of the Off-Broadway theaters.

CHRISTOPHER STREET

BLEECKER STREET

BEDFORD STREET

JONES

BARROW STREET

SEVENTH AVENUE STREET

MORTON STREET

START

ST LUKE'S PLACE

This beautiful row of Italianate houses, called St. Luke's Place, was built in the 1850s.

Did You Know?

Friends is set largely in Greenwich Village but the TV series was shot entirely in LA.

Built in 1848 to house waiters from the Brevoort Hotel, Patchin Place was later home to the poet E. E. Cummings and other famous writers of the 1920s and 1930s.

Locator Map
For more detail see p126

PERRY ST

GREENWICH STREET

CHARLES STREET

W 10TH STREET

GREENWICH AVENUE

SIXTH AVENUE

WASHINGTON PLACE

FINISH

Jefferson Market Courthouse was built in 1877, and has been voted the fifth most beautiful building in the US It was designed by Calvert Vaux, who co-designed Central Park (p238). The building was converted into a public library in 1967.

Gay Street attracted many aspiring artists, writers, and musicians during the 1920s. It was the setting for Ruth McKenney's novel My Sister Eileen and the film Carlito's Way (1993).

The Northern Dispensary began offering free medical care to the poor in 1831. Edgar Allan Poe (1809–49) was treated for a cold here in 1837. Since 1998, the building has been unoccupied.

0 meters 100
0 yards 100
N

Apartments line Greenwich Village's Gay Street ↓

Bar-hoppers enjoying drinks in East Village bar Bua

EAST VILLAGE

Home to a country estate owned by Peter Stuyvesant in the 17th century, the East Village neighborhood only really took shape in the early 1900s. The Irish, Germans, Jews, Poles, Ukrainians, and Puerto Ricans all left their mark on the area, not least in the form of Manhattan's most varied and least expensive ethnic restaurants. In the 1950s, low rents attracted the "Beat Generation," and, ever since, music clubs and theaters have abounded in the area. From the 1990s, the culinary and bar scene here blossomed, making this one of the city's most fashionable districts. To the west lies NoHo (north of Houston), while to the east, avenues lettered A–D form "Alphabet City," a trendy district of restaurants and gardens.

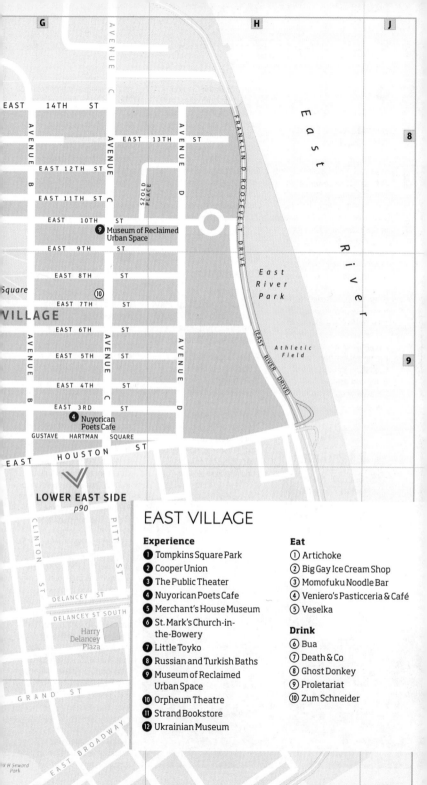

EAST VILLAGE

Experience

1. Tompkins Square Park
2. Cooper Union
3. The Public Theater
4. Nuyorican Poets Cafe
5. Merchant's House Museum
6. St. Mark's Church-in-the-Bowery
7. Little Toyko
8. Russian and Turkish Baths
9. Museum of Reclaimed Urban Space
10. Orpheum Theatre
11. Strand Bookstore
12. Ukrainian Museum

Eat

1. Artichoke
2. Big Gay Ice Cream Shop
3. Momofuku Noodle Bar
4. Veniero's Pasticceria & Café
5. Veselka

Drink

6. Bua
7. Death & Co
8. Ghost Donkey
9. Proletariat
10. Zum Schneider

EXPERIENCE

❶ Tompkins Square Park

⚲ G9 **Ⓢ 2 Av (F), 1 Av (L)**
🚌 M8, M9, M14A

This English-style park has the makings of a peaceful spot, but its past has more often been dominated by strife. It was the site of America's first organized labor demonstration in 1874. Almost 100 years later, during the 1960s, this was the main gathering place for the neighborhood's hippies, and, in 1988, it was an arena for violent riots when the police tried to evict homeless people who had taken over the grounds.

The square also contains a poignant monument to the neighborhood's greatest tragedy. A small statue of a boy and a girl looking at a steamboat commemorates the deaths of over 1,000 local residents in the *General Slocum* steamer disaster. On June 15, 1904, the boat caught fire during a pleasure cruise on the East River. It was crowded with women and children from this then-German neighborhood and many local men lost their entire families and moved away, leaving the area and its memories behind.

---

❷ Cooper Union

⚲ E9 **🏠 7 East 7th St**
Ⓢ Astor Pl (6) **🕐 Sep–May: 11am–7pm Mon–Fri, 11am–5pm Sat 🕐 Jun–Aug, Federal hols** **🌐 cooper.edu**

Peter Cooper had no formal schooling but went on to build the first US steam locomotive, make the first steel rails, and become a partner in the first transatlantic cable venture. In 1859, the wealthy industrialist founded New York's first free, non-sectarian coeducational college specializing in design, engineering, and architecture. Though no longer free, the college still inspires intense competition for places. The six-story building, renovated in 1973–4, was the first to be constructed with a steel frame, made from Cooper's own rails. The Great Hall, which was inaugurated by Mark Twain in 1859, hosts lectures and concerts.

---

❸ The Public Theater

⚲ E9 **🏠 425 Lafayette St**
Ⓢ Astor Pl (6) **🌐 publictheater.org**

This large red-brick and brownstone building began its life in 1854 as the Astor Library, New York City's first free library, made possible through a bequest from millionaire John Jacob Astor. It is one of the foremost examples in the United States of German Romanesque Revival style.

When the building was threatened with demolition in 1965, Joseph Papp, founder of the New York Shakespeare Festival, which became The Public Theater, persuaded New York City to buy it as a home for the company. Renovation began in 1967, and much of the handsome interior was preserved during its conversion into six theaters. Although much of the work shown is experimental, the theater was the original home of the hit musicals *A Chorus Line* and *Hamilton* and sponsors the very popular Shakespeare in the Park event (in Central Park) every summer.

Did You Know?

The Public Theater's Mobile Unit performs in prisons and homeless shelters.

← Tompkins Square Park, buzzing with locals enjoying the greenery

DRINK

Bua

Open-fronted (in summer) for people-watching, this bar has a great happy hour.

📍 F9 🏠 122 St. Mark's Pl
🌐 buabar.com

Death & Co

Lauded cocktail bar with a charming, speakeasy theme.

📍 F9 🏠 433 East 6th St 🌐 deathandcompany.com

Ghost Donkey

Cozy tequila and mezcal cocktail bar.

📍 F9 🏠 4 Bleecker St
🌐 ghostdonkey.com

Proletariat

Long, narrow bar with quality ales and craft beers.

📍 F9 🏠 102 St. Mark's Pl
🌐 proletariatny.com

Zum Schneider

Lively Bavarian *bierhaus*, serving *steins* and *wursts*, with an indoor garden.

📍 G9 🏠 107 Av C
🌐 zumschneider.com

④

Nuyorican Poets Cafe

📍 G9 🏠 236 East 3rd St
Ⓢ 2 Av (F) 🕐 For performances only
🌐 nuyorican.org

Originally founded in the apartment of Puerto Rican writer and poet Miguel Algarín in 1973, this seminal Latin American arts venue moved here in 1981. It's a lively hub for live poetry readings, play and film-script readings, open mics, jazz and hip-hop shows, plays, and visual art exhibits.

⑤ 🎨 🎭 🛍

Merchant's House Museum

📍 E9 🏠 29 East 4th St
Ⓢ Astor Pl (6), Bleecker St (6)
🕐 Noon–5pm Mon & Fri–Sun, noon–8pm Thu
🌐 merchantshouse.org

This remarkable, Federal-style brick town house, improbably tucked away on an East Village block, is a time capsule of a vanished way of life. It retains its original fixtures, and is filled with the actual furniture, ornaments, and utensils of the family who lived here. Built in 1832, it was bought in 1835 by Seabury Tredwell, a wealthy merchant, and stayed in the family until Gertrude Tredwell,

↑ Performance venue and cultural hub Nuyorican Poets Café

the last member, died in 1933. A relative then opened the house as a museum in 1936. The first-floor parlors reveal how well New York's merchant class lived during the 1800s.

---

⑥

St. Mark's Church-in-the-Bowery

📍 F8 🏠 131 East 10th St
Ⓢ Astor Pl (6) 🕐 10am–4pm Mon–Fri (hours may vary)
🌐 stmarksbowery.org

One of New York's oldest churches, this 1799 building replaced a 1660 church on the *bouwerie* (farm) of Governor Peter Stuyvesant. He is buried here, along with seven generations of his descendants and many other prominent early New Yorkers.

In 1878, a grisly kidnapping took place when the remains of department store magnate A. T. Stewart were removed from the site and held for a $20,000 ransom.

The church rectory at 232 East 11th Street dates from 1900 and is by Beaux Arts architect Ernest Flagg, who achieved renown for his Singer Building.

Weathered apartment buildings in the East Village

EAT

Artichoke

Fabulous late-night pizza slices to go, including the signature artichoke-spinach.

📍F8 🏠321 East 14th St 🌐artichoke pizza.com

$⑤⑤⑤

Big Gay Ice Cream Shop

Addictive ice cream with naughty names; try the "salty pimp."

📍F9 🏠125 East 7th St 🌐biggay icecream.com

$⑤⑤⑤

Momofuku Noodle Bar

Celebrity chef David Chang's steamed pork buns and pork ramen noodles are not to be missed.

📍F8 🏠171 First Av 🌐momofuku.com

$⑤⑤⑤

Veniero's Pasticceria & Café

Old-school Italian gem dating back to 1894; think ricotta cheesecake and cannoli.

📍F8 🏠342 East 11th St 🌐venieros pastry.com

$⑤⑤⑤

Veselka

Ukrainian diner offering traditional favorites like *borscht*, *kielbasa* sausage and *pierogi* since 1954.

📍F9 🏠144 Second Av 🌐veselka.com

$⑤⑤⑤

7

Little Tokyo

📍F8 🏠East 9th and 10th sts (between 3rd and 1st avs) Ⓢastor Pl (6)

Located on and around East 9th and 10th streets, this tiny locality is peppered with colorful Japanese stores, steamy noodle shops, packed supermarkets, and quality sushi bars, such as Hasaki at 210 East 9th Street. Sunrise Mart is a popular Japanese supermarket at 4 Stuyvesant Street, while Toy Tokyo at 91 Second Avenue sells all sorts of Japanese anime figures, collectibles, and toys. Top restaurants in the area include Ippudo (at 65 Fourth Avenue), the first overseas outpost of Fukuoka-based "ramen king" Shigemi Kawahara, and Ikinari Steak (90 E 10th Street), a Japanese steakhouse chain. Authentic Tokyo *izakaya* Kenka (25 St. Mark's Place) features wooden benches, small plates of tempting Japanese snacks, and quality sake.

8

Russian and Turkish Baths

📍F8 🏠268 East 10th St Ⓢ1 Av (L), Astor Pl (6) 🕐Daily (times vary, check website) 🌐russianturkish baths.com

One of the few old-school experiences remaining in the East Village, these steam rooms have been active since 1892 and remain popular. There's the Steam Room, the Turkish Room, and the Russian Sauna (the hottest). Admission includes a towel, robe, soap, and slippers.

9

Museum of Reclaimed Urban Space

📍G8 🏠155 Av C Ⓢ3 Av (L) 🕐11am-7pm Tue, Thu-Sun 🌐morusnyc.org

This tiny museum, housed in a 19th-century tenement and run solely by volunteers, honors the neighborhood's

Labyrinthine Strand Bookstore, a New York landmark

This tiny locality is peppered with colorful Japanese stores, steamy noodle shops, packed supermarkets, and quality sushi bars.

long tradition of urban activism and charts its history, covering events such as the Tompkins Square Park riot (p142), development of community gardens, and squatting in the East Village. Check online for guided tour information (usually Sat and Sun at 3pm).

10 ⊘ 🏛 Orpheum Theatre

📍 F9 🏠 126 2nd Ave
🚇 Astor Pl (6) 🕐 For shows
only 🌐 stomponline.com

One of the East Village's biggest (and oldest) theaters has been the home of the innovative percussion group *Stomp* since 1994. The show,

which began in Brighton, England, sees its cast use everyday objects and their own bodies to make music and entertaining, foot-tapping rhythms.

A theater has been on this site since at least 1904, when the whole area became known as the Yiddish Theater District. Years later, several landmark productions had Off-Broadway premieres here, including comedy rock musical *Little Shop of Horrors* (1982), Sandra Bernhard's *Without You I'm Nothing* (1988) and David Mamet's *Oleanna* (1992).

11 🏛 Strand Bookstore

📍 E8 🏠 828 Broadway
🚇 Union Sq (4, 5, 6, L, N, Q, R, W) 🕐 9:30am–10:30pm daily 🌐 strandbooks.com

The last remaining bookstore on "Book Row," the Strand is a delight, with some 18 miles (29 km) of remaindered, new and used books at discount prices. It's estimated the store contains some 2.5 million books in total. It first opened in 1927 and was named after the London street, before moving into this labyrinthine space in 1957. Authors such as Junot Díaz, Paul Auster, and Nicole Krauss regularly hold readings here.

12 ⊘ 🏛 Ukrainian Museum

📍 F9 🏠 222 East 6th St
🚇 Astor Pl (6) 🕐 11:30am–5pm Wed–Sun 🌐 ukrainianmuseum.org

Founded in 1976, this small but beautifully maintained museum pays homage to what was once a major Ukrainian enclave in New York City. The exhibits are primarily folk costumes and textiles, but there is also modern art from lauded Ukrainian artists. There is also a range of traditional crafts, including the famously pretty painted Easter eggs, known as *pysanky*.

ST. MARK'S PLACE

East 8th Street is known to locals as St. Mark's Place - the cultural, rebellious heart of the 'hood since the 1960s. It's now lined with souvenir stalls, hippie-chic fashion stores, and Asian restaurants. Don't miss St. Mark's Comics at No. 11, nor Physical Graffitea at No. 96, which is based in the tenement featured on the eponymous Led Zeppelin album cover.

A SHORT WALK
EAST VILLAGE

Distance 1.25 mile (2 km) **Nearest subway** Astor Pl
Time 25 minutes

History abounds in the East Village. At the spot where 10th and Stuyvesant streets now intersect, Governor Peter Stuyvesant's country house once stood, and many other homes were built here between 1871 and 1890. This makes for a picturesque place to explore today – but it's not all beauty and charm. The East Village is one of New York's hottest neighborhoods, and the Manhattan of popular imagination. Here you'll find weathered apartments papered with fliers, locals chatting on stoops, and a buzzing bar and restaurant scene.

Astor Place saw rioting in 1849. English actor William Macready, playing Hamlet at the Astor Place Opera House, criticized American actor Edwin Forrest. Forrest's fans revolted, and there were 34 deaths.

Alamo is the title of the 15-ft (4.6-m) steel cube in Astor Place designed by Bernard Rosenthal. It revolves when pushed.

Built in the Greek Revival style in the 1830s, the buildings of Colonnade Row were once expensive town houses. The houses, of which only four are left, are unified by one facade in the European style. The Astor Place Theatre, which is located here, has been home to the Blue Man Group since 1991.

In 1965, the late Joseph Papp convinced the city to buy the Astor Library (1849) as a home for The Public Theater (p142).

The Merchant's House Museum displays Federal, American Empire, and Victorian furniture (p143).

Astor Pl subway (line 6)

START

E 8TH ST
ASTOR PLACE
LAFAYETTE STREET
STABLE COURT
FOURTH AVENUE
BOWERY

0 meters 100
0 yards 100
N ↑

← Astor Place, with Clinton Hall at its heart

← McSorley's Old Ale House, an East Village icon

EAST VILLAGE

Locator Map
For more detail see p140

Cooper Union is known for its art and engineering programs, and provided free education to its students until 2014 (p142).

Renwick Triangle is a group of 16 houses built in the Italianate style in 1861.

The Stuyvesant-Fish House (1803–4) was constructed out of brick. It is a classic example of a Federal-style house.

St. Mark's Church-in-the-Bowery was built in 1799, and the steeple was added in 1828 (p143).

Stuyvesant Polyclinic was built in 1884 as the German Dispensary and was in use until 2007. The facade is adorned with the busts of famous physicians and scientists.

Little Tokyo is a belt of noodle shops, sushi bars, and Japanese businesses, around East 9th Street (p146).

E 10TH STREET

STUYVESANT ST

FINISH

THIRD AVENUE

ST MARK'S PLACE

E 7TH STREET

SECOND AVENUE

E 9TH STREET

E 6TH STREET

St. Mark's Place was once the epicenter of hippie life and remains an East Village icon. Many shops can now be found here (p147).

McSorley's Old Ale House still serves its own ale in surroundings virtually unchanged since it opened in 1854. There are just two beer options here: "light" and "dark."

St George's Ukrainian Catholic Church is set in Little Ukraine, home to around 25,000 Ukrainians and the Ukrainian Museum (p147).

Did You Know?

When you order beer at McSorley's, you get two smallish glass mugs, rather than one.

The innovative and iconic Flatiron Building

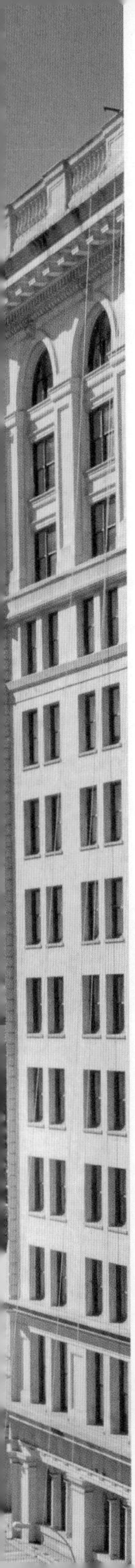

GRAMERCY AND THE FLATIRON DISTRICT

Four squares were laid out in this area by real estate developers in the 1830s and 1840s to emulate the quiet, private residential quarters in many European cities. Chief among them is Union Square, a bustling space that hosts New York's best farmers' market. To the northeast lies Gramercy, with its private clubs and posh town houses, designed by Calvert Vaux and Stanford White. Gertrude Vanderbilt Whitney's bronze statue of Peter Stuyvesant, overlooked by the stately St. George Episcopal Church, stands in tranquil Stuyvesant Square. Finally, at the north end of the Flatiron District is Madison Square Park.

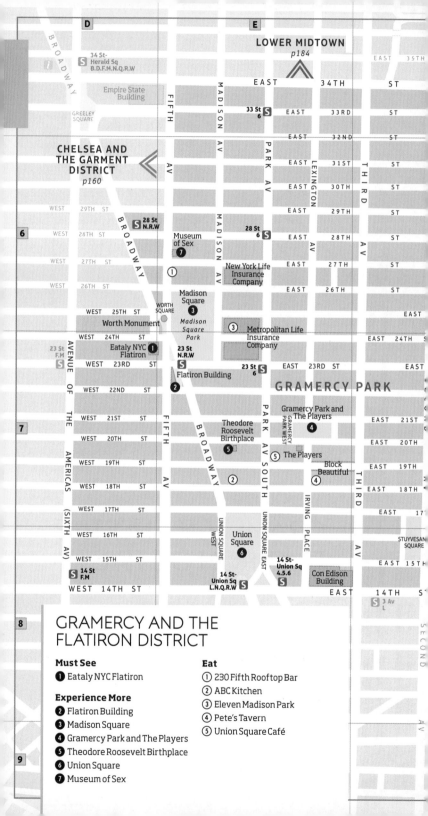

LOWER MIDTOWN
p184

34 St-
Herald Sq
S B.D.F.M.N.Q.R.W

Empire State
Building

GREELEY
SQUARE

EAST   35TH

EAST   34TH   ST

33 St **S**   EAST   33RD   ST
6

EAST   32ND   ST

**CHELSEA AND
THE GARMENT
DISTRICT**
p160

FIFTH AV

MADISON AV

PARK AV

LEXINGTON

THIRD

EAST   31ST   ST

EAST   30TH   ST

WEST   29TH   ST

S 28 St
N.R.W

WEST   28TH   ST

WEST   27TH   ST

WEST   26TH   ST

Museum
of Sex
7

①

EAST   29TH   ST

28 St **S**   EAST   28TH   ST
6

New York Life
Insurance
Company

EAST   27TH   ST

EAST   26TH   ST

Madison
Square
3

WORTH
SQUARE

WEST   25TH   ST

Worth Monument

Madison
Square
Park

EAST

③ Metropolitan Life
Insurance
Company

EAST   24TH   S

WEST   24TH   ST

23 St
F.M
S

AVENUE

Eataly NYC
Flatiron **1**

WEST   23RD   ST

Flatiron Building
2

23 St
N.R.W
S

23 St **S**
6

EAST   23RD   ST

EAST

GRAMERCY PARK

WEST   22ND   ST

OF

THE

AMERICAS

(SIXTH

AV)

WEST   21ST   ST

WEST   20TH   ST

WEST   19TH   ST

WEST   18TH   ST

WEST   17TH   ST

WEST   16TH   ST

WEST   15TH   ST

FIFTH AV

BROADWAY

Theodore
Roosevelt
Birthplace
5

②

PARK AV SOUTH

GRAMERCY PARK WEST

Gramercy Park and
The Players
4

⑤ The Players

Block
Beautiful
4

IRVING PLACE

THIRD

EAST   21ST

EAST   20TH

EAST   19TH

EAST   18TH   ST

EAST   17

STUYVESAN
SQUARE

S 14 St
F.M

WEST   14TH   ST

UNION SQUARE WEST

Union
Square
6

14 St-
Union Sq
S

UNION SQUARE EAST

14 St-
Union Sq
4.5.6
S

Con Edison
Building

EAST   15T

EAST   14TH   S

S 3 Av
L

SECOND AV

GRAMERCY AND THE
FLATIRON DISTRICT

Must See

1 Eataly NYC Flatiron

Experience More

2 Flatiron Building
3 Madison Square
4 Gramercy Park and The Players
5 Theodore Roosevelt Birthplace
6 Union Square
7 Museum of Sex

Eat

① 230 Fifth Rooftop Bar
② ABC Kitchen
③ Eleven Madison Park
④ Pete's Tavern
⑤ Union Square Café

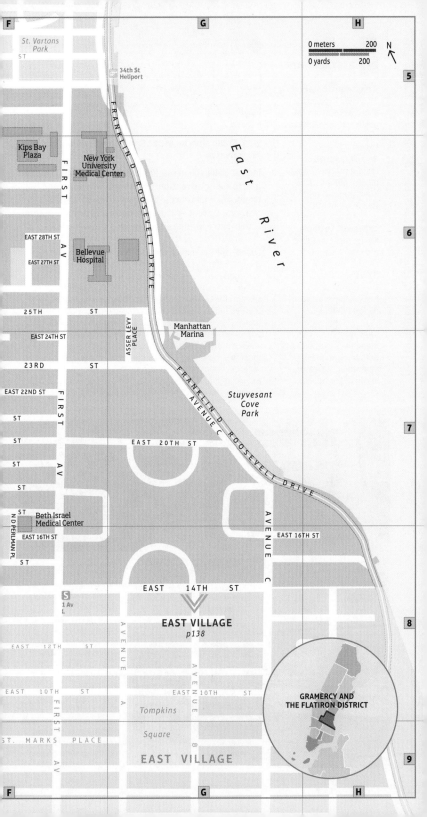

St. Vartans Park
ST

0 meters 200
0 yards 200
N

5

Kips Bay Plaza

New York University Medical Center

F I R S T   A V

E a s t

34th St Heliport

F R A N K L I N   D   R O O S E V E L T   D R I V E

EAST 28TH ST

EAST 27TH ST

Bellevue Hospital

R i v e r

6

25TH   ST

EAST 24TH ST

23RD   ST

ASSER LEVY PLACE

Manhattan Marina

EAST 22ND ST

F I R S T

Beth Israel Medical Center

Stuyvesant Cove Park

A V

N D PERLMAN PL

ST

ST

ST

ST

EAST 20TH ST

F R A N K L I N   D   R O O S E V E L T   D R I V E

A V E N U E   C

7

ST

EAST 16TH ST

A V E N U E   C

EAST 16TH ST

ST

S
1 Av
L

EAST   14TH   ST

EAST VILLAGE
p138

8

EAST   12TH   ST

A V E N U E   A

A V E N U E   B

EAST 10TH ST

EAST   10TH   ST

F I R S T

Tompkins

GRAMERCY AND THE FLATIRON DISTRICT

ST. MARKS   PLACE

A V

Square

EAST VILLAGE

9

TOP 5 EATALY RESTAURANTS

Il Pastaio di Eataly
Fresh Italian pasta bar showcasing artisanal pasta-making traditions.

Manzo
Butcher-focused restaurant celebrating meat of all kinds, plus a bar specializing in Italian vermouth.

La Pizza & La Pasta
Naples-style pizza and al dente pasta.

Il Pesce
Serves fresh and responsibly sourced fish and shellfish.

La Piazza
Standing-only *enoteca*, with fresh *antipasti*, cured meats, cheeses, and a host of wines.

① 🍴 🖥 🏠

EATALY NYC FLATIRON

📍D7 **🏠200 Fifth Av** **🚇E 23 St (N, R, W)** **🕐7am–11pm daily**
🌐eataly.com

Indoor Italian food market Eataly has become a major gastronomic attraction, sparking a New York food hall trend. The market comprises a variety of sit-down restaurants, food and drink counters, and grocery stores, with mouthwatering scents drifting throughout.

Founded by Italian entrepreneur Oscar Farinetti in 2007, the first Eataly debuted in Turin. Part-restaurant complex, part-food market, Eataly NYC Flatiron opened in 2010, followed by Eataly NYC Downtown in 2016. The market section offers a huge range of rare Italian wines, unusual cheeses, freshly baked breads, and seafood and meats sourced locally or flown in from Italy. Sample fresh *gelato* and *sorbetto* at Il Gelato, sip espresso at Caffè Vergnano, indulge in sweet treats at La Pasticceria or stand at the tables in La Piazza and nibble on cured meats and cheeses, washed down with a fine Chianti. There's also a cooking school, homewares section, and bookstore, so you can take a little bit of Italy home with you.

① The entrance to covered food market Eataly NYC Flatiron, just down the block from the Flatiron Building.

② For those not dining at one of Eataly's self-contained restaurants, the covered food market has places to sit, which get exceptionally busy at peak times.

③ Loaves galore at Eataly's bakery. All of the store's artisanal breads are freshly baked on site in a wood-burning, hand-rotated oven, using natural yeast and stone-ground flour.

↑ Rooftop pop-up SERRA by
Birreria, inspired by the
Italian countryside

EXPERIENCE MORE

② Flatiron Building

📍E7 🏛175 Fifth Av
🚇23 St (N, R, W) ⛔Closed to the public

Possibly one of New York City's most famous sights, the Flatiron's elegant, triangular exterior draws crowds, all vying for that perfect photo. Originally named the Fuller Building after the construction company that owned it, this building by Chicago architect Daniel Burnham was one of the tallest in the world when completed in 1902 and one of the first to use a steel frame. This innovative construction of 20-stories was a precursor to the skyscrapers to come.

Although called the Flatiron for its unusual tapered shape, some called it "Burnham's folly," predicting that the ground level winds created by the building's frame would knock it down. Some even placed bets, convinced it would topple. It has, however, withstood the test of time.

The stretch of Fifth Avenue to the south of the building has chic stores such as Michael Kors and Paul Smith, adding cachet to the area now called the Flatiron District.

③ Madison Square

📍E6 🚇23 St (N, R, W)

Planned as the center of a fashionable residential district, this square became a popular entertainment hub after the Civil War. It was bordered by the elegant Fifth Avenue Hotel, the Madison Square Theater, and Stanford White's Madison Square Garden. The torch-bearing arm of the Statue of Liberty was exhibited here in 1884.

The Shake Shack is a top lunchtime spot for neighborhood office workers, while the surrounding park makes for a leisurely stroll to admire the sculptures. The 1880 statue of Admiral David Farragut, hero of a Civil War sea battle, is by Augustus Saint-Gaudens, its pedestal by Stanford White. Figures representing Courage and Loyalty are carved on the base. The statue of Roscoe Conkling commemorates a US senator who died during the great blizzard of 1888. The Eternal Light flagpole, by Carrère and Hastings, honors fallen soldiers of World War I.

Did You Know?

The Flatiron Building is destined to become a luxury hotel when its current leases expire.

④ Gramercy Park and The Players

📍E7 🏛Irving Pl, between East 20th and 21st sts 🚇14 St-Union Sq (L, N, R, W, 4, 5, 6) 🌐nationalarts club.org 🌐theplayersnyc.org

Laid out in the 1830s and 1840s to attract society residences uptown, this is the city's only private park. Residents of the surrounding buildings have keys to the gate. Famous key-holders have included Uma Thurman, Julia Roberts, and several Kennedys and Roosevelts. The handsome brownstone at 15 Gramercy Park South houses the National Arts Club. Members have included most leading American artists of the late 19th and early 20th centuries, who were asked to donate a painting or sculpture in return for life membership; these gifts form the National Arts Club's permanent collection. The club is open to the public for exhibitions only.

←

Madison Square Park, in the heart of the Flatiron District

↑ Flowers and fresh produce stalls at Union Square Greenmarket

The Players at 18 Gramercy Park South was once the home of actor Edwin Booth, brother of John Wilkes Booth, President Lincoln's assassin. Architect Stanford White remodeled the building as a club in 1888. Intended primarily for actors, members have also included White himself, author Mark Twain, publisher Thomas Nast, and Winston Churchill, whose mother, Jennie Jerome, was born nearby. A statue of Booth playing Hamlet is across the street in Gramercy Park itself.

5
Theodore Roosevelt Birthplace

◊ E7 28 East 20th St **⑤** 14 St-Union Sq (L, N, R, W, 4, 5, 6), 23 St (6) **◎** 9am–5pm Wed-Sun (last adm 4pm) **◙** Federal hols **◻** nps.gov/thrb

The reconstructed boyhood home of the colorful 26th president displays everything from the toys with which the young Teddy played to campaign buttons and emblems of the trademark "Rough Rider" hat that Roosevelt wore in the Spanish- American War. One exhibit features his explorations and general interests; the other covers his political career.

6
Union Square

◊ E8 **⑤** 14 St-Union Sq (L, N, W, R, 4, 5, 6)

Created in the 1830s, this park is an inviting public space, best known for its enormous greenmarket. Held from 8am to 6pm on Monday, Wednesday, Friday, and Saturday, the market sells all sorts of seasonal produce. Statues here include those of George Washington and a Lafayette by Bartholdi, and the square is flanked by restaurants, gourmet supermarkets, and department stores. Nearby are the Decker Building, to which Andy Warhol moved his studio in 1968, and the Union Square Theatre, once HQ of the Democratic Party.

7
Museum of Sex

◊ E6 233 Fifth Av at 27th St **⑤** 28 St (N, R, W, 6) **◎** 10:30am–11pm Sun-Thu, 10:30am–midnight Fri-Sat **◻** museumofsex.com

This is the only New York museum for visitors aged 18 and over. Through thought-provoking changing exhibits, and a permanent collection of over 20,000 artifacts (including works of art, photography, costumes, and technological inventions), the Museum of Sex means to promote serious discourse surrounding sex and sexuality. Temporary exhibits hold court on the first floor.

EAT

230 Fifth Rooftop Bar
Swish bar and roof garden serving international fare. Come for the sensational views of the Empire State Building.

◊ E6 230 Fifth Av **◻** 230-fifth.com

$$$

ABC Kitchen
New American cuisine from Jean-Georges Vongerichten.

◊ E7 35 East 18th St **◻** abchome.com/dine/abc-kitchen

$$$

Eleven Madison Park
Gorgeous Art Deco space for contemporary American fine dining.

◊ E6 11 Madison Av **◻** L Mon-Thu **◻** elevenmadison park.com

$$$

Pete's Tavern
Atmospheric bar, open since 1864, known for being writer O. Henry's local. Serves hearty burgers and Italian staples.

◊ E7 129 East 18th St **◻** petestavern.com

$$$

Union Square Café
Danny Meyer's famous restaurant produces exquisite contemporary American cuisine.

◊ E7 101 East 19th St **◻** unionsquare cafe.com

$$$

A SHORT WALK
GRAMERCY PARK

Distance 1.4 mile (2.25 km) **Nearest subway** 23 St
Time 30 minutes

Gramercy Park and nearby Madison Square tell a tale of two cities. Madison Square, ringed by offices and traffic, is used mainly by those working nearby, but the surrounding commercial architecture make it worth visiting. It was once the home of Madison Square Garden, where revelers always thronged. Gramercy Park, meanwhile, retains the air of dignified tranquility it has long been known for. Homes and clubs remain, set around the last private park, accessible only to those living on the square.

The Knickerbocker Club played baseball here, at Madison Square, in the 1840s. Today, office workers enjoy the park's statues (p156).

23 St subway (lines N, R, W)

S START

A sidewalk clock in front of 200 Fifth Avenue marks the end of the once-fashionable shopping area known as Ladies' Mile.

The triangle made by Fifth Avenue, Broadway, and 22nd Street is the site of one of New York's most famous early skyscrapers, the Flatiron Building. When it was built in 1903, the Flatiron was the world's tallest building (p156).

23 St subway (lines N, R, W)

Broadway from Union Square to Madison Square was once New York's finest shopping area, called Ladies' Mile.

Theodore Roosevelt Birthplace is a replica of the house in which the 26th American president was born (p157).

BROADWAY (LADIES' MILE)

E 23RD STREET

E 22ND STREET

E 21ST STREET

E 19TH STREET

E 17TH STREET

IRV

The National Arts Club is a private club for the arts, on the south side of the park (p156).

↑ Springtime flowers bloom in Madison Square Park

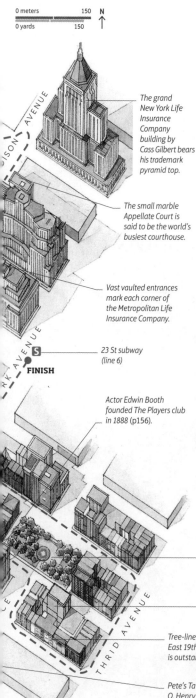

The grand New York Life Insurance Company building by Cass Gilbert bears his trademark pyramid top.

The small marble Appellate Court is said to be the world's busiest courthouse.

Vast vaulted entrances mark each corner of the Metropolitan Life Insurance Company.

23 St subway (line 6)

S **FINISH**

Actor Edwin Booth founded The Players club in 1888 (p156).

Only residents can go into Gramercy Park itself, but everyone can enjoy the peace and charm of the area around it (p156).

The Brotherhood Synagogue was a Friends' Meeting House from 1859 to 1975, when it became a synagogue.

Tree-lined Block Beautiful stretches along East 19th Street. Though no particular house is outstanding, the street as a whole is lovely.

Pete's Tavern has been here since 1864. O. Henry wrote The Gift of the Magi in the second booth (p157).

GRAMERCY AND THE FLATIRON DISTRICT

Locator Map
For more detail see p152

↑ Pete's Tavern, a haunt of locals and writers alike

The elevated High Line busy with walkers

CHELSEA AND THE GARMENT DISTRICT

Developed on former farmland, this area really began to take shape in 1830. This was largely thanks to Clement Clarke Moore, who wrote *'Twas the Night Before Christmas* – his estate comprised most of what is now Chelsea. After a long period as a rather gritty area, a new and fashionable Chelsea emerged. When Macy's arrived at Herald Square, garment and retail districts sprouted around it. Some of New York's best art galleries flourished in the early 1990s, and the transformation of the High Line has triggered the development of major condo conversions, affluent town houses, and stores of every variety.

A | B

WEST 40TH ST
WEST 39TH ST
LINCOLN TUNNEL
WEST 38TH ST
WEST 37TH ST
WEST 36TH ST
WEST 35TH ST
WEST 34TH ST

ELEVENTH AV
TENTH AV
HUDSON BLVD E

Jacob K Javits Convention Center

CHELSEA AND THE GARMENT DISTRICT

PIER 76

TWELFTH AV

34 St-Hudson Yards S
WEST 33RD ST 7

HIGH LINE
WEST 30TH ST
Port Authority
West 30 St Heliport
WEST 29TH ST
WEST 28TH ST
WEST 27TH ST
WEST 26TH ST

Hudson River

PIER 66

ELEVENTH AV
TENTH AV
HIGH LINE

High Line 2

Chelsea Art Galleries 11
WEST 25TH ST
WEST 24TH ST

CHELSEA AND THE GARMENT DISTRICT

Chelsea Waterside Park

WEST 23RD ST

Empire Diner
22ND

WEST

Must Sees
1 Empire State Building
2 High Line

PIER 62

WEST 21ST

WEST 20TH

Experience More
3 Marble Collegiate Reformed Church
4 Herald Square
5 Macy's
6 Madison Square Garden
7 Museum at the FIT
8 Chelsea Market
9 Rubin Museum of Art
10 St. John the Baptist Church
11 Chelsea Art Galleries

PIER 61

Chelsea Piers

PIER 60

PIER 59

ELEVENTH AV

Chelsea Historic
WEST 19TH
District
WEST 18TH
WEST 17TH
WEST 16TH

Chelsea Market 8
WEST 15TH

Eat
1 BCD Tofu House
2 Cho Dang Gol
3 Mandoo Bar
4 New Wonjo
5 Woorijip Authentic Korean Food

14th Street Park

PIER 57

Shop
6 Chelsea Flea Market
7 Flower District

B

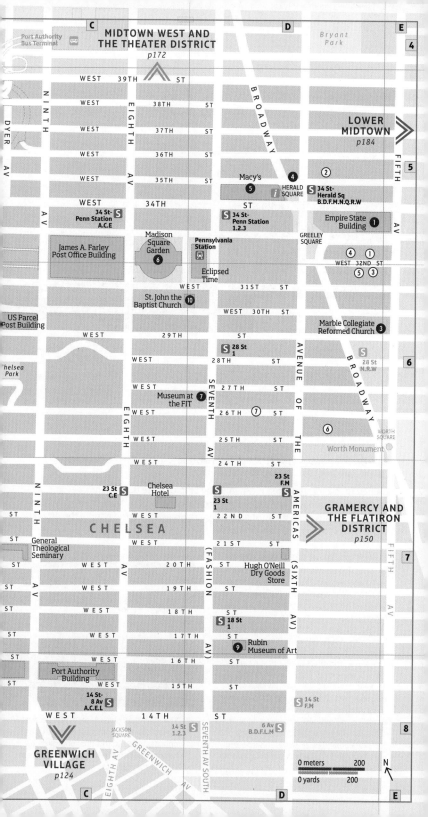

C

Port Authority
Bus Terminal

MIDTOWN WEST AND
THE THEATER DISTRICT
p172

D

E

*Bryant
Park*

4

WEST 39TH ST

WEST 38TH ST

WEST 37TH ST

WEST 36TH ST

WEST 35TH ST

WEST 34TH ST

BROADWAY

NINTH AV

EIGHTH AV

DYER AV

FIFTH AV

LOWER
MIDTOWN
p184

5

Macy's ❹

HERALD
SQUARE

❺ i

34 St-
Herald Sq
B.D.F.M.N.Q.R.W

②

34 St-
Penn Station
A.C.E

34 St-
Penn Station
1.2.3

Empire State
Building ❶

GREELEY
SQUARE

④ ①

WEST 32ND ST

⑤ ③

Madison
Square
Garden ❻

Pennsylvania
Station

James A. Farley
Post Office Building

Eclipsed
Time

WEST 31ST ST

St. John the
Baptist Church ❿

WEST 30TH ST

US Parcel
Post Building

Chelsea
Park

WEST 29TH ST

Marble Collegiate
Reformed Church ❸

WEST 28TH ST

28 St
1

AVENUE OF THE AMERICAS

28 St
N.R.W

BROADWAY

6

WEST 27TH ST

Museum at
the FIT ❼

SEVENTH AV

WEST 26TH ST ⑦

WEST 25TH ST

⑥

WORTH
SQUARE

EIGHTH AV

WEST 24TH ST

Worth Monument

23 St
C.E

Chelsea
Hotel

23 St
F.M

23 St
1

WEST 22ND ST

AMERICAS (SIXTH

GRAMERCY AND
THE FLATIRON
DISTRICT
p150

7

CHELSEA

NINTH ST

General
Theological
Seminary

WEST 21ST ST

WEST 20TH ST

Hugh O'Neill
Dry Goods
Store

AV (FASHION

FIFTH AV

ST

AV

WEST 19TH ST

ST

WEST 18TH ST
1

ST

WEST 17TH ST

Rubin ❾
Museum of Art

AV)

Port Authority
Building

WEST 16TH ST

WEST 15TH ST

14 St-
8 Av
A.C.E.L

WEST 14TH ST

14 St
F.M

8

GREENWICH
VILLAGE
p124

JACKSON
SQUARE

GREENWICH AV

14 St
1.2.3

SEVENTH AV SOUTH

6 Av
B.D.F.L.M

14 St
B.D.F.L.M

EIGHTH AV

0 meters 200

0 yards 200

N

C

D

E

The Empire State Building, dominating the city's skyline ↑

① 🖐 🍴 🛍

EMPIRE STATE BUILDING

1,454 ft

The height of the Empire State Building with its mast (443 m).

📍 D5 🏠 350 Fifth Ave 🚇 34 St (A, B, C, D, E, F, N, Q, R, W, 1, 2, 3) 🚌 M1-5, M16, M34, Q32 🕐 8am-2am (last adm: 1:15am) 🌐 esbnyc.com

Named for New York state's nickname, the Empire State Building has become an enduring symbol of the city since its completion in 1931. More than 3.5 million people visit the country's most iconic skyscraper every year to admire the dizzying views from the building's observatories.

Construction of the Skyscraper

Construction of the city's most evocative skyscraper began in March 1930, not long after the Wall Street Crash. The building was designed for ease and speed of construction; everything possible was prefabricated and slotted into place at a rate of about four stories a week. By the time the skyscraper opened in 1931, reaching the heady heights of 102 stories, space was so difficult to rent that it was nicknamed "the Empty State Building." Only the popularity of the observatories saved the building from bankruptcy. Art Deco touches run throughout, such as in the Fifth Avenue Entrance Lobby, which includes a relief image of the building superimposed on a map of New York State. The skyscraper is a natural lightning conductor and is struck up to 100 times a year.

↑ The 86th-floor observatory offers superb views from its indoor galleries and its outdoor deck. The 102nd-floor observatory requires an extra fee (payable online or at the Visitors' Center).

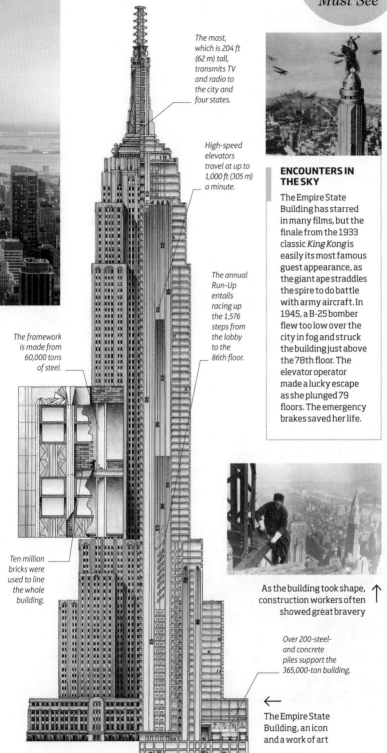

The mast, which is 204 ft (62 m) tall, transmits TV and radio to the city and four states.

High-speed elevators travel at up to 1,000 ft (305 m) a minute.

The annual Run-Up entails racing up the 1,576 steps from the lobby to the 86th floor.

The framework is made from 60,000 tons of steel.

Ten million bricks were used to line the whole building.

Over 200-steel-and concrete piles support the 365,000-ton building.

ENCOUNTERS IN THE SKY

The Empire State Building has starred in many films, but the finale from the 1933 classic *King Kong* is easily its most famous guest appearance, as the giant ape straddles the spire to do battle with army aircraft. In 1945, a B-25 bomber flew too low over the city in fog and struck the building just above the 78th floor. The elevator operator made a lucky escape as she plunged 79 floors. The emergency brakes saved her life.

As the building took shape, ↑ construction workers often showed great bravery

← The Empire State Building, an icon and a work of art

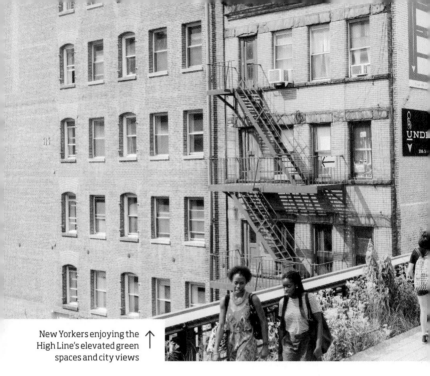

New Yorkers enjoying the ↑
High Line's elevated green
spaces and city views

HIGH LINE

📍B6 🏠From Gansevoort St (Meatpacking District) to West 34th St (between 10th and
12th avs) Ⓢ14 St (A, C, E, L), 34 Street-Hudson Yards (7) 🕐Jun-Sep: 7am-11pm daily;
Apr-May & Oct-Nov: 7am-10pm daily; Dec-Mar: 7am-7pm daily 🌐thehighline.org

The High Line has rapidly become one of New York's signature attractions. Once an
elevated railroad, now an urban park, this sensational addition to the city offers
green spaces and unique perspectives as it cuts through blocks and across streets.

The High Line snaking ↑
through buildings on
Manhattan's west side

New York's Elevated Greenway

An ambitious urban renewal project that
links Midtown, Chelsea, and the Meatpacking
District, the innovative High Line has transformed a disused railroad into a 1.45-mile
(2.33-km) long landscaped park. The railroad
had been abandoned for years when, in 1999,
two local residents created the Friends of the
High Line organization to save the structure
from demolition. Extending from Gansevoort
Street to 34th Street, the park has since played
an important role in the gentrification of the
west side of Manhattan. Designed by top architects, the outstanding elevated promenade-
cum-public-park stands 30 ft (9 m) high above
the streets and cuts through swathes of buildings. At intervals, there are art installations and
food vendors, along with water features, areas
for seating, and countless attractive flower beds.

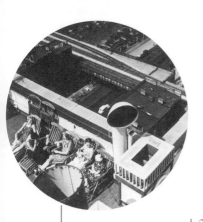

Viewpoints on the High Line

There are countless stunning views along the High Line, but there are a number of viewpoints that shouldn't be missed. These include the overlook at Gansevoort Street, 15th Street Bridge (which offers views of the 1930 skybridge crossing West 15th Street), 10th Avenue Overlook, 23rd Street Bridge (where the 1931 London Terrace Gardens can be seen), 26th Street Viewing Spur, and the final section along 12th Avenue (which has views of Hudson Yards and the Hudson River).

Timeline

1934
▲ The High Line opens to trains.

1980
▽ Last train runs on the line; track is abandoned.

2004
James Corner Field Operations, Diller Scofidio + Renfro, and Piet Oudolf selected to lead redevelopment.

2009
Section 1 opens.

2011
Section 2 opens.

2014
▽ Third and final section opens.

←

The Marble Church and Empire State Building reaching skyward on Fifth Avenue

SHOP

Chelsea Flea Market

Year-round weekend market with up to 135 vendors of antiques, arts and crafts, toys, furniture, vintage clothing, jewelry, and all sorts of old bits and pieces, generally sold for cash only. Admission $1.

◉ D6 ⬛ West 25th St, between Broadway and Sixth Av ◷ 6:30am–6pm Sat & Sun
🌐 annexmarkets.com

Flower District

This area has warehouses and storefronts selling a huge array of beautiful potted plants, small trees, and cut flowers.

◉ D6 ⬛ West 28th St, between Sixth and Seventh avs ◷ 5:30am–5pm (generally)

EXPERIENCE MORE

③

Marble Collegiate Reformed Church

◉ D6 ⬛ 1 West 29th St ⓢ 28 St (N, R, W) ◷ 8:30am–8:30pm Mon–Fri, 9am–4pm Sat, 8am–3pm Sun
🚫 Federal hols
🌐 marblechurch.org

This church is best known for its former pastor, Norman Vincent Peale, who wrote *The Power of Positive Thinking*. Another positive thinker, future US president Richard M. Nixon, attended services here when he was a lawyer in his pre-White House days.

The church was built in 1854 using the marble blocks that give it its name. Fifth Avenue was then no more than a dusty country road, and the cast-iron fence was there to keep wandering livestock out. The original white-and-gold interior walls were replaced with a stenciled gold fleur-de-lis design on a soft rust background. Two stained-glass Tiffany windows, depicting Old Testament scenes, were placed in the south wall in 1900 and 1901.

④

Herald Square

◉ D5 ⬛ Sixth Av at at W 32nd St ⓢ 34 St-Herald Sq (B, D, F, N, Q, R, W)

Named after the *New York Herald*, which occupied a fine arcaded, Italianate Stanford White building here from 1893 to 1921, the square was the hub of the rowdy Tenderloin District in the 1870s and 1880s. Theaters such as the Manhattan Opera House, dance halls, hotels, and restaurants kept the area humming with life until reformers clamped down on sleaze in the 1890s. The ornamental Bennett clock, named for James Gordon Bennett Jr., publisher of the *Herald*, is now all that is left of the Herald Building.

The Opera House was razed in 1901 to make way for Macy's and, soon after, other department stores followed, making the square a mecca for shoppers. One such store was the now-defunct Gimbel

↑ Macy's storefront, with its famous red star logo

Brothers Department Store, once arch-rival to Macy's. (The rivalry was affectionately portrayed in the New York Christmas movie *A Miracle on 34th Street*.) In 1988, the store was converted into a vertical mall with a glittery neon front. Herald Square is still a key shopping district, with chain stores and a traffic-free plaza.

5 🖥 🏛

Macy's

📍 D5 🏠 151 West 34th St 🚇 34 St-Penn Station (1, 2, 3), 34 St-Herald Sq (B, D, F, N, Q, R, W) ⏰ 10am–10pm Mon–Sat, 11am–9pm Sun 🌐 macys.com

The "world's largest store" covers a square block, and the merchandise inside includes any item you could imagine in every price range. Perhaps most famously, the department store sponsors New York's Thanksgiving Day parade *(p55)*, which sees soaring balloons and spectacular floats travel through the streets of Manhattan, along with the Fourth of July fireworks. The store's popular Spring Flower Show also draws thousands of visitors.

Macy's was founded by a former whaler named Rowland Hussey Macy, who opened a small store on West 14th Street in 1858. The store's red star logo came from his tattoo, a souvenir of his sailing days.

By the time Macy died in 1877, his little store had grown to a row of 11 buildings, and at the turn of the century it had outgrown its 14th Street premises. In 1902 it moved to its present site, which covers a staggering 2 million sq ft (186,000 sq m). The eastern facade has a modern entrance but retains the bay windows and pillars of the 1902 design. The 34th Street facade has its original caryatids guarding the entrance, along with the clock, canopy, and lettering. Inside, many of the early wooden escalators are still in working order. Unsurprisingly, Macy's is a designated National Historic Landmark.

6 🚶 Ⓜ️

Madison Square Garden

📍 C5 🏠 4 Pennsylvania Plaza 🚇 34 St-Penn Station (1, 2, 3, A, C, E) ⏰ Daily (for games, shows, and tours) 🌐 msg.com

This is the 20,000-seat home of the NBA's New York Knicks (basketball) and New York Rangers (hockey) teams.

A packed calendar of other events includes rock concerts, championship tennis and boxing, outrageously staged wrestling, and the Westminster Kennel Club Dog Show. There is also a 5,600-seat theater. Tours are available daily, except during games and shows.

There's only one good thing to be said for the razing of the extraordinarily lovely McKim, Mead & White Pennsylvania Station building in favor of this undistinguished complex: it so enraged city preservationists that they formed an alliance to ensure that such a thing would never be allowed to happen again.

KNICKS BASKETBALL AT MADISON SQUARE GARDEN

Madison Square Garden is the home of the Knicks, New York's fanatically supported NBA basketball team. Their last championship win was in 1973, despite star players such as Carmelo Anthony and Jeremy Lin. Fans hope Latvian Kristaps Porziņģis will turn things around. Tickets are nonetheless very hard to get and often astronomically expensive, thanks to an enthusiastic fan base that includes a lot of celebrities, such as Tom Hanks and Katie Holmes.

Gourmet Chelsea Market, selling spices galore *(inset)* ↑

7 Ⓜ 🖥 🏛
Museum at the FIT

📍 D6 🏠 227 West 27th St
🚇 28 St (1) 🕐 Noon–8pm
Tue–Fri, 10am–5pm Sat
🌐 fitnyc.edu/museum

The Fashion Institute of Technology (FIT) is one of the world's top fashion schools, affiliated with the State University of New York, and Norma Kamali, Calvin Klein, and Michael Kors are among its alumni. In the institute's Shirley Goodman Resource Center, the museum hosts changing exhibits. The Fashion and Textile History Gallery, on the main floor, rotates selections from its collection of over 50,000 garments and accessories, and 30,000 textiles. All the major designers are here, including Balenciaga, Coco Chanel, Christian Dior, Yves Saint Laurent, Vivienne Westwood, and Manolo Blahnik. The Gallery FIT shows student and faculty exhibitions.

HOTEL CHELSEA

Arguably Chelsea's most famous building, Hotel Chelsea (222 West 23rd St) was partly converted to a hotel in 1903. It became notorious as the home of literary and music rebels. Jack Kerouac supposedly typed *On the Road* here in 1951, and Dylan Thomas was resident when he died suddenly in 1953. Andy Warhol and protégées Nico and Brigid Berlin holed up here during the filming of *Chelsea Girls* in 1966, and Sid Vicious stabbed Nancy Spungen to death in 1978. It is set to reopen as a luxury hotel sometime in 2019.

8 🏛 🖥
Chelsea Market

📍 B8 🏠 75 Ninth Av
between 15th and 16th sts
🚇 14 St (A, C, E) 🕐 7am–9pm
Mon–Sat, 8am–8pm Sun
🌐 chelseamarket.com

This unmissable destination for foodies incorporates an enclosed food court and shopping mall and the Food Network's TV production facility. A range of gourmet ingredients, exotic food-stuffs, and charming gifts are on offer here, with retail options including Li-lac Chocolates (established in 1923 in the West Village); Chelsea Wine Vault, for a global choice of wines; and Bowery Kitchen Supply, for

> Attracted by low rents, the many galleries that set up shop in Chelsea during the 1990s were a driving force in this area's resurgence.

professional-quality equipment. Some high-end purveyors make and bake on site, cooking up only the freshest, most tempting treats. Google bought Chelsea Market for more than $2.4 billion in 2018.

Rubin Museum of Art

📍D7 🏠150 West 17th St Ⓢ14 St (1, 2, 3), 18 St (1) 🕐11am–5pm Mon & Thu, 11am–9pm Wed, 11am–10pm Fri, 11am–6pm Sat & Sun 🌐rubinmuseum.org

This museum may be a lesser-known treasure, but it has a collection of 2,000 paintings, sculptures, and textiles from the Himalayas, Tibet, India, and the neighboring regions. The Tibetan Buddhist Shrine Room recreates an authentic shrine with flickering lamps and an exhibit on the four Tibetan religious traditions, which rotates every two years.

The museum also hosts captivating travel exhibitions and programs, with concerts, debates, and films. Tours take place daily, at 1 and 3pm. Café Serai, on the first floor, serves Himalayan food.

St. John the Baptist Church

📍D6 🏠210 West 31st St 📞(212) 564-9070 Ⓢ34 St–Penn Station (1, 2, 3, A, C, E) 🕐6:15am–6pm daily

Founded in 1840 to serve a congregation of newly arrived immigrants, this small Roman Catholic church, with a single spire, is today almost lost in the heart of the Fur District. Although the brownstone facade on 30th Street is dark with city soot, many treasures lie within this dull exterior. The entrance is through the modern Friary on 31st Street.

The sanctuary by Napoleon Le Brun is a marvel of Gothic arches in glowing white marble surmounted by gilded capitals. Painted reliefs of religious scenes line the walls and sunlight streams through the stained-glass windows. Also off the Friary is the small Prayer Garden, a peaceful oasis with religious statuary, a fountain, and stone benches.

Chelsea Art Galleries

📍B6 🏠Between West 19th St and West 27th St, around 10th and 11th avs Ⓢ23 St (C, E) 🕐Usually 10am–6pm Tue–Sat 🌐nygallerytours.com

Attracted by low rents, the many galleries that set up shop in Chelsea during the 1990s were a driving force in this area's resurgence. Some 150 to 200 venues exhibit work by emerging artists in various media. Check out P.P.O.W. or David Zwirner, with reputations for provocative work. Avoid Saturdays, which get busy.

↑ Beautiful stained-glass in St. John the Baptist Church

EAT

BCD Tofu House
Specializing in home-made tofu – served on its own, in meat dishes, and in soups.

📍D5 🏠5 West 32nd St 🌐bcdtofu.com

$$$$$

Cho Dang Gol
This place is best known for tofu and *jjigae*, spicy Korean hotpots and soups.

📍D5 🏠55 West 35th St 🌐chodanggol nyc.com

$$$$$

Mandoo Bar
Mouthwatering, Korean-style "mandoo" dumplings are freshly made all day in the store window up front.

📍D6 🏠2 West 32nd St 📞(212) 279-3075

$$$$$

New Wonjo
Korean barbecue is the specialty here, with charcoal-fueled grills under every table.

📍D5 🏠23 West 32nd St 🌐new wonjo.com

$$$$$

Woorijip Authentic Korean Food
This cafeteria is very popular for its bargain lunch buffets and *bibimbop*.

📍D6 🏠12 West 32nd St 📞(212) 244-1115

$$$$$

Times Square glowing with neon lights

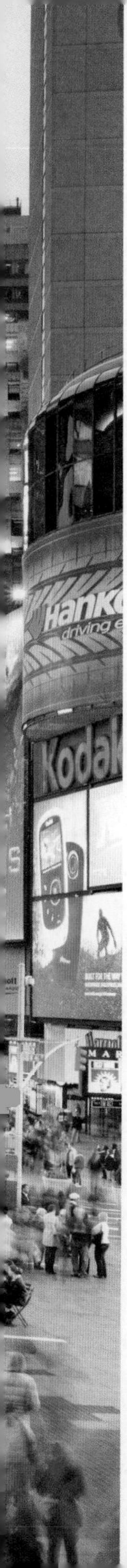

MIDTOWN WEST AND THE THEATER DISTRICT

At the heart of Midtown lies Times Square, where huge neon displays flash and crowds bustle. The Theater District lies north of 42nd Street, and offers a fabulous concentration of live theater. It was the move of the Metropolitan Opera House to Broadway at 40th Street, in 1883, that first drew theaters and restaurants here. In the 1920s, movie palaces added the glamor of neon to Broadway, the signs getting bigger and brighter, until eventually the street came to be known as the "Great White Way." After World War II, the draw of the films waned, and the glitter was replaced by grime. Fortunately, since the 1990s, regeneration has brought back the public and the bright lights of Broadway.

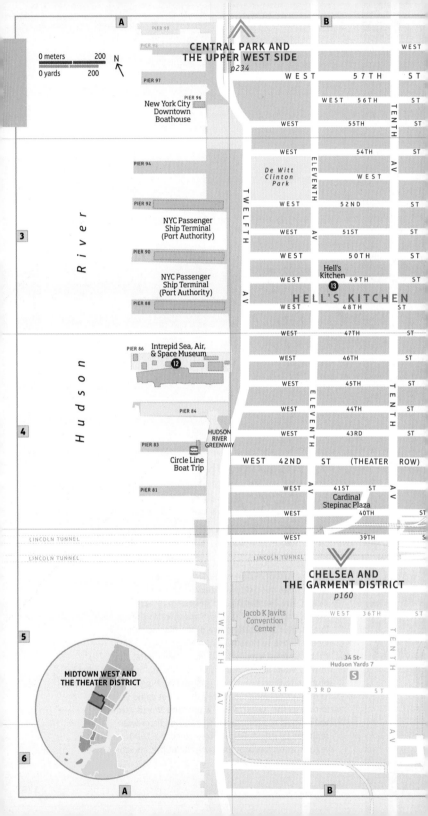

MIDTOWN WEST AND THE THEATER DISTRICT

Must Sees

1. Rockefeller Center
2. New York Public Library

Experience More

3. Times Square
4. SPYSCAPE
5. New York City Center and Alvin Ailey American Dance Theater
6. Bryant Park
7. Carnegie Hall
8. Madame Tussauds New York
9. Museum of Arts and Design
10. Gulliver's Gate
11. National Geographic Encounter
12. Intrepid Sea, Air & Space Museum
13. Hell's Kitchen

Eat

1. Le Bernardin
2. Rainbow Room
3. Russian Tea Room

Shop

4. Drama Book Shop

1 🖥 🏛

ROCKEFELLER CENTER

📍 D3 🏢 30 Rockefeller Plaza 🚇 47–50 St-Rockefeller Ctr (B, D, F, M)
🕐 Top of the Rock: 8am–midnight daily 🌐 rockefellercenter.com

This massive Art Deco complex has been at the heart of Midtown since the 1930s. Today it's home to TV studios, restaurants, and one of the city's highest observation decks, Top of the Rock, not forgetting the famous ice rink during the holiday season.

The Heart of New York

The Art Deco complex was commissioned by tycoon John D. Rockefeller Jr. and designed by a team headed by Raymond Hood. Rockefeller had leased the site in 1928, seeing it as a new home for the Met Opera, but the 1929 Wall Street Crash scuttled those plans. Today the center encompasses Radio City Music Hall, the 850-ft- (259-m-) tall 30 Rockefeller Plaza (or "30 Rock"), an underground shopping mall, Rainbow Room, and the sunken Lower Plaza.

↑ Illuminated cityscapes, as seen from the Top of the Rock

Rockefeller went ahead with his own development. The 14 buildings erected between 1931 and 1940 provided jobs for up to 225,000 people during the Depression; by 1973, there were 19 buildings.

Did You Know?

The Rockefeller Christmas tree is lit by 30,000 environmentally friendly lights.

← The famous Rockefeller Christmas tree beside the ice-skating rink

The Rink at Rockefeller Center

Every winter since 1936, the Lower Plaza at Rockefeller Center transforms into an ice-skating rink. Skating is on a first-come, first-served basis, so arrive early to avoid a long wait (open daily 8:30am to midnight; www.therinkatrockcenter.com). From late November to early January, the Christmas Tree, known for having featured in a number of shows and movies, overlooks the rink above Paul Manship's *Prometheus* sculpture.

---

30 ROCK

30 Rockefeller Plaza has long been the home of the NBC television network. See where *Saturday Night Live, The Tonight Show Starring Jimmy Fallon,* and *The Today Show* are filmed on the NBC Studio Tour (www.thetouratnbcstudios.com). You can be a part of *The Today Show* outdoor audience by simply turning up before 7am on a weekday.

Water features lining ↑
the Art Deco Rockefeller
Center complex

2 (icons)

NEW YORK PUBLIC LIBRARY

D4 476 Fifth Av 42 St-Bryant Park (B, D, F, M) 10am-8pm Tue & Wed, 10am-6pm Thu-Sat, 1-5pm Sun nypl.org

The New York Public Library is one of the city's most beloved public buildings. It's an attraction as much for its lavish architecture and decor as for its extensive book collections, changing exhibits, and cultural events.

New York's Beaux Arts Gem

In 1897, the coveted job of designing New York Public Library Main Branch (now the Stephen A. Schwarzman Building) was awarded to architects Carrère & Hastings. The library's first director envisaged a light, quiet, airy place for study, where millions of books could be both stored and available to readers as promptly as possible. In the hands of Carrère & Hastings, his vision came true in what is considered the epitome of New York's Beaux Arts period. The library opened in 1911 to immediate acclaim. The vast, paneled Rose Main Reading Room stretches two full blocks and is suffused with daylight from the two interior courtyards. Below it are 88 miles (142 km) of shelves, holding over seven million volumes.

The DeWitt Wallace Periodicals Room is adorned with 13 murals by Richard Haas, honoring New York's great publishing houses. The similarly opulent Map Room is home to one of the largest public map collections in the world. There are also public exhibitions on wide-ranging subjects filling several galleries. Free guided tours (11am and 2pm Mon–Sat) are a great way to take in these spaces.

→ The New York Public Library facade, designed by Carrère & Hastings architects

THE REAL POOH BEAR

Visit the Children's Center to see the real stuffed toy animals that inspired the beloved Winnie-the-Pooh stories by A. A. Milne. Pooh, Eeyore, Piglet, Kanga, and Tigger were originally owned by Christopher Robin Milne in the 1920s, and acquired by the Library in 1987.

The Map Room

Aside from its stunning map room, the library's map division houses an astounding 433,000 sheet maps and some 20,000 books and atlases, from the 16th to the 21st centuries. Staff are on hand to produce any cartographic print, from British strongholds during the Revolution and German maps used during World War II to historic maps of New York itself.

→

The ornate Map Room, where historic maps are available for viewing

↓ The spectacular Rose Main Reading Room

EXPERIENCE MORE

3

Times Square

📍D4 🚇Times Sq-42 St
(N, R, 1, 2, 3, 7) 🎫Broadway
Plaza, between 43rd and
44th sts; 9am-6pm daily
🌐timessquarenyc.org

Broadway traditions coexist
with modern innovations
here and, thanks to a 1990s
transformation, this iconic
New York address is now a
vibrant hub bustling with
activity. Buildings such as
1540 Broadway (formerly
known as the Bertelsmann),
and the fashionably
minimalist Condé Nast offices
sit alongside the classic
Broadway theaters.

Although *The New York
Times* has moved from its
original headquarters at the
south end of the square to
a site opposite the Port
Authority, its famous
glittering ball (of Waterford
crystal) still drops at midnight
on New Year's Eve to great
fanfare, as it has since the
building opened in 1906.

Broadway's fortunes have
also revived. Many theaters
have been renovated and are
again hosting contemporary
productions; theater-goers
throng the area's bars and
restaurants each evening.

One of the landmarks is the
Westin Hotel, a 57-story
skyscraper designed by Miami

architects Arquitectonica, that
tops the E-Walk entertainment and retail complex at
42nd Street and Eighth
Avenue. Other attractions
include a Madame Tussauds at
42nd Street (*p182*), a massive
Disney Store, a traffic-free
plaza, and M&M World at
1600 Broadway.

4

SPYSCAPE

📍C2 🏠928 Eighth Ave
🚇50th St (A, C, E) 🕐10am-
9pm Mon-Fri, 9am-9pm Sat
& Sun 🌐spyscape.com

This fun experience – part-
spy museum and part-
interactive adventure – is
targeted at adults and teens.
Exhibits include a copy of the
famed Enigma machine (you
can try coding and decoding
messages), lie detectors
(you can have a go), and a
hacking bar. There's also a
laser tunnel (the "Special Ops
Challenge") and the chance to
have your very own personal
spy profile developed by a
former head of training at
British Intelligence services.

5

New York City
Center and Alvin
Ailey American
Dance Theater

📍D2 🏠131 West 55th St
🚇57 St (N, O, R, W)
🕐For performances only
🌐nycitycenter.org

This highly ornate Moorish
structure, with its dome of
Spanish tiles, was designed
in 1924 as a Masonic Shriners'
Temple. After Mayor La Guardia
saved it from developers, it
became home to the New
York City Opera (1944–64)
and Ballet (1948–66). City
Center lived on as a venue for

Did You Know?

Drama Book Shop
closed in 2019, but Lin-
Manuel Miranda and
friends are looking for
new premises.

dance after the companies
moved to the Lincoln Center,
instead becoming the home
of the Manhattan Theatre
Club and the highly respected
Alvin Ailey American Dance
Theater, which specializes in
modern dance.

6

Bryant Park

📍D4 🚇5 Av (7), 42 St-
Bryant Pk (B, D, F, M)
🕐Daily; hours vary, check
website for details
🌐bryantpark.org

This park is a welcome oasis
of calm wedged between

💬 INSIDER TIP
Ticket Bargains

The Times Square
TKTS booth (*www.tdf.
org*), located beneath
the red steps at
Broadway and West
47th Street, is still the
primary go-to spot for
discounted tickets to
stellar Broadway shows.
Lines are long, but it's
worth it for the discount.

↑ Alfresco summer-time dining in pretty Bryant Park

Midtown's towering sky-scrapers. It hosts a range of activities all year round in its lush gardens, including fitness classes, literary and contemporary dance events, open-air screenings of classic movies in the summer, and a free ice-skating rink in winter. There are also food kiosks and restaurants dotted around the park, making it the perfect place to while away an afternoon or make a rest stop. Many people don't realise that the New York Public Library (p178) keeps over a million books from its collections in temperature-controlled storage beneath the park.

In 1853, Bryant Park (then known as Reservoir Park) housed a dazzling Crystal Palace, built for the World's Fair of the same year. This precipitated one of the first tourist booms New York had seen, attracting over one million visitors. Sadly the palace burnt down in 1858.

In 1989, the park was renovated and reclaimed for workers and visitors to enjoy.

7 Ⓜ 🛍

Carnegie Hall

📍D2 🏛154 West 57th St 🚇57 St-7 Av (N, Q, R) ⏰For concerts 🌐carnegie hall.org

Financed by millionaire philanthropist Andrew Carnegie, New York's first great concert hall opened in 1891, with guest conductor Tchaikovsky. For many years it was home to the New York Philharmonic, under conductors such as Arturo Toscanini, Bruno Walter, and Leonard Bernstein. Playing Carnegie Hall quickly became an international symbol of success for musicians, and today the corridors are lined with memorabilia of artists who have performed here.

A 1950s campaign by violinist Isaac Stern saved the site from developers, and in 1964 it became a national landmark, planting it firmly in the city's consciousness as a place of cultural importance.

If you aren't able to watch a concert, you can join a tour; check the website for details.

THEATERS OF BROADWAY

Many of Broadway's original theaters have gone, but 25 of those that remain are designated Historic Landmarks. The 1903 Lyceum (149 West 45th St) was the first to receive the designation and is the city's oldest active theater. When it opened in 1903, the New Amsterdam (214 West 42nd St) was the most opulent theater in the US. The first with an Art Nouveau interior, it was owned by Florenz Ziegfeld, of Ziegfeld Follies fame. The 1912 Helen Hayes (240 West 44th St) is Broadway's smallest theater, while the celebrated Shubert (225 West 44th St) has a magnificent interior that belies its simple exterior.

8

Madame Tussauds New York

C4 **234 West 42nd St** **Times Sq-42 St (N, Q, R, S, 1, 2, 3, 7)** **10am-10pm Fri & Sat, 10am-8pm Sun-Thu** **madametussauds.com/new-york**

This global tourist franchise operates a large branch just off Times Square, with the usual line-up of amazingly realistic wax models of movie stars, celebrities, royalty, and politicians. Extras (which you must pay extra for) include the "Ghostbusters: Dimension Virtual Reality Experience," which allows you to dress up like the movie's characters and catch a ghost. There's also the "Marvel 4D Cinema Experience," where superheroes, including the Hulk, are brought to life with wax figures and 4D film.

9

Museum of Arts and Design

C2 **2 Columbus Circle** **59 St-Columbus Circle (A, B, C, D, 1)** **10am-6pm Tue-Sun (to 9pm Thu)** **Federal hols** **madmuseum.org**

The leading American cultural institution of its kind, this museum, housed in a modern, eye-catching building, is dedicated to contemporary

↑ Waxwork of *Ghostbusters* actress Leslie Jones at Madame Tussauds

THE DIAMOND DISTRICT

New York's Diamond District (47th Street, between Fifth and Sixth avenues) features window displays of glittering gold and diamonds, the buildings filled with booths and workshops where jewelers vie for customers. The district was born in the 1930s, when Jewish diamond-cutters fled Europe to escape Nazism. It deals mainly in wholesale, but individuals are welcome. Bring cash, compare prices, and haggle – but only if you know something about the value of diamonds.

objects in an array of media, from clay and wood to metal and fiber. The permanent collection has over 2,000 artifacts by international craftspeople and designers.

About four exhibitions a year are complemented by selected pieces from the Tiffany & Co. Foundation Jewelry Gallery. Items by top-class American artisans are for sale in The Store at MAD.

10

Gulliver's Gate

D4 **216 West 44th St** **Times Sq-42 St (N, Q, R, W, S, 1, 2, 3, 7)** **10am-8pm daily (last adm: 1 hour before closing)** **gulliversgate.com**

Encompassing some 50,000 sq ft (6,645 sq m), this is a family-friendly, interactive world of miniature cities from five continents. An astounding 102 bridges, 967 buildings, and 233 cars have been reproduced to mimic real-life places. The first exhibit, naturally, is New York City, with its most iconic buildings and landmarks represented. This includes the Brooklyn Bridge, the Empire State Building, Central Park, Staten Island Ferry Building, and

Grand Central Station. There are tiny, realistic touches at "street level": familiar graffiti tags, sunbathers on fire escapes, cops investigating crimes, and pigeons fluttering on rooftops.

Latin America features the Panama Canal, Iguazu Falls, Machu Picchu, and Chichen Itza, while the Taj Mahal, Angkor Wat, the Great Wall, and Forbidden City represent Asia. Paris and Venice both feature in Europe's section, and there's a stunning model of Jerusalem's Old City. Buy timed tickets online to save time (and money).

11

National Geographic Encounter

C4 **226 44th St** **Times Sq-42 St (N, Q, R, S, W, 1, 2, 3, 7)** **10am-9pm Sun-Thu, 10am-10pm Fri & Sat** **natgeoencounter.com**

Opened in 2017, the spectacular National Geographic Encounter: Ocean Odyssey is a vast complex that utilizes

→

The opulent Russian Tea Room serving up a sense of opulence

advanced technology to simulate a walk across the ocean. Specifically, visitors can "walk" from the South Pacific to the coast of California. Immersive sounds, touch screens, and holograms create virtual interaction with sea lions, dolphins, and 50-foot (15-m)humpback whales. There's even a battle between two Humboldt squids.

Allow at least two hours for this attraction. It's also advisable to buy timed tickets online in advance.

⑫ Intrepid Sea, Air & Space Museum

🟢 A4 🏠 Pier 86, West 46th St 🚇 Times Sq-42 St (N, Q, R, S, W, 1, 2, 3, 7) 🚌 M42, M50 ⏰ Apr-Oct: 10am-5pm Mon-Fri, 10am-6pm Sat, Sun and hols; Nov-Mar: 10am-5pm daily 🌐 intrepidmuseum.org

Exhibits on board this World War II aircraft carrier include fighter planes from the 1940s; the A-12 Blackbird, the world's fastest spy plane;

an original Concorde; and the USS *Growler*, a guided-missile submarine launched in 1958 at the height of the Cold War.

The museum's family-friendly Exploreum Hall contains two G-Force flight simulators, a 4D motion ride theater, a Bell 47 helicopter, and an interactive submarine. There is also the Space Shuttle Pavilion, which houses the historic spacecraft *Enterprise*.

⑬ 🍴 Hell's Kitchen

🟢 B3 🚇 50 St (C, E)

West of Times Square, roughly between 30th and 59th streets, lies Clinton, more commonly called Hell's Kitchen. Now known for its culinary reputation, in the late 1800s the area was a poor Irish enclave, and one of New York's most violent neighborhoods, as African-Americans, Greeks and Puerto

Did You Know?

Madonna worked in coat-check at the Russian Tea Room in 1982.

Ricans moved in and tensions rapidly developed. Such rivalries were glamorized in the musical *West Side Story*, the movie of which was filmed in New York and released in 1957. The area has been cleaned up, with rents skyrocketing and Ninth Avenue especially crammed with restaurants, bars, and delis. There's also a strong gay community, with as many gay bars as in Chelsea or the West Village. These moved in here as Chelsea and the West Village became gentrified and, as a result, expensive.

Elegant interiors at Grand Central Terminal

LOWER MIDTOWN

From Beaux Arts to Art Deco, this section of Midtown boasts some fine architecture, chic boutiques, and towering skyscrapers, primarily scattered along Fifth, Madison, and Park avenues. Quiet, residential Murray Hill, between East 34th and East 40th streets, was named for a country estate that once occupied the site. By the turn of the 20th century, it was home to many of New York's first families, including the financier J. P. Morgan, whose library, now a museum, reveals the grandeur of the age. The commercial pace quickens at 42nd Street, near Grand Central Terminal, where tall office blocks line the streets. However, few of the newer buildings equal the Beaux Arts Terminal, Art Deco gems such as the Chrysler Building, or the Modernist United Nations complex overlooking the East River.

MIDTOWN

MIDTOWN WEST AND
THE THEATER DISTRICT
p172

Helmsley
Building **9**

MetLife
Building
6

Grand
Central
Terminal
1
① ② ③

Bowery Savings
Bank Building **5**

Grand Central-
42 St
S.4.5.6.7

Fred F.
French
Building

Bryant
Park

New York
Public
Library

PERSHING
SQUARE

Morgan Library
& Museum
13

Church of the
Incarnation **11**

LOWER MIDTOWN

Must Sees
1 Grand Central Terminal
2 United Nations

Experience More
3 Chrysler Building
4 Chanin Building
5 Bowery Savings Bank Building
6 MetLife Building
7 Daily News Building
8 Ford Foundation Center for
   Social Justice
9 Helmsley Building
10 Japan Society
11 Church of the Incarnation
12 Sniffen Court
13 Morgan Library & Museum

Eat
① Grand Central Oyster Bar
② Great Northern Food Hall
③ The Campbell

Stay
④ Library Hotel

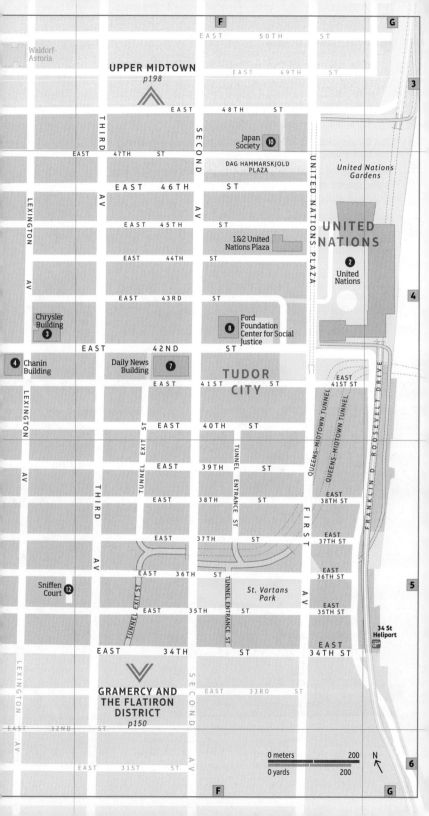

❶ Ⓜ️ 🍴 🖥️ 🛍️

GRAND CENTRAL TERMINAL

📍 E4 🏛️ East 42nd St at Park Av 🚇 Grand Central (S, 4, 5, 6, 7) 🚌 M1–5, M42, M50, M101–103, Q32 🕐 5:30am–2am daily 🌐 grandcentralterminal.com

Since it opened in 1913, this Beaux Arts gem has been a gateway to and symbol of the city. The terminal's glory is its soaring main concourse, along with its fabulous Oyster Bar.

EXPERIENCE Lower Midtown

In 1871, Cornelius Vanderbilt (1794–1877) opened a railway station on 42nd Street. Although often revamped, it was never large enough and was finally demolished. Grand Central Terminal as we see it today opened in 1913. The building has a steel frame covered with plaster and marble. Reed & Stern were in charge of the logistical planning; Warren & Wetmore, the overall design. The restoration by architects Beyer Blinder Belle is outstanding, and transports both railway travelers and tourists to a bygone era.

← Sun beams pour through the terminal's main concourse, c. 1930

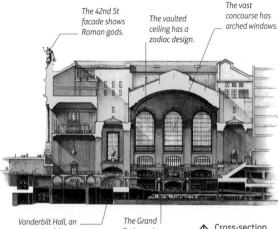

The 42nd St facade shows Roman gods.

The vaulted ceiling has a zodiac design.

The vast concourse has arched windows.

Vanderbilt Hall, an example of Beaux Arts architecture.

The Grand Staircase is based on Paris's opera house.

↑ Cross-section of Grand Central Terminal's interior

EAT

**Grand Central
Oyster Bar**
Sample fresh oysters at
this seafood palace
below Grand Central.
Open since 1913, it's
crowned by grand,
vaulted ceilings. The
chefs opt for simple
preparation – a squeeze
of lemon or a hand-
plucked garnish –
allowing the fresh fish,
clam chowder, steamed
Maine lobster, and
sweet Kumamoto
oysters to shine on their
own delectable merit.

⬛E4 🏠Lower level,
Grand Central Terminal
📅Sun 🌐oyster
barny.com

$$⑤

↑ The impressive main
terminal concourse
and exterior *(inset)*

Secretariat Building

The Conference Building

↑ Called Colors of the World, flags of member nations fly before the UN

Colors of the World

General Assembly

Security Council

Trusteeship Council

Economic and Social Council

WORKS OF ART AT THE UN

The UN Building has acquired numerous works of art; most have either a peace or international friendship theme. These include a mosaic by Norman Rockwell, a Henry Moore sculpture in the grounds, and a Peace Bell gifted by Japan.

Rose Garden

The United Nations complex, including its gardens ↑

↑ The General Assembly in session, with murals by Fernand Leger

2 (Ⓜ) (🖥) (🏛)

UNITED NATIONS

📍 F4 **🏠 First Av at 46th St** **🚇 42 St-Grand Central (S, 4, 5, 6, 7)**
🚌 M15, M42, M50 **🕘 9am–4:45pm daily** **🚫 Federal hols, Eid**
🌐 visit.un.org

Visitors' entrance

Many visitors to New York don't realize that the city is the home of international humanitarian organization the United Nations. The 193 member nations aim to preserve world peace, and aid economic and social well-being around the globe.

The UN was founded in 1945 with just 51 members. John D. Rockefeller Jr. donated $8.5 million for the purchase of the site. Today, the UN comprises five forums. The General Assembly holds regular sessions to discuss international problems September through December, and all member states are represented with an equal vote. It cannot enact laws, but its recommendations strongly influence world opinion. The most powerful body is the Security Council, which strives to achieve peace and security, intervening in international crises, such as conflict. It is the only body whose decisions member states must obey, as well as the only one in continuous session. China, France, the Russian Federation, the UK, and the US are permanent Council members; ten non-permanent members are elected by the General Assembly for two-year terms.

The 54 members of the Economic and Social Council work to improve the standard of living and social welfare around the world, including economic issues and human rights abuses. The Secretariat has some 16,000 international workers and carries out the day-to-day work of the UN It's headed by the Secretary General, who is a spokesperson in the organization's peace-keeping efforts. Finally, the International Court of Justice settles disputes between member states.

Tours of the UN take place Monday through Friday and booking is essential.

↑ The Security Council, where delegates confer, overlooked by murals by artist Per Krohg

EXPERIENCE MORE

❸ Chrysler Building

📍E4 🏠405 Lexington Av
📞(212) 682-3070 🚇42 St-
Grand Central (S, 4, 5, 6, 7)
🕐Lobby: 7am–6pm

William Van Alen's 77-story Chrysler Building, topped by its shining crown, is one of New York City's best-known and most-loved landmarks. It was built for Walter P. Chrysler, a former Union Pacific Railroad machinist, whose passion for the motor car helped him rise swiftly to the top of this industry to found the corporation bearing his name in 1925. His wish for a headquarters in New York that symbolized his company led to a building that will always be linked with the golden age of motoring. The stainless-steel Art Deco spire resembles a car radiator grille; the series of stepped setbacks are emblazoned with winged radiator caps, wheels, and stylized automobiles; and gargoyles are modeled on hood ornaments from the 1929 Chrysler Plymouth.

The crowning spire, kept a secret until the last moment, was built in the fire shaft, then raised into position through the roof, ensuring that the 1,046-ft (320-m) building would be higher than the just-completed Bank of Manhattan by Van Alen's great rival, H. Craig Severance. Just a few months later, it was overtaken by the Empire State Building.

Van Alen was poorly rewarded. Chrysler accused him of accepting bribes from contractors and refused to pay him. Van Alen's career never recovered from the slur.

The stunning lobby, once a car showroom, is lavish, with patterned marble and granite and a chromed steel trim. A vast painted ceiling by Edward Trumball shows scenes of late-1920s transportation.

Although it was never the Chrysler Corporation's HQ, their name remains.

↑ The Chanin Building, a splendid example of Art Deco style

❹ Chanin Building

📍E4 🏠122 East 42nd St
🚇42 St- Grand Central (S, 4, 5, 6, 7) 🕐Office hours

Once the headquarters of Irwin S. Chanin, one of New York's leading real estate developers and a self-made man, the 56-story 1929 tower, by Sloan & Robertson, was the first skyscraper in the Grand Central area, and is one of the best examples of the Art Deco period. A wide bronze band, with bird and fish motifs, runs the length of the facade and the terra-cotta base features a tangle of stylized plantlife. Sculptor René Chambellan's interior includes reliefs in the vestibule charting Chanin's career.

❺ Bowery Savings Bank Building

📍E4 🏠110 East 42nd St
🚇42 St-Grand Central (S, 4, 5, 6, 7) 🕐By appt only
🌐cipriani.com

Many consider this 1923 building the best work of bank architects York & Sawyer, who chose the style of a Romanesque basilica for the offices of the venerable bank (now part of Capital One Bank). An arched entrance leads into the vast banking room, with a high-beamed ceiling, mosaic floors, and marble columns on which stone arches soar overhead.

Between the columns are unpolished mosaic panels of marble from France and Italy. The building, now an event space, is also home to Cipriani restaurant, whose opulent decor lures high rollers for celebratory dinners.

← The distinctive Chrysler Building, a monument to the early days of motoring

6

MetLife Building

E4 **200 Park Av** **S** 42 St-Grand Central (S, 4, 5, 6, 7) **Office hours**

When this colossus was built, as the Pan Am Building, in 1963, its status as the largest commercial building in the world was somewhat over-shadowed by the loss of the view from Park Avenue of the

EAT

Great Northern Food Hall

Nordic-inspired food market inside Grand Central, with seasonal menus that showcase the New York region's best produce. Stalls include organic bakery Meyers Bageri, coffee shop Brownsville Roasters, gourmet hot dogs at Danish Dogs, and vegetable-driven menus at Almanak.

E4 **Vanderbilt Hall West, Grand Central Terminal** **w** great northernfood.com

$$$

The Campbell

This is one of New York's most elegant cocktail bars, in the style of a Florentine palace. Serving good lunches and bar food, the real draws here are the drinks and the setting. The adjacent Campbell Palm Court offers views into the terminal. No casual wear after 4pm.

E4 **15 Vanderbilt Av (off 43rd St), Grand Central Terminal** **w** thecampbellnyc.com

$$$

sculptures atop the Grand Central Terminal. Designed in the Modernist style by Walter Gropius, Emery Roth and Sons, and Pietro Belluschi, it dwarfed the terminal and aroused universal dislike. The building's rooftop heliport was abandoned in 1977 after a freak accident showered debris onto the surrounding streets. In 1981, the building was sold to the Metropolitan Life organization, and then on to Tishman Speyer Properties.

It is ironic that the New York skies were blocked by Pan Am, a company that had opened up the skies as a means of travel. When the company began in 1927, Charles Lindbergh, fresh from his solo transatlantic flight, was one of its pilots and an adviser on new routes. By 1936, Pan Am introduced the first trans-Pacific route, and in 1947 their first round-the-world route was launched, though it ceased operations in 1991.

7

Daily News Building

F4 **220 East 42nd St** **S** 42 St-Grand Central (S, 4, 5, 6, 7) **8am–6pm Mon–Fri**

The *Daily News* was founded in 1919 and by 1925 it was a million-seller, known, rather scathingly, as "the servant girl's bible," for its focus on scandals, celebrities and

> **William Van Alen's 77-story Chrysler Building, topped by its shining crown, is one of New York City's best-known and most-loved landmarks.**

murders, its readable style, and heavy use of illustration. Over the years it has stuck to what it does best, and this formula has paid off handsomely. It revealed stories such as the romance of Edward VIII and Mrs Simpson, and has become renowned for its punchy headlines. Its circulation figures are still among the highest in the United States.

Its former headquarters (the offices are now at 4 New York Plaza), designed by Raymond Hood in 1930, have vertical stripes of brown and black brick alternating with windows. Hood's lobby is familiar to many as that of the *Daily Planet* in the 1980s *Superman* movies. It includes the world's largest interior globe, and bronze lines on the floor indicate the direction of world cities and the position of the planets. At night, the intricate detail over the front entrance of the building is illuminated from within by neon. The building has now been designated as a National Historic Landmark.

Giant globe in the ↑ lobby of the Daily News Building

8
Ford Foundation Center for Social Justice

F4 **320 East 43rd St** **42nd St-Grand Central (S, 4, 5, 6, 7)** **8am-6pm Mon-Fri**

Built in 1968, this building was designed by architect Kevin Roche, and featured the first of the atria now common across Manhattan. The atrium resembles an enormous greenhouse, supported by towering columns of granite, and was one of the first attempts at a natural environment within a building. It is fringed by two walls of offices, visible through windows, and yet the enclave is incredibly tranquil. The din outside disappears and all that remains is the echo of voices, trickle of fountains, and sound of shoes on brick walkways.

The Ford Foundation Center underwent a major renovation, which was completed at the end of 2018.The improved space includes an atrium garden (with 39 plant species) plus a new auditorium.

9
Helmsley Building

E4 **230 Park Av** **42 St-Grand Central (S, 4, 5, 6, 7)** **Office hours**

One of the great New York views looks south down Park Avenue to the Helmsley Building, straddling the busy traffic flow beneath. There is just one flaw – the monolithic MetLife Building (p193) towers behind it, replacing the former backdrop, the sky.

Built by Warren & Wetmore in 1929, the Helmsley Building was originally the headquarters of the New York Central Railroad Company. Its namesake, the late Harry Helmsley, was a billionaire who began his career as a New York office boy for $12 per week. His wife, Leona, was a prominent feature in all the advertisements for their hotel chain – until her imprisonment in 1989 for tax evasion on a grand scale. Many observers believe that the extravagant glitter of the building's facelift was due to Leona's overblown taste in decor.

Did You Know?

When Leona Helmsley died in 2007, she left a $12 million trust fund for her pet Maltese, called Trouble.

10
Japan Society

F3 **333 East 47th St** **42 St-Grand Central (S, 4, 5, 6, 7)** **M15, M50** **japansociety.org**

The headquarters of the Japan Society, founded in 1907 to foster understanding and cultural exchange between Japan and the US, was built with the help of John D. Rockefeller III, who underwrote costs of some $4.3 million. The striking black building, with its delicate sun grilles, was designed by Tokyo architects Junzo Yoshimura and George Shimamoto in 1971. It includes a museum gallery (open Tuesday to Sunday in October through to June), an auditorium, a language

---

MIDTOWN MANHATTAN

The skyline here is graced with some of the city's most spectacular towers and spires, from the familiar beauty of the Empire State Building's Art Deco pinnacle to the dramatic wedge of Citibank's modern headquarters. As the shoreline progresses uptown the architecture becomes more varied. The United Nations complex dominates a long stretch before Beekman Place begins a strand of exclusive residential enclaves offering the rich and famous some seclusion in this busy part of the city.

Empire State Building

United Nations

Chrysler Building

← Attractive and leafy setting of John Sniffen's carriage houses

center, a research library, and traditional Oriental gardens.

Changing exhibits include a variety of Japanese arts, from swords to kimonos to scrolls. The society offers programs of Japanese performing arts, lectures, language classes and many business workshops for American and Japanese executives and managers.

11

Church of the Incarnation

📍 E5 🏠 209 Madison Av
Ⓢ 42 St-Grand Central (S, 4, 5, 6, 7), 33rd Street (6)
🕐 11:30am- 2pm Mon-Fri, 8am-1pm Sun 🌐 churchof theincarnation.org

This Episcopal church dates from 1864, when Madison Avenue was home to the elite. Its patterned sandstone and brownstone exterior is typical of the period. The interior has an oak communion rail by Daniel Chester French; a chancel mural by John La Farge; and stained-glass windows by La Farge, Tiffany, William Morris, and Edward Burne-Jones.

12

Sniffen Court

📍 E5 🏠 150-158 East 36th St
Ⓢ 33 St (6)

This is a delightful, intimate courtyard of ten brick Romanesque Revival carriage houses, built by John Sniffen in the 1850s. They are perfectly and improbably preserved off a busy block in modern New York. The house at the south end was the studio of sculptor Malvina Hoffman, whose plaques of Greek horsemen decorate the exterior wall.

13

Morgan Library & Museum

📍 E5 🏠 225 Madison Av
Ⓢ 33 St (6) 🕐 10:30am-5pm Tue-Thu, 10am-9pm Fri, 10am-6pm Sat, 11am-6pm Sun 🌐 themorgan.org

One of the world's finest collections of rare manuscripts, drawings, prints, books, and bindings is on display here, accumulated by legendary banker J. P. Morgan (1837–1913). A stunning piazza-style central atrium, created by Renzo Piano, links several Morgan properties. The magnificent palazzo-style building in which Morgan originally stored his collection, completed in 1906, contains his immaculately maintained personal library and study. The 1928 Annex was designed in similar fashion (replacing Morgan's old town house) and now houses the Morgan Stanley galleries. The 1850s Italianate brownstone home of J. P. Morgan Jr., who lived here from 1905 to 1943, now features the Morgan Dining Room and Morgan Shop. A 2006 renovation also doubled the exhibition space. The collection has over 10,000 drawings and prints by the likes of Da Vinci and Dürer, rare literary manuscripts by Austen and Dickens, and priceless copies of the Gutenberg Bible (three of the eleven that survive).

A SHORT WALK
LOWER MIDTOWN

Distance 1.25 mile (2 km) **Nearest subway**
Grand Central-42 St **Time** 25 minutes

A walk in Lower Midtown is a great way to fully
appreciate New York's eclectic mix of architectural
styles. Step back to take in the contours of the
tallest skyscrapers, and step inside to experience
the many fine interiors; from modern atriums,
such as those in the Ford Foundation Center for
Social Justice, to the ornate details of the Bowery
Savings Bank Building, and the soaring spaces
of Grand Central Terminal.

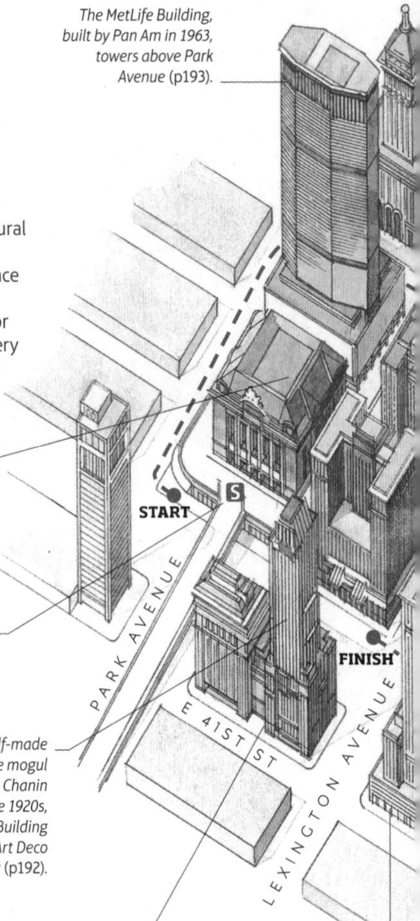

*The MetLife Building,
built by Pan Am in 1963,
towers above Park
Avenue (p193).*

*The vast, vaulted interior of Grand
Central Terminal is a splendid
reminder of the heyday of train
travel. This historic building also
features specialty shops and
gourmet restaurants (p188).*

START S

*Grand Central-42
St subway (lines
S, 4, 5, 6, 7)*

FINISH

PARK AVENUE

E 41ST ST

LEXINGTON AVENUE

3,862
windows on the
Chrysler Building.

*Built for self-made
real estate mogul
Irwin S. Chanin
in the 1920s,
the Chanin Building
has a fine Art Deco
lobby (p192).*

*Formerly the headquarters of the
Bowery Savings Bank, this is one
of the finest bank buildings in
New York. Architects York &
Sawyer designed it to resemble a
Romanesque palace (p192).*

*The Mobil Building has
a self-cleaning stainless
steel facade that is
embossed in geometric
patterns to prevent it
from warping. It was
built in 1955.*

← Magnificent
interior of Grand
Central Terminal

For more detail see p186

Locator Map
For more detail see p186

Straddling Park Avenue between 45th and 46th streets, the Helmsley Building has an ornate entrance symbolizing the wealth of its first official occupants, New York Central Railroad (p194).

Ornamented with automotive motifs, the Chrysler Building is an Art Deco delight. It was built in 1930 for the Chrysler car company (p192).

→
Tudor City
apartment block,
Lower Midtown

The Ford Foundation Center for Social Justice is the headquarters of the philanthropic Ford Foundation. It has a lovely interior garden surrounded by a cube-shaped building made of pinkish-gray granite, glass, and steel (p194).

THIRD AVENUE

E 43RD STREET

E 42ND STREET

SECOND AVENUE

FIRST AVENUE

Ralph J. Bunche Park

Tudor City is a 1928 private residential complex and has 3,000 apartments. Built in the Tudor style, it features fine stonework details.

The Daily News Building, the former home of the eponymous newspaper, is Art Deco in style and has a revolving globe in the lobby (p193).

UPPER MIDTOWN

Upscale New York in all its diversity is here, in this district of churches and synagogues, clubs and museums, grand hotels and famous stores, and trendsetting skyscrapers. Upper Midtown was once home to society names such as Astor and Vanderbilt. The Waldorf Astoria Hotel, completed in 1931, is where the Waldorf salad originated and, in 1934, the Bloody Mary was first served at the King Cole Bar in the St. Regis Hotel. In the 1950s, architectural history was made when the Lever and Seagram buildings were erected. The undisputed highlight of Upper Midtown, however, is the Museum of Modern Art (MoMA), one of the greatest art galleries in the world.

UPPER MIDTOWN

Must Sees
1. Museum of Modern Art (MoMA)
2. St. Patrick's Cathedral

Experience More
3. Fifth Avenue
4. Waldorf Astoria
5. Tiffany & Co
6. Paley Center for Media
7. Central Synagogue
8. General Electric Building
9. St. Bartholomew's Church
10. Seagram Building
11. Citigroup Center
12. Lever House
13. Roosevelt Island
14. Franklin D. Roosevelt Four Freedoms Park

Eat
1. The Modern at MoMA
2. Palm Court
3. The Pool
4. 21 Club

Drink
5. King Cole Bar
6. P.J. Clarke's

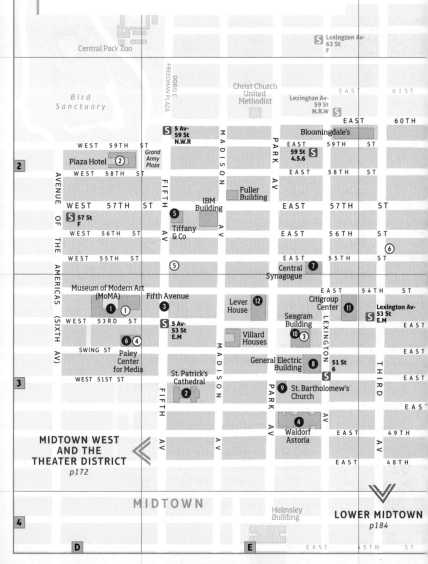

MIDTOWN WEST AND THE THEATER DISTRICT p172

LOWER MIDTOWN p184

① ⊘ ⊘ ⑨ ⊜ ⑪

MUSEUM OF MODERN ART (MOMA)

📍 D3 🏛 11 West 53rd St between Fifth Av & Av of the Americas 🚇 5th Av-53rd St (E,M) 🚌 M1-5, M50, Q32
🕐 10:30am-5:30pm daily (to 8pm Fri) 🌐 moma.org

Affectionately shortened to MoMA, this modern art powerhouse contains one of the world's most comprehensive collections of late 19th and 20th- century art.

Founded in 1929, the Museum of Modern Art set the standard for museums of its kind. The first museum dedicated solely to modern art moved from a small premises on Fifth Avenue to its current location in 1939. Extensions have been added to the building across the decades, including an expansion program completed in 2004, and another in 2019. Stretches of glass across the museum allow for abundant natural light to penetrate the building, and to bathe the Abby Aldrich Rockefeller Sculpture Garden. MoMA houses almost 200,000 works of art by more than 18,000 artists, ranging from Post-Impressionist classics to an unrivaled collection of modern and contemporary art, as well as fine examples of design and early masterpieces of photography and film. Tours are available for groups; check the website for more information.

Gallery Rooms

First Floor

▽ From the entrance on 53rd Street, visitors will find the lobby, store, restaurant, and Sculpture Garden, which contains works by Picasso, Matisse, and Calder. The Sculpture Garden is open free of charge 9-10:15am, though it closes in bad weather.

Second Floor

Along with a store and café, the second floor houses Contemporary Galleries, Prints and Illustrated Books, Media, and special exhibitions. The Education Center can also be found here.

Third Floor

Galleries here include Architecture and Design, Drawings, and Photography. Special exhibitions are also displayed here.

↑ MoMA's sleek exterior
and *(inset)* Pablo Picasso's
*Les Demoiselles
d'Avignon* (1907)

**THE DARING
LADIES**

MoMA was primarily
conceived by three
remarkable women.
Abby Aldrich
Rockefeller (wife of
John D. Rockefeller Jr.),
Lillie P. Bliss, and Mary
Quinn had become
friends through their
love of modern art,
but the Met refused
to show contemporary
artwork in the 1920s.
Without J.D.'s help
(he hated modern art),
the three women were
able to raise the funds
and hire the staff
for the first modest
museum at 730 Fifth
Avenue in 1929.

Fourth Floor

The core of the collection, which
follows on from the floor above,
can be found on the fourth floor.
Named Painting and Sculpture II,
these galleries are numbered 15-26
and span the 1940s to 1980.

Sixth Floor

Special exhibitions are
displayed on the sixth
floor. There's also
another store here.

Fifth Floor

◁ Preceding the fourth floor in
years, Painting and Sculpture I
displays works from the
1880s through to the
1940s across its galleries
numbered 1-14. Along
with masterpieces such as
Dance (1) by Henri Matisse
(1909, *inset*), visitors
will also find a café here.

MUSEUM'S UPPER LEVELS

MoMA's core collection comprises the Painting and Sculpture galleries, which can be found on the upper levels.

Painting and Sculpture I covers the 1880s through to the 1940s, and can be found on the fifth floor. Paul Cézanne's monumental *The Bather* and Vincent van Gogh's *Portrait of Joseph Roulin* are two of the seminal works in the museum's collection of late 19th-century painting. Fauvism and Expressionism are well represented with works by Matisse, Derain, Kirchner, and others, while Pablo Picasso's *Les Demoiselles d'Avignon* marks a transition to the Cubist style of painting.

The collection also has an unparalleled number of Cubist paintings, providing an over-view of a movement that radically challenged our perception of the world. Among the vast range are Picasso's *Girl with a Mandolin*, Georges Braque's *Man with a*

FILM DEPARTMENT

With more than 22,000 films and four million stills, the collection offers a wide range of programs and exhibits. Film conservation is a key to the department's work and many directors have donated copies of their films to help fund it.

Guitar and Soda, and *Guitar and Glasses* by Juan Gris. Works by the Futurists, who brought color and movement to Cubism, include *Dynamism of a Soccer Player* by Umberto Boccioni, plus works by Balla, Carrà, and Jacques Villon. The geometric abstract art of the Constructivists is included in a strong representation of El Lissitzky, Malevich, and Rodchenko. There is a large body of work by Matisse, such as *Dance (I)* and *The Red Studio*. Dalí, Miró, and Ernst feature among the bizarre, strangely beautiful Surrealist works.

Painting and Sculpture II covers the 1940s through to 1980, and can be found on the fourth floor. The post-War art includes works by Bacon and Dubuffet, and has a particularly strong represent-ation of American artists. Abstract Expressionist art here includes Jackson Pollock's *One: Number 31*, Willem de Kooning's *Women, I*, Arshile Gorky's *Agony*, and *Red, Brown, and Black* by Mark Rothko. Other notable works include Jasper Johns' *Flag*, Robert Rauschenberg's *First Landing Jump*, composed of urban refuse, and *Bed*. Pop Art here

includes Roy Lichtenstein's *Girl with Ball* and *Drowning Girl*, Andy Warhol's famous *Gold Marilyn Monroe*, and Claes Oldenburg's *Giant Soft Fan*. Works after 1965 include pieces by Judd, Flavin, Serra, and Beuys.

Did You Know?
—
Renovations in 2004, led by Japanese architect Yoshio Taniguchi, doubled exhibition space.

TOP 5 UNMISSABLE ARTWORKS

The Starry Night
Vincent van Gogh (1889). Magical re-imagining of the view from his asylum room.

Les Demoiselles d'Avignon
Pablo Picasso (1907). A landmark in Cubism.

Reflections of Clouds on the Water-Lily Pond
Claude Monet (c. 1920). Monumental triptych.

Persistence of Memory
Salvador Dalí (1931). Perhaps the most famous Surrealist work.

Campbell's Soup Cans
Andy Warhol (1962). Key piece in the Pop Art movement.

↑ *The Dream* (1910), painted from Henri Rousseau's imagination

MUSEUM'S LOWER LEVELS

Floors one, two, and three host a number of galleries. The second floor houses a wonderful collection of Prints and Illustrated Books. All significant art movements from the 1880s onward are represented, providing a fascinating overview of printed art. With more than 50,000 items in the department's holdings, there are wide-ranging examples of historical and contemporary printmaking. There are some particularly fine examples of works by Andy Warhol, who is widely considered to be the most important printmaker of the 20th century.

There are also many illustrations and prints by other artists including Munch, Matisse, Dubuffet, Johns, Lichtenstein, Freud, and Picasso.

On the third floor, visitors will find the Architecture and Design galleries. MoMA was the first art museum to incorporate utilitarian objects in its collection. These range from household appliances, such as stereo equipment, furniture, lighting, textiles, and glassware, to industrial ball bearings and silicon chips. Architecture is represented in the collection through photographs, scale models, and drawings of buildings that have been or might have been built.

The photography galleries begin with the invention of the medium around 1840, and include pictures by artists, journalists, and amateur photographers. Highlights include some of the best-known works by American and European photographers including Atget, Stieglitz, Lange, Arbus, Steichen, Cartier-Bresson, and Kertesz.

In the Drawings galleries, more than 7,000 artworks range in size from tiny preparatory pieces to large mural-sized works. Many drawings use conventional materials; however, there are also collages and mixed-media. The collection gives an overview of Modernism, and features drawings by artists such as Picasso, Miró, and Johns, alongside emerging artists.

← *Reflections of Clouds on the Water-Lily Pond* by Claude Monet

ST. PATRICK'S CATHEDRAL

📍 E3 🏛 Fifth Av and 50th St 🚇 51 St (6), Lexington Av/ 53 St (E, M) 🚌 M1-5, M50, Q32 🕐 6:30am-8:45pm daily 🌐 saintpatrickscathedral.org

Splendid and Gothic, this is among America's largest Catholic cathedrals. The magnificent house of worship, built during the Civil War, is best appreciated inside, where beautiful details await.

The Roman Catholic Church originally intended this site for use as a cemetery but, in 1850, Archbishop John Hughes decided to build a cathedral instead. Many thought that it was foolish to build so far beyond the (then) city limits, but Hughes went ahead anyway. The result was New York's finest Gothic Revival building, and one of the largest Catholic cathedrals in the US. The cathedral, which seats 2,500 people, was completed in 1878, though the spires were added between 1885 and 1888. It cost a whopping $2 million to build.

The Lady Chapel honors the Blessed Virgin.

The exterior wall is built of white marble. The spires rise 330 ft (101 m) above the sidewalk.

1 The facade of St. Patrick's Cathedral.

2 The great baldachin, made entirely of bronze, rises over the high altar and is adorned with statues of the saints and prophets.

3 The bronze doors weigh 20,000 lb (9,000 kg) and depict religious figures.

SAINT ELIZABETH ANN SETON

Elizabeth Ann Seton (1774-1821) was the first American to be canonized by the Catholic Church. Born in New York, she lived in Lower Manhattan from 1801 to 1803 and founded the American Sisters of Charity. St. Patrick's houses a statue and screen depicting her life.

A Pietà, created by sculptor William O. Partridge in 1906, can be found by the Lady Chapel.

The baldachin

Gothic Revival St. Patrick's Cathedral
↓ in Midtown

Stations of the Cross reliefs won first prize at the Chicago World's Fair in 1893.

The great bronze doors

Measuring 26 ft (8 m) in diameter, the rose window shines above the great organ.

EXPERIENCE MORE

③
Fifth Avenue

📍 E3 🚇 5 Av-53 St (E, M), 5 Av-59 St (N, R, W)

In 1883, when William Henry Vanderbilt built his mansion at Fifth Avenue and 51st Street, he started a trend that led to palatial residences stretching as far as Central Park. One of the few that remains is Cartier at No. 651, once home to millionaire Morton F. Plant, commodore of the New York Yacht Club. As retailers swept north up the avenue – a trend that began in 1906 – high society began to move uptown. In 1917, Plant traded his home to Pierre Cartier for a perfectly matched string of pearls.

Fifth Avenue has long been synonymous with luxury goods. From Cartier to Henry Bendel and Tiffany to Bergdorf Goodman, there are many brands symbolizing wealth and social standing, just as Astor and Vanderbilt once did.

---

④
Waldorf Astoria

📍 E3 🏠 301 Park Av
🚇 Lexington Av, 53 St (E, M)
🔧 For renovation 🌐 waldorf astoria3.hilton.com

Still deservedly one of New York's most prestigious hotels, this Art Deco classic, which covers an entire city block, is also a reminder of a more glamorous era in the city's history. Designed by Schultze & Weaver in 1931, the 625-ft (190-m) twin towers, where Cole Porter, Frank Sinatra, and Marilyn Monroe once lived, have hosted numerous celebrities, including every US president since 1931. A huge renovation project, and partial conversion to condos, is underway and the hotel is likely to be closed until at least 2021.

---

⑤
Tiffany & Co

📍 E2 🏠 727 Fifth Av
🚇 5 Av-53 St (E, M), 5 Av-59 St (N, R, W) 🕐 10am-7pm Mon-Sat, noon-6pm Sun
🌐 tiffany.com

Immortalized by Truman Capote in his famous 1958 novel *Breakfast at Tiffany's*, this prestigious jewelry store, founded in 1837, is a must-see for fans of the book and film buffs alike. The famous Tiffany Diamond is usually on display; the 128.54-carat yellow diamond, discovered in South Africa

---

NEW YORK'S CLASSIC DEPARTMENT STORES

Bloomingdale's, founded in 1872, remains synonymous with the good life, though it had a bargain-basement image until the 1960s. Bergdorf Goodman, luxurious, elegant and understated since 1928, sells contemporary European designer fashions at high prices and is the king of Christmas window decorations. Saks Fifth Avenue has been known for style and elegance since 1924, while Lord & Taylor is the place for classic, conservative fashions.

← The Waldorf Astoria, popular with celebrities and dignitaries since the 1930s

entertainment and sports documentaries, from radio and television's earliest days to the present. Pop fans can watch the Beatles on the Ed Sullivan Show in 1964 or a young Elvis Presley making his television debut. Comedy fans can enjoy shows such as those made by 1960s television star Lucille Ball, and sports enthusiasts can relive classic Olympic Games moments. World War II footage might be chosen by students of history. Six choices at any one time can be selected from a computer catalog that covers a library of more than 50,000 items. The selections are then played in small private areas. Larger screening rooms are also available, as well as a theater seating 200 for the center's program of retrospectives of artists and directors, and for guest events. There are also photography exhibits and memorabilia.

The museum was the brainchild of William S. Paley, a former head of the CBS TV network. It opened in 1975 as the Museum of Broadcasting on East 53rd Street and was so popular that, in 1991, it moved to this hi-tech $50 million home.

Did You Know?

The 21 Club is where Humphrey Bogart took Lauren Bacall on their first date.

in 1877, was acquired by founder Charles Tiffany a year later. With weathered wood and green marble interiors, the store is still best described by Capote's fictional Holly Golightly: "It calms me down right away . . . nothing very bad could happen to you there." *Breakfast at Tiffany's* is now a reality; head for the Blue Box Café on the 4th floor (reservations are recommended).

6 ⬦ Ⓜ 🏛

Paley Center for Media

🔲 D3 🏠 25 West 52nd St 🚇 5 Av-53 St (E, M) 🕐 Noon-6pm Wed-Sun (to 8pm Thu) 🚫 Federal hols 🌐 paley center.org

In this one-of-a-kind museum, visitors can watch and listen to a collection of

7 Ⓜ

Central Synagogue

🔲 E2 🏠 652 Lexington Av 🚇 Lexington Av-53 St (E, M) 🕐 Noon-2pm Tue & Wed 🌐 central synagogue.org

This is New York's oldest building in continuous use as a synagogue. It was designed in 1870 by Silesian-born Henry Fernbach, America's first prominent Jewish architect. He also designed some of SoHo's

EAT

Palm Court

Soaring palms under an elegant stained-glass dome mark this iconic spot for afternoon tea.

🔲 D2 🏠 Fifth Ave at Central Park South (The Plaza) 🌐 theplazany.com

$$$

The Pool

Replacing the legendary Four Seasons in 2017, this sophisticated spot serves quality seafood. Tables are arranged around a small marble pool festooned with foliage depending on the season.

🔲 E3 🏠 99 East 52nd St 🚫 Sun 🌐 thepool newyork.com

$$$

21 Club

An institution since 1929, surviving Prohibition, when staff pulled hidden levers to sweep bottles from shelves and down a chute. Head here for classic and contemporary American cuisine. Note that jeans are not permitted and jackets are required.

🔲 D3 🏠 21 West 52nd St 🚫 Sun 🌐 21club.com

$$$

finest cast-iron buildings (p121). Restored after a 1999 fire, the synagogue is considered the city's best example of Moorish-Islamic Revival architecture. The congregation was founded in 1846 as Ahawath Chesed (Love of Mercy) by 18 immigrants, most of them from Bohemia, on Ludlow Street on the Lower East Side.

8

General Electric Building

📍 E3 🏠 570 Lexington Av
🚇 51 St (6) 🚫 Closed to the public

In 1931, architects Cross & Cross were challenged to design a skyscraper in keeping with neighboring St. Bartholomew's Church. It was not an easy task, but the result won acclaim. The colors were chosen to blend and contrast, and the tower complemented the church's polychrome dome. Viewing the pair from the corner of Park Avenue and 50th Street reveals how well it works. The General Electric is no mere backdrop to the church, but a work of art in its own right and a favorite part of the city skyline. It is an Art Deco gem, from its chrome and marble lobby to its spiky "radio waves" crown.

One block north on Lexington Avenue is a place much cherished by movie fans. Here is the spot where Marilyn Monroe memorably stood in a white frock, which billowed in the breeze from the Lexington Avenue subway grating in the movie *The Seven Year Itch*.

↑ The church of St. Bart's flanked by Midtown skyscrapers

9

St. Bartholomew's Church

📍 E3 🏠 325 Park Av 🚇 51 St (6) 🕐 9am–6pm daily (to 7:30pm Thu, 8:30pm Sun) 🌐 stbarts.org

Known fondly to New Yorkers as "St. Bart's," this Byzantine structure, with its ornate detail, pinkish brick, open terrace, and a polychromed gold dome, brought color and variety to Park Avenue in 1919.

Architect Bertram Goodhue incorporated the Romanesque entrance portico created by Stanford White for the original 1903 St. Bartholomew's on Madison Avenue, and marble columns from that church were used in the chapel.

St. Bartholomew's program of concerts is well known, as is its theater group, which mounts three productions in the church each year.

10

Seagram Building

📍 E3 🏠 375 Park Av 🚇 5 Av-53 St (E, M) 🕐 9am–5pm Mon–Fri

Samuel Bronfman, the late head of Seagram distillers,

← The General Electric Building, crowned with Gothic spires and fanciful carvings

was prepared to put up an ordinary commercial building until his architect daughter, Phyllis Lambert, intervened and persuaded him to go to the best – Mies van der Rohe. The result, which is widely considered the finest of the many Modernist buildings of the 1950s, consists of two rectangles of bronze and glass that let the light pour in.

11

Citigroup Center

📍 E3 🏠 601 Lexington Av 🚇 5 Av-53 St (E, M) 🕐 7am–11pm daily. St. Peter's Lutheran Church: 619 Lexington Ave 🕐 8:30am–8pm daily 🌐 saintpeters.org

An aluminum-clad tower built on ten-story stilts and with a 45-degree angled roof, the Citigroup Center caused a sensation when it was completed in 1978. The slanting top never functioned as a solar panel as intended,

← Cable car crossing the river to Roosevelt Island

HIDDEN GEM
East River Cable Car

Even if Roosevelt Island isn't on your bucket list, the breathtaking views on the three-minute aerial tramway ride, soaring rapidly to 250 ft (76 m) above the East River, make the visit worthwhile.

but it is an unmistakable landmark on the skyline.

The unusual base design accommodates St. Peter's Lutheran Church, which sits underneath the northwest corner of the building. Step inside to see the striking interior and the Erol Beker Chapel by sculptor Louise Nevelson. The church is well-known for its jazz vespers, theater presentations, and organ concerts (generally on Wednesdays at noon).

12

Lever House

📍 E3 🏠 390 Park Av
🚇 5 Av-53 St (E, M)
🚫 Closed to the public

Imagine a Park Avenue lined with sturdy, residential buildings – and then imagine the sensation when they were suddenly reflected here in the first of the city's glass-walled skyscrapers, one of the most influential buildings of the modern era. The Skidmore, Owings & Merrill design is simply two rectangles of stainless steel and glass, one horizontal, the other standing tall above it, to allow light in from every side. The crisp, bright design was intended to symbolize the Lever Brothers' soap products; in 1930, Lever merged to form Unilever.

Revolutionary in 1952, Lever House is now dwarfed by its many imitators, but its importance as an architectural pacesetter is undiminished. The Casa Lever restaurant is a VIP scene.

13

Roosevelt Island

📍 G2 🚇 59 St Tram; Roosevelt Island (F)
🌐 rioc.ny.gov

An often-overlooked corner of New York, Roosevelt Island sits in the East River, and is home to around 13,000 people. Known as Minnahannock by indigenous peoples, it was renamed Blackwell's Island when ownership passed to the English farmer Robert Blackwell in 1686.

Although it became known as Welfare Island in 1921, much of the island was deserted and forgotten by the 1950s.

It was redeveloped in the 1970s, and eventually became a popular residential neighborhood. Today, it has a breezy promenade with fabulous views of Midtown. A Swiss cable car departing from Second Avenue at 60th Street has offered a quick, thrilling ride across the river since 1976.

14

Franklin D. Roosevelt Four Freedoms Park

📍 G3 🏠 1 FDR Four Freedoms Park, Roosevelt Island 🚇 Roosevelt Island (F) 🕐 Apr-Sep: 9am-7pm Mon, Wed-Sun; Oct-Mar: 9am-5pm Mon, Wed-Sun
🌐 fdrfourfreedomspark.org

Lying at the southern end of Roosevelt Island, the Franklin D. Roosevelt Four Freedoms Park was designed by architect Louis Kahn in the 1970s but was only completed in 2012. With 120 linden trees lining the park, the triangular expanse ends with a bronze portrait of the 32nd president. Nearby, there is an engraving of his "four freedoms" on slabs of granite. In a speech delivered in 1941, these four tenets were described as the freedom of speech, freedom of worship, freedom from want, and freedom from fear.

A SHORT WALK

UPPER MIDTOWN

Distance 1 mile (1.5 km) **Nearest subway** 5 Av, 51 St **Time** 20 minutes

The luxury stores synonymous with Fifth Avenue first blossomed as society moved on uptown. In 1917, Cartier acquired the mansion of banker Morton F. Plant, supposedly in exchange for a string of pearls, setting the style for other retailers to follow. But this stretch of Midtown is not simply for shoppers looking to splash their cash. There are some distinctive museums and a diverse assembly of architectural styles to enjoy, too.

Carriage rides have long been replaced with rickshaws and iconic yellow taxis along Fifth Avenue, offering tourists more leisurely ways to view some of the main sights (p208).

The University Club was built in 1899 as an elite club for gentlemen.

The Museum of Modern Art (MoMA) is one of the world's finest collections of modern art (p202).

Much of the interior carving of St. Thomas Church was designed by sculptor Lee Lawrie.

Exhibitions, seasons of special screenings, live events, and a vast library of historic broadcasts are offered at the Paley Center for Media (p209).

5 Av subway (lines E, M)

Saks Fifth Avenue has offered goods in impeccable taste to generations of New Yorkers.

St. Patrick's Cathedral is one of the largest Catholic cathedrals in the United States and a magnificent Gothic Revival building (p206).

Olympic Tower combines offices, apartments, and a skylit atrium within its sleek walls.

Villard Houses comprise five handsome brownstone houses that form part of the Lotte New York Palace Hotel.

↑ St. Patrick's Cathedral, incongruous in busy Upper Midtown

0 meters 100
0 yards 100

N ↑

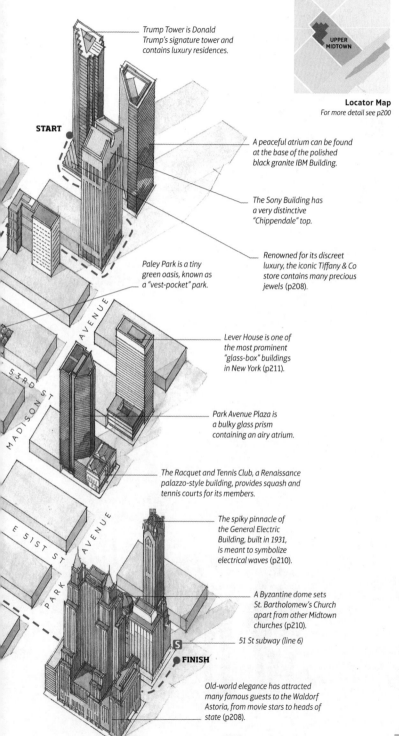

Trump Tower is Donald Trump's signature tower and contains luxury residences.

Locator Map
For more detail see p200

UPPER MIDTOWN

START

A peaceful atrium can be found at the base of the polished black granite IBM Building.

The Sony Building has a very distinctive "Chippendale" top.

Renowned for its discreet luxury, the iconic Tiffany & Co store contains many precious jewels (p208).

Paley Park is a tiny green oasis, known as a "vest-pocket" park.

MADISON ST

53RD ST

AVENUE

Lever House is one of the most prominent "glass-box" buildings in New York (p211).

Park Avenue Plaza is a bulky glass prism containing an airy atrium.

The Racquet and Tennis Club, a Renaissance palazzo-style building, provides squash and tennis courts for its members.

E 51ST ST

PARK AVENUE

The spiky pinnacle of the General Electric Building, built in 1931, is meant to symbolize electrical waves (p210).

A Byzantine dome sets St. Bartholomew's Church apart from other Midtown churches (p210).

51 St subway (line 6)

FINISH

Old-world elegance has attracted many famous guests to the Waldorf Astoria, from movie stars to heads of state (p208).

A gallery of treasures at the Metropolitan Museum of Art

UPPER EAST SIDE

An enclave of New York's upper class since the 1890s, the area was once home to dynasties such as the Astors, Rockefellers, and Whitneys. Many of their Beaux Arts mansions are now museums and embassies, such as the Met and the buildings on Museum Mile, but the well-to-do still occupy apartment buildings on Fifth and Park avenues. Chic stores and galleries line Madison Avenue. Farther east lies what is left of German and Hungarian Yorkville in the East 80s, and little Bohemia, with its Czech population, below 78th Street. Although many of these ethnic groups no longer occupy the area, their churches, restaurants, and stores still remain.

UPPER EAST SIDE

N

P

Q

HARLEM AND
MORNINGSIDE HEIGHTS
p250

EAST 105TH ST

18 Museum of the
City of New York

S 103 St
6

EAST 104TH ST
EAST 103RD ST

5

Wards Island
Footbridge

EAST 102ND ST
EAST 102ND ST

Mount Sinai
Medical Center

EAST 101ST ST
EAST 101ST ST

H a r l e m

EAST 100TH ST
EAST 100TH ST

**CENTRAL
PARK AND THE
UPPER WEST
SIDE**
p234

EAST 99TH ST
EAST 99TH ST

15

EAST 98TH ST

R i v e r

St. Nicholas Russian
Orthodox Cathedral

EAST 97TH ST

Mill
Rock Park

96 St **S**
6

EAST 96TH ST

6

EAST 95TH ST
EAST 95TH ST

EAST 94TH ST
EAST 94TH ST

Jewish
Museum
6

EAST 93RD ST
EAST 93RD ST

EAST 92ND ST
EAST 92ND ST

4 Cooper Hewitt,
Smithsonian Design Museum

EAST 91ST

Solomon R. Guggenheim
Museum
1

EAST 90TH ST
EAST 90TH

16

EAST 89TH ST
EAST 89TH

Gracie
Mansion

EAST 88TH ST
EAST 88TH

Church of the
Holy Trinity **14**

EAST 87TH ST

86 St **S**
4.5.6

EAST 87TH

7

Neue Galerie
New York **1**

EAST 86TH ST

EAST 86TH ST

Carl
Schurz
Park

5

EAST 85TH ST
EAST 85TH ST

EAST 84TH ST
EAST 84TH ST

EAST 83RD ST
EAST 83RD ST

9

EAST 82ND ST
EAST 82ND

2
The
Metropolitan
Museum of Art

EAST 81ST ST
EAST 81ST ST

EAST 80TH ST
EAST 80TH ST

Ukrainian
Institute

EAST 79TH ST
EAST 79TH ST

10

4

EAST 78TH ST
EAST 78TH

John
Jay Park

8

Lenox Hill
Hospital

8 **7**

S **77 St**
6

EAST 77TH ST
EAST 77TH

6

EAST 76TH ST
EAST 76TH

17
The Met
Breuer

EAST 75TH ST
EAST 75TH ST

*Conservatory
Water*

EAST 74TH ST
EAST 74TH ST

EAST 73RD ST
EAST 73RD ST

Frick
Collection
3

EAST 72ND ST
EAST 72ND ST

EAST 71ST ST

7
Asia
Society

EAST 70TH ST
EAST 70TH

NYP
Hospital

Hunter
College

S 68 St-
Hunter College
6

EAST 69TH ST
EAST 69TH ST

Memorial
Hospital

9

EAST 67TH ST

13
Park
Avenue Armory

EAST 66TH ST

9

Temple
Emanu-El

2

EAST 65TH ST

EAST 64TH ST

Society of
Illustrators
8

S Lexington Av-
63 St
F.Q

EAST 63RD ST

Mount Vernon
Hotel Museum

11

Christ Church
United Methodist
12

EAST 62ND ST

3 **5**
EAST 60TH ST

N

P

Q

**UPPER
EAST
SIDE**

FRANKLIN D ROOSEVELT DRIVE (EAST RIVER DRIVE)

FIFTH AVENUE

MADISON AVENUE

PARK AVENUE

LEXINGTON AVENUE

THIRD AVENUE

SECOND AVENUE

FIRST AVENUE

YORK AVENUE

END AVENUE

(MUSEUM MILE)

Interior, designed by
Frank Lloyd Wright ↑

① SOLOMON R. GUGGENHEIM MUSEUM

Did You Know?

The museum's modern design was controversial when it opened on the genteel Upper East Side in 1959.

📍 N7 🏛 1071 Fifth Av at 89th St 🚇 86 St (Q, 4, 5, 6) 🚌 M1-4 🕐 10am-5:45pm Fri-Wed (to 7:45pm Sat) 🌐 guggenheim.org

Home to one of the world's finest collections of modern and contemporary art, the building itself, designed by Frank Lloyd Wright, is perhaps the Guggenheim's greatest masterpiece. Inside, the spiral ramp curves down and inward from the dome, passing works by major 19th-, 20th-, and 21st-century artists along the way.

This seminal museum was named after its founder, mining magnate and abstract art collector Solomon R. Guggenheim. In 1937, he founded the Guggenheim Foundation, which displayed his art collection in rented spaces, before Frank Lloyd Wright was commissioned to design a permanent space in 1942. During his time, Wright was considered the great innovator of American architecture, though the Guggenheim commission was his only New York building. It was completed in 1959 after both his and Guggenheim's deaths. The museum has continued to grow since it opened, today housing works by the likes of Kandinsky, Calder, Picasso, Pollock, Degas, Cézanne, Van Gogh, and Manet.

↑ The museum's famous, shell-like facade, a veritable New York landmark

←

Woman Ironing (1904), from Picasso's Blue Period, conveying real hard work and fatigue

Black Lines (1913) by Kandinsky, part of the Guggenheim's collection

MUSEUM GUIDE

The Great Rotunda features special exhibitions. The Small Rotunda shows some of the museum's Impressionist and Post-Impressionist holdings. The Tower galleries (also known as The Annex) hold exhibitions of works from the permanent collection, as well as contemporary pieces. The permanent collection is shown on a rotating basis, and only parts of it are on display at any one time.

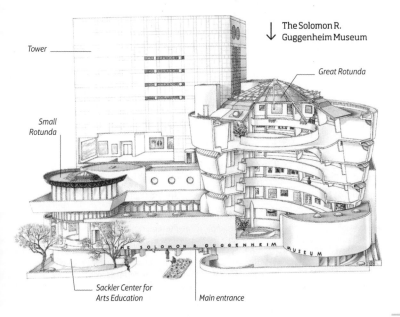

The Solomon R. Guggenheim Museum

Tower

Great Rotunda

Small Rotunda

THE SOLOMON R. GUGGENHEIM MUSEUM

Sackler Center for Arts Education

Main entrance

The grand exterior of the Met ↑

2 ⬦ 🚫 🍴 🖥 🛍

THE METROPOLITAN MUSEUM OF ART

📍 N8 🏠 1000 Fifth Av 🚇 86 St (Q, 4, 5, 6) 🚌 M1-4 🕐 10am-5:30pm Sun-Thu, 10am-9pm Fri & Sat 🚫 Thanksgiving 🌐 metmuseum.org

The jewel in New York City's crown, and one of the most prestigious collections in the world, the Met houses more than two million treasures.

Generally referred to as "the Met," this museum's comprehensive collection was founded in 1870 by a group of artists and philanthropists who dreamed of an American art institution to rival those of Europe. The museum opened here in 1880 and today a staggering variety of objects and artifacts, dating from prehistoric times to the present, can be found across its sprawling galleries. You could spend days here, particularly as the museum also houses a number of excellent dining options. A guided tour is a great way to take in the museum and its stellar attractions. Tours are included with museum admission; visit the website for more information.

Did You Know?

The Met has a residential florist who arranges the impressive bouquets in the Great Hall.

Gallery Rooms

First Floor

▽ From the stunning Great Hall, visitors can explore Egyptian Art, Greek and Roman Art, Medieval Art, Modern and Contemporary Art, and the American Wing.

Third, Fourth, and Fifth Floors

▽ Asian Art and the American Wing both continue onto the third floor. The fourth floor is home to the Dining Room, and the fifth floor has the Cantor Roof Garden.

Second Floor

△ Modern and Contemporary Art and the American Wing both continue onto the second floor. Here visitors can also find galleries dedicated to European Paintings (1250–1800), Musical Instruments, Asian Art, and much more.

17,000

drawings by the likes of Michelangelo and Da Vinci are in the Met's collection.

↑ The Temple of Dendur busy with visitors

MUSEUM'S LOWER LEVELS

EAT

The American Wing Café

With views of Central Park on one side, and the beautiful Charles Engelhard Court – adorned with American sculptures – on the other, this is the best of the Met's light bites.

📍N8 🏛The Charles Engelhard Court, First Floor

💲💲💲

The Dining Room

Undeniably the Met's most elegant dining option, this restaurant overlooks Central Park. It offers a seasonal fixed-price lunch on weekdays and pricier tasting menus, with creative themes like "spring in Italy," throughout the week.

📍N8 🏛Fourth Floor
🕐D Sun

💲💲💲

The Great Hall is a suitably grand entrance to the Met, and the nerve center from which the wings and galleries are connected.

One of the museum's best-loved areas, just off the Great Hall, is the Egyptian Art wing, which displays every one of its holdings – from the prehistoric period to the 8th century AD. Objects range from the fragmented jasper lips of a 15th-century BC queen to the massive Temple of Dendur.

A Roman sarcophagus from Tarsus, donated in 1870, was the first work of art in the Met's collections. It can still be seen in the museum's Greek and Roman galleries, along with wall panels from a villa that was buried under the lava of Vesuvius in AD 79, Roman portrait busts, and Greek vases.

The Met's Medieval Art collection includes works dating from the 4th to the 16th centuries, roughly from the fall of Rome to the beginning of the Renaissance.

The collection is split between here and its uptown branch, the Cloisters (p290). In the Met, you'll find a chalice once thought to be the Holy Grail.

What had been one of the finest private art collections in the world, that of investment banker Robert Lehman, was donated to the museum in 1969. The Lehman Wing is a dramatic glass pyramid, crossing the ground and first floors, and houses an extraordinarily varied collection rich in Old Masters, drawings, and Post-Impressionists.

→ Marble statue of an old market woman

MUSEUM'S UPPER LEVELS

The Met's colossal collection continues upward. Spanning the first, second and third floors is the American Wing, which holds not only one of the world's finest collections of American painting and sculpture but also of decorative arts from Colonial times to the beginning of the 20th century. Period rooms, with their original decorative woodwork and furnishings, include the saloon hall in which George Washington celebrated his last birthday.

Also crossing the first and second floors are the Modern and Contemporary Art galleries. Since its foundation, the museum has been acquiring contemporary art,

but it was not until 1987 that a permanent home for 20th-century art was built – the Lila Acheson Wallace Wing. Other museums have larger collections of modern art, but this display space is considered among the finest. European and American works from 1900 onward are featured, including works by Picasso and Kandinsky. Each year the Cantor Roof Garden at the top of the wing features a new installation of contemporary sculpture, especially dramatic against the backdrop of the city and Central Park.

The second floor also houses Asian Art, including Chinese, Japanese, Korean, Indian, and Southeast Asian masterpieces, dating from the second millennium BC to the 20th century. The museum also has one of the finest collections of Song and Yuan dynasty paintings in the world, Chinese Buddhist monumental sculptures, Chinese ceramics and jade, and an important display of the arts of ancient China.

↑ *The Last Communion of Saint Jerome* (c. 1490), by Botticelli

MUSEUM GUIDE

We have collated the ground and first floors under "Lower Levels," and the second to fifth floors under "Upper Levels." Most artworks are housed on the first and second floors, with some additional collections featuring on the ground, third, and fifth levels. The fourth level doesn't feature any artworks.

TOP 5 **UNMISSABLE ARTWORKS**

Madonna and Child
Duccio (c. 1290-1300). Delicately crafted, early-Renaissance piece.

Harvesters
Pieter Bruegel the Elder (1565). This captures an agricultural scene.

Washington Crossing the Delaware
Emanuel Leutze (1851). Shows Washington's surprise attack in 1776.

Bridge over a Pond of Water Lilies
Claude Monet (1899). The Met's most popular Impressionist painting.

White Flag
Jasper Johns (1955). This was inspired by a dream.

↑ *Washington Crossing the Delaware* (1851) by Emanuel Leutze

EXPERIENCE MORE

3 🎨 🎭 🖥️ 🏛️

Frick Collection

📍 N9 🏛️ 1 East 70th St
🚇 68 St (6) 🕐 10am–6pm
Tue–Sat, 11am–5pm Sun
🌐 frick.org

The remarkable art collection of steel magnate Henry Clay Frick (1849–1919) is exhibited amid the furnishings of his opulent mansion built for him in 1914. The residential setting provides a rare glimpse of how the extremely wealthy lived in New York's gilded age. Henry Frick intended the collection to be a memorial to himself, and on his death he bequeathed the entire house to the nation.

The collection includes important Old Master paintings, major works of sculpture, French furniture, rare Limoges enamels, and beautiful Oriental rugs. Highlights include Vermeer's *Officer and Laughing Girl* (c. 1657) and the 18th-century Boucher Room, smothered in florid Rococo panels by François Boucher. The Living Hall contains a real masterpiece, Giovanni Bellini's *St. Francis in the Desert*. Stunningly well preserved, it depicts Francis's vision of Christ. Here also are two famous works by Hans Holbein the Younger, portraits of old adversaries Thomas Cromwell and Sir Thomas More.

The two are separated by El Greco's restrained *St. Jerome*. In the West Gallery, the identity of the subject in *The Polish Rider*, by Rembrandt (around 1655), is unknown. The somber, rocky landscape creates an eerie atmosphere of unknown danger.

---

4 🎨 🎭 🖥️ 🏛️

Cooper Hewitt, Smithsonian Design Museum

📍 N7 🏛️ 2 East 91st St
🚇 86 St (Q, 4, 5, 6), 96 St (Q, 6) 🚌 M1–4 🕐 10am–6pm
(to 9pm Sat) 🌐 cooper
hewitt.org

Housed in the former mansion of industrialist Andrew Carnegie, this museum underwent a massive redevelopment project, completed in 2014. The modern galleries are now scattered around the original staircase, with the mansion's wooden interiors and parquet floors still intact. On the second floor is the Carnegie Library, which features an array of intricate teak carvings.

The museum offers a varied and engaging range of displays, from digitally printed fruit to steel necklaces, rubber chairs, and porcelain chess sets. It also has the largest ensemble of paintings by the American artists Frederic Edwin Church and Winslow Homer. Aside from the permanent collection, the museum hosts a number of temporary exhibitions each year.

← Modern piece by Mathias Bengtsson at Cooper Hewitt, Smithsonian Design Museum

Did You Know?

Portrait of Adele Bloch-Bauer I was bought by the Neue in 2006 for a record-breaking $135 million.

5 🎨 🖥️ 🏛️

Neue Galerie New York

📍 N7 🏛️ 1048 Fifth Av at East 86th St 🚇 86 St (Q, 4, 5, 6) 🚌 M1–4 🕐 11am–6pm
Thu–Mon 🌐 neue galerie.
org

Founded by art dealer Serge Sabarsky and philanthropist Ronald Lauder, the Neue Galerie's objective is to collect, research, and exhibit early 20th-century fine and decorative arts of Germany and Austria.

The Louis XIII-style Beaux Arts structure was completed in 1914 by Carrère & Hastings, who also designed the New York Public Library *(p178)*. Once home to Mrs Cornelius Vanderbilt III, the mansion was purchased by Lauder and Sabarsky in 1994. The first floor has a bookstore and café; the second is devoted to works by Klimt and Schiele, and Wiener Werkstätte objects. The upper floors feature works from Der Blaue Reiter (Klee, Kandinsky), the Bauhaus (Feininger, Schlemmer), and Die Brücke (Mies van der Rohe, Breuer). Klimt's *Portrait of Adele Bloch-Bauer I* (1907) is the star of the museum. From his "Golden Period," the portrait depicts Adele Bloch-Bauer, a member of one of Vienna's richest Jewish families. Stolen by the Nazis in 1938, the painting's story was told in the 2015 movie *Woman in Gold*, starring Helen Mirren.

DRINK

Bar Pléiades

This stylish Art-Deco hotel bar and jazz venue is a homage to Chanel.

📍N8 🏠The Surrey, 20 East 76th St
🌐bar pleiades.com

Bemelmans Bar

Best known for Ludwig Bemelmans' exuberant murals and gold ceiling.

📍P8 🏠Carlyle Hotel, 35 East 76th St
🌐rosewoodhotels.com

Café Carlyle

Clarinet-playing Woody Allen and jazz band on most Monday nights, with others performing throughout the week.

📍P8 🏠Carlyle Hotel, 35 East 76th St
🕐Sun, Jul-Dec
🌐rosewoodhotels.com

Roof Garden Bar

Romantic spring and summertime spot, with the best views of Central Park and the city.

📍N7 🏠The Met, 1000 Fifth Av
🕐Mid-Oct-mid-Apr
🌐metmuseum.org

↑ The Asia Society bookstore and its wide range of books

6

Jewish Museum

📍N6 🏠1109 Fifth Av
🚇86 St (Q, 4, 5, 6), 96 St (6, Q) 🕐11am-5:45pm Thu-Tue (to 8pm Thu; Mar-Nov: to 4pm Fri) 🕐Jewish and Federal hols 🌐thejewish museum.org

The exquisite, château-like residence of Felix M. Warburg, financier and leader of the Jewish community, was designed by C. P. H. Gilbert in 1908. It now houses one of the world's largest collections of Jewish fine and ceremonial art, and historical Judaica. The stonework in an extension is by the stonemasons who built the Cathedral of St. John the Divine (p254) in Harlem.

The objects that form the collection have been brought here from all over the world, sometimes at great risk of persecution to the donors. Covering some 4,000 years of Jewish history, nearly 30,000 works of art and artifacts include Torah crowns, candelabras, Kiddush cups, plates, scrolls, and silver ceremonial objects.

There is a Torah ark from the Benguiat Collection, the exquisite faience entrance wall of a 16th-century Persian synagogue, along with the powerful *Holocaust* by sculptor George Segal. Regularly changing exhibitions reflect Jewish life and experience around the world and the museum hosts talks and film screenings.

Note that admission to the museum is free on Saturday and "pay what you wish" on Thursday from 5 to 8pm.

7 🎨🎭💻🛍

Asia Society

📍P9 🏠725 Park Av
🚇68 St (6) 🕐11am-6pm Tue-Sun (Sep-Jun: to 9pm Fri) 🌐asiasociety.org

Founded by John D. Rockefeller III in 1956 to increase understanding of Asian culture, the society is a forum for 30 countries in the Asia-Pacific region, from Japan to Iran and from Central Asia to Australia.

The 1981 eight-story building was designed by Edward Larrabee Barnes and constructed with red granite. After a renovation in 2001, the museum has increased gallery space. One gallery is devoted to Rockefeller's own collection of Asian sculptures, which he and his wife amassed on their frequent trips to Asia. It includes Chinese ceramics from the Song and Ming periods, and a copper Bodhisattva statue inlaid with precious stones from Nepal.

Changing exhibits show a wide variety of Asian arts, and the society has a full program of films, dance, concerts, and lectures. There is also a well-stocked bookstore.

↑ Exhibits at the Society of Illustrators include the signatures of some of its notable members *(inset)*

8

Society of Illustrators

♀ P9 **♠ 128 East 63rd St** **Ⓢ Lexington Av-63 St (F, Q)** **🕐 10am-8pm Tue & Thu, 10am-5pm Wed & Fri, 11am-5pm Sat** **Ⓦ society illustrators.org**

Established in 1901, this society was formed to promote the illustrator's art. Its notable members have included Charles Dana Gibson, N. C. Wyeth and Howard Pyle. At first concerned with education and public service, it still holds monthly lectures. In 1981, the Museum of American Illustration opened in two galleries. Changing thematic exhibitions show the history of book and magazine illustration, with an annual exhibition of the year's finest American illustrations.

9

Temple Emanu-El

♀ N9 **♠ 1 East 65th St** **Ⓢ 68 St (6), Lexington Av-63 St (F, Q)** **🕐 10am-4:30pm Sun-Thu** **Ⓦ emanuelnyc.org**

This impressive limestone edifice of 1929 is one of the largest synagogues in the world, with seating for 2,500 in the main sanctuary alone. It is home to the city's longest established (and richest) Reform congregation.

Among many fine details are the Ark's bronze doors, which represent an open Torah scroll, and stained glass depicting biblical scenes and the tribal signs of the houses of Israel. These signs also appear on a great recessed arch framing the magnificent wheel window that dominates the Fifth Avenue facade.

The synagogue is on the site of the palatial home of famed society hostess

Mrs William Astor, who moved to the Upper East Side after a feud with her nephew, who previously lived next door to her. Her wine cellar and three marble fireplaces remain at the synagogue.

10

Ukrainian Institute

♀ N8 **♠ 2 East 79th St** **Ⓢ 86 St (Q, 4, 5, 6)** **🚌 M1-4** **🕐 Noon-6pm Tue-Sat** **Ⓦ ukrainianinstitute.org**

Inevitably overshadowed by the Met up the road, this cultural center, with its intriguing art collection, is well worth a visit. Temporary exhibits from modern Ukrainian artists are on the second floor, while the upper levels exhibit abstract work by Alexander Archipenko, paintings by David Burliuk, the "father of Russian Futurism," and huge Soviet Socialist Realist canvases.

Built for the banker Isaac Fletcher in 1899, it is more famous for being the home, in the 1920s, of industrialist and scandal-prone oilman Harry Sinclair.

Mount Vernon Hotel Museum

Q9 **421 East 61st St** **Lexington Av-59 St (N, R, W), 59 St (4, 5, 6)** **11am-4pm Tue-Sun** **mvhm.org**

Built in 1799, the Mount Vernon Hotel Museum was once a retreat into the country for New Yorkers who needed an escape from the crowded city, then covering only the south end of the island. The stone building sits on land once owned by Abigail Adams Smith, daughter of President John Adams.

Acquired by the Colonial Dames of America, a women's patriotic society, in 1924 it was turned into a charming re-creation of a Federal home. Costumed guides show visitors through eight rooms, which exhibit Chinese porcelain, Sheraton chests, and a Duncan Phyfe sofa. One bedroom even contains a baby's cradle and children's toys. An attractive, 18th-century-style garden has also been planted around the house.

The imposing Park Avenue Armory, now a cultural hub ↓

DYNASTIES OF NEW YORK

The Upper East Side has long been associated with New York's most wealthy and influential families. John Jacob Astor amassed a fortune, and in 1853 his grandson, William Backhouse Astor Jr., married Caroline Schermerhorn, of New York's Dutch aristocracy - their grand mansion was at 65th Street and Fifth Avenue. In 1937, John D. Rockefeller Jr. moved to 740 Park Avenue (where Jacqueline Kennedy Onassis grew up) and his son Nelson lived at 810 Fifth Avenue. Eleanor Roosevelt moved to 49 East 65th Street in 1908, then to 55 East 74th in 1959. The Vanderbilt family had huge mansions on Fifth Avenue in the 19th century, and socialite Grace Vanderbilt later moved to what is now the Neue Galerie (*p224*).

Christ Church United Methodist

P9 **524 Park Av** **5 Av-59 St (N, R, W)** **7am-6pm Mon-Fri, 8:30am-2pm Sun** **christchurchnyc.org**

With deceptively simple exteriors, this dazzling Romanesque structure was designed and built in 1931 by influential architect Ralph Adams Cram. Gold-leaf mosaics fill the stunning vaulted ceiling and apse, while parts of the choir screen date from 1660 and were once owned by Tsar Nicholas II of Russia. The altar is Spanish marble and the nave columns are veined, purple Levanto marble.

Park Avenue Armory

P9 **643 Park Av** **68 St (6)** **For tours; days vary, check website for details** **armoryonpark.org**

From the War of 1812 through two World Wars, the Seventh Regiment, an elite corps of "gentlemen soldiers" from prominent families, has played a vital role. Within the fortress-like exterior of their armory are extraordinary rooms filled with lavish Victorian furnishings and objets d'art, along with a collection of regimental memorabilia.

The design, by Charles W. Clinton, a veteran of the regiment, had offices facing Park Avenue, with a vast drill hall stretching behind to Lexington Avenue. The reception rooms include the Veterans' Room and the Library by Louis Comfort Tiffany. The drill hall is now the site of the Winter Antiques Show and a favorite venue for charity balls. The Armory hosts a large number of cultural performances, from modern dance displays to concerts by the New York Philharmonic Orchestra.

Visitors are able to view the interiors of this landmark building as part of a tour. Check online for specific dates, and to make a reservation, which is compulsory.

The remarkable exterior of the Guggenheim

⑭ Church of the Holy Trinity

📍 Q7 🏠 316 East 88th St
🚇 86 St (Q, 4, 5, 6)
🕐 Opening times vary;
check website for details
🌐 holy trinity-nyc.org

Delightfully placed in a serene garden setting, this church was built in 1899. It' built of glowing golden brick and terra-cotta and has one of New York's best bell towers, with a handsome wrought-iron clock. The arched doorway is richly carved with images of saints and prophets.

Serena Rhinelander (1830-1914) was the church benefactor, memorializing her father and grandfather. The church was on part of the family farmland, and their Rhinelander Mansion still stands at 867 Madison Avenue (today it's owned by Ralph Lauren).

⑮ St. Nicholas Russian Orthodox Cathedral

📍 N6 🏠 15 East 97th St
📞 (212) 726-4229 🚇 96 St (Q, 6) 🕐 By appt

A unique and unexpected find on a side street in this staid part of Manhattan, St. Nicholas Russian Orthodox

---

GREAT CHURCHES OF THE UPPER EAST SIDE

The richest and most opulent churches in the city can be found in the Upper East Side, including Christ Church United Methodist *(p227)* and Church of the Holy Trinity. Episcopal St. James' Church (1885) at 865 Madison Avenue has an elegant gilded reredos above the marble altar by Ralph Adams Cram. At 184 East 76th Street, St. Jean Baptiste Church (1913), built for the French-Canadian community, has a magnificent dome and rare stained-glass windows. Neo-Gothic Park Avenue Christian Church (1911), on 1010 Park Avenue, was built by Ralph Adams Cram to mimic the regal Sainte-Chapelle in Paris.

Cathedral (1902), in Muscovite Baroque style, has five onion domes crowned with crosses, and blue and yellow tiles on a red-brick and white-stone facade. Inside, the high central sanctuary has marble columns with blue and white trim above, and ornate wooden screens trimmed with gold enclose the altar.

Among the early worshipers here were White Russians, who had fled the Russian Revolution. They were mostly intellectuals and aristocrats who soon became a part of New York society. Later, there were further waves of refugees, dissidents, and defectors.

The cathedral now serves a scattered community, and the congregation is small. Mass is celebrated in Russian with great pomp and dignity.

---

⑯ 🚶 🚲 🏛 Gracie Mansion

📍 Q7 🏠 East End Av at 88th St 🚇 86 St (Q, 4, 5, 6)
🚌 M31, M79, M86 🕐 10am, 11am & 5pm Mon 🌐 nyc.gov/gracie

This gracious, balconied, wooden 1799 country home is the official mayor's residence. Built by wealthy merchant Archibald Gracie, it is one of the city's best Federal houses.

Acquired by the city in 1896, it was the first home of the Museum of the City of New York. When Fiorello La Guardia moved in after nine years in office, he said that even the modest Gracie Mansion was too fancy for him.

The mansion is open for pre-booked, guided tours only.

---

⑰ 🚶 🚲 🖥 🏛
The Met Breuer

📍 P8 🏠 945 Madison Av
🚇 77 St (6) 🕐 10am-5:30pm Tue-Thu & Sun, 10am-9pm Fri & Sat 🌐 metmuseum.org

An extension of The Metropolitan Museum of Art, The Met Breuer occupies the former premises of the Whitney Museum of American

←

The dining room at Gracie Mansion featuring wallpaper made by Zuber in the 1830s

The Met Breuer holds contemporary and modern art

EAT

Café Sabarsky
Classic Viennese café with aromatic coffees and Austrian food.

⬛N7 🏠Neue Galerie, 1048 Fifth Av
🌐kurtguten brunner.com

$$$

Daniel
Opulent restaurant of chef Daniel Boulud.

⬛P9 🏠60 East 65th St 🕐Lunch, Sun
🌐danielnyc.com

$$$

Dylan's Candy Bar
Iconic candy store, with a chocolate fountain.

⬛P9 🏠1011 Third Av
🌐dylanscandy bar.com

$$$

Lady M
Posh cake shop with a cult following.

⬛P8 🏠41 East 78th St 🌐ladym.com

$$$

Serendipity 3
Café and ice-cream parlor, known for "frrozen" hot chocolate.

⬛P9 🏠225 East 60th St
🌐serendipity3.com

$$$

> **Created by architect Marcel Breuer, the building's Brutalist design was a controversial addition to the town houses of the Upper East Side in 1966.**

Art. Created by architect Marcel Breuer, the building's Brutalist design was a controversial addition to the town houses of the Upper East Side in 1966. It provides exhibition space for 20th- and 21st-century art, along with educational programs and unique performances.

🔘18 ⬡ ⬡ ⬡ ⬡

Museum of the City of New York

⬛N5 🏠1220 Fifth Av at 103rd St 🚇103 St (6)
🕐10am–6pm daily
🌐mcny.org

Founded in 1923, and at first housed in Gracie Mansion, this museum is dedicated to New York's development from its earliest

beginnings to the present, and on to the future.

Housed in a handsome Georgian Colonial building since 1932, the museum has expanded its public space, with special exhibitions throughout the year on subjects such as fashion, architecture, theater, social and political history, and photography. In addition to all of this there is a fantastic and expansive collection of toys from different areas, including the famous Stettheimer Dollhouse, containing original works of art in miniature painted by such luminaries as Marcel Duchamp and Albert Gleizes.

A core exhibit of the museum is the fascinating film *Timescapes: A Multimedia Portrait of New York*. Shown every 30 mins, from

10:15am to 4:45pm, this uses various images from the museum's collection, along with historic maps charting the growth of New York City, from its earliest days as a tiny settlement to its current status as one of the largest cities in the world.

A SHORT WALK
MUSEUM MILE

Distance 1.25 mile (2 km) **Nearest subway**
96 St, 86 St-Lexington Av **Time** 25 minutes

Many of New York's museums are clustered on the
Upper East Side, in homes ranging from the former
Frick and Carnegie mansions to the modernistic
Guggenheim; it's worth exploring this neighborhood
for the palatial architecture of these world-famous
museums alone. If you're visiting the museums
themselves, you'll find the displays are as varied as
the architecture, running the gamut from Old Masters
to photographs, to decorative arts. Presiding over
the scene is the vast Metropolitan Museum of Art,
New York's answer to Paris's Louvre.

↑ Frank Lloyd Wright's
stunning Guggenheim
Museum

Did You Know?

Museum Mile has deals
on entry fees, with
"pay what you wish"
on specified days.

The most extensive collection
of Judaica in the world is
housed at the Jewish Museum.
It includes coins, archaeo-
logical objects, and
ceremonial and religious
artifacts (p225).

Ceramics, glass, furniture,
and textiles are well
represented at the Cooper
Hewitt, Smithsonian
Design Museum (p224).

The Church of the Heavenly
Rest was built in 1929 in the
Gothic style. The Madonna in
the pulpit is by sculptor
Malvina Hoffman.

Architect Frank Lloyd Wright's
Guggenheim is in the form of a
spiral, and is floodlit at dusk.
To best appreciate one of the
world's premier collections of
modern and contemporary art,
take the elevator to the top and
walk down (p218).

FIFTH AVENUE (MUSEUM MILE)

MADISON AVENUE

93RD S

92ND ST

91ST ST

90TH ST

89TH ST

FINISH

START

Graham House is an
apartment building
with a splendid Beaux
Arts entrance. It was
built in 1892.

Locator Map
For more detail see p216

UPPER
EAST
SIDE

The facade of the Squadron A Armory is all that remains of the original building. It is now the west wall of the playground of Hunter College High School. The school was built to complement the style of the armory.

Public basketball court

The William G. Loew Mansion (1931), now part of the Spence School, is in the "American Adams" style.

The Synod of Bishops of the Russian Orthodox Church Outside of Russia is housed in a lovely 1918 mansion.

Night Presence IV (1972), a modern work in rusting steel, was created by Louise Nevelson. Some New Yorkers feel it is out of place among its staid, old-fashioned neighbors on Park Avenue.

PARK AVENUE

LEXINGTON AVENUE

At 120 and 122 East 92nd Street are two of the few wooden houses left in Manhattan. Built in 1859 and 1871 respectively, they have a charming Italianate air.

The Marx Brothers spent their childhood in a three-bedroom apartment in a modest rowhouse at 179 East 93rd Street.

← Manhattan's few remaining wooden houses, on East 92nd Street

CENTRAL PARK AND THE UPPER WEST SIDE

The city's "backyard" was officially opened in 1876 and it's difficult to imagine New York without it. Over the years, Central Park has blossomed, with playgrounds, skating rinks, ball fields, and spaces for every other activity, not to mention hills, lakes, and meadows. In 1868, when the Ninth Avenue railroad made commuting to Midtown possible, the city streets were levelled and graded. Buildings sprang up on Central Park West and Broadway and the Upper West Side remains mainly residential today, with a blend of highrises and old brownstones. The Lincoln Center complex has made the area something of a cultural hub, while the American Museum of Natural History is one of the city's most popular family-friendly attractions.

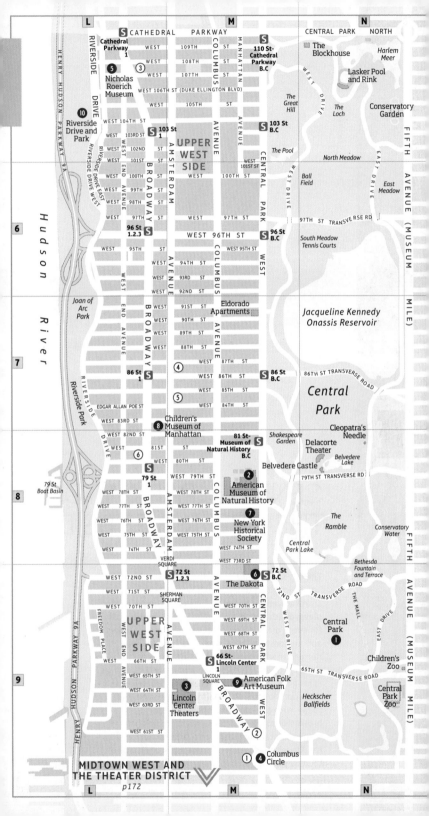

Q

5

CENTRAL PARK AND
THE UPPER WEST SIDE

EAST 105TH ST

EAST 104TH ST

S 103 St
6

EAST 102ND ST

Wards Island
Footbridge

EAST 99TH ST

EAST 99TH ST

96 St S EAST 96TH ST
6

6

SECOND AVENUE

CAST 91ST ST

FIRST AVENUE

YORK AVENUE

EAST 87TH ST

Harlem

Mill
Rock Park

River

Gracie
Mansion

86 St S
4.5.6

MADISON AVENUE

PARK AVENUE

LEXINGTON AVENUE

THIRD AVENUE

Carl
Schurz
Park

7

EAST END AVENUE

EAST 83RD ST

0 meters   500   N

0 yards   500

77 St S
6

UPPER
EAST SIDE

PARK AVENUE

EAST 72ND ST

LEXINGTON AVENUE

THIRD AVENUE

SECOND AVENUE

S 68 St-
Hunter College
6

8

Park
Avenue
Armory

AVENUE

AVENUE

S

CENTRAL PARK AND
THE UPPER WEST SIDE

Must Sees

1. Central Park
2. American Museum of Natural History

Experience More

3. Lincoln Center Theaters
4. Columbus Circle
5. Nicholas Roerich Museum
6. The Dakota
7. New York Historical Society
8. Children's Museum of Manhattan
9. American Folk Art Museum
10. Riverside Drive and Park

Eat

1. Per Se
2. Jean-Georges
3. Absolute Bagels
4. Barney Greengrass
5. Jacob's Pickles
6. Zabar's Café

9

1 🍴 ☕

CENTRAL PARK

📍 N9 🚇 Between 59th St, Fifth Av, 110th St and Eighth Av 🚇 59 St-Columbus Circle (A, B, C, D, 1), 5 Av-59 St (N, Q, R, W), 72nd St (B, C) 🕐 6am-1am daily
🌐 centralparknyc.org

Few New Yorkers today could imagine their city without this expansive and beloved park, which lies at the heart of New York. With a wealth of green spaces, numerous sights to explore, and various activities to entertain, Central Park has something for everyone, and a different story to tell with each season.

Central Park is a green paradise for both New Yorkers and visitors to the city. It attracts bird-watchers and naturalists, swimmers and skaters, picnickers and sunbathers, runners and cyclists, and festival-goers in the summer. After a fierce competition, Frederick Law Olmsted and Calvert Vaux were chosen to create Central Park in the 1850s. The area had been largely desolate, pockmarked with shantytowns and pig farms, and the transformation was a huge undertaking. It opened to the public in 1876 under the proviso that it was a "people's park." Today the southern section of the park contains most of the popular attractions, including the Delacorte Theater, where Shakespeare in the Park is staged, and the Wollman Rink during the holiday season. But the northern tract (above 86th Street) is well worth a visit for its wilder natural setting and a dramatically quieter ambience.

Green and leafy Central Park contrasting with the city skyline ↑

City's Coolest Spot

Central Park tends to be cooler than the rest of the city in the summer months, so it's good to head here if you're visiting June–August; it's also colder in winter, meaning photogenic snow lasts longer here than anywhere else.

↑ The Sheap Meadow, in the southern part of Central Park

Seasonal Guide

Spring

The park returns to life at the end of March, with cherry trees blossoming around the Reservoir and birds chirping on their spring migration. Check out model boat races at the Boat Pond (10am–1pm Sat).

Summer

The park becomes a shady respite in summer, while sunbathers bask in the Sheep Meadow. For many, it's all about the free festivals: Shakespeare in the Park, SummerStage, the Met Opera Summer Recital Series, and New York Philharmonic Concerts.

Fall

With 20,000 trees turning red and gold, plus milder temperatures, Central Park is at its most beautiful in the fall. Birds again visit, with hawks best spotted from Belvedere Castle.

Winter

Most of the trees are bare and the winds are biting cold, but winter can be a magical time in Central Park. Snow often blankets the lawns and woods long after it has melted from the streets, and you'll have large swaths of the park to yourself. Don't miss ice-skating at the Wollman Rink or Lasker Rink (Nov–Mar).

← Cyclists enjoying Central Park in the warm summer months

① The Dairy

🕙 **10am–5pm daily**

Central Park's visitor center is the place to begin. Maps and event information can be obtained here, and visitors can rent chess sets too.

② Strawberry Fields

This is Yoko Ono's tribute to her husband, John Lennon. Gifts for the garden came from all over the world.

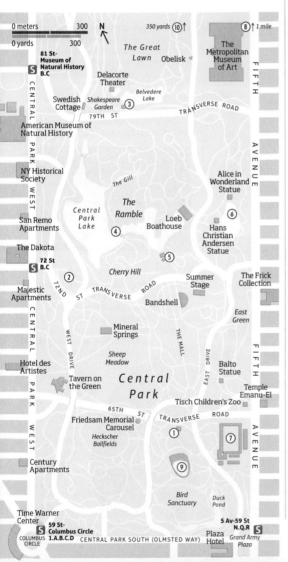

↑ Pedestrians crossing Bow Bridge, while boaters enjoy the lake

③ Belvedere Castle

🕙 **10am–5pm daily**

This stone castle atop Vista Rock, complete with tower and turrets, offers some of the best views of the park. Inside is the Henry Luce Nature Observatory, with a delightful exhibit about the surprising variety of wildlife to be found in the park.

④ Bow Bridge

This is one of the park's original cast-iron bridges, and was designed as a bow tying together sections of the lake. In the 19th century, when the lake was used for skating, a hoisted red ball signalled that the ice was safe. The bridge offers expansive park views.

Map labels:

0 meters 300
0 yards 300
N
350 yards ⑩ ↑

⑧ ↑ 1 mile

81 St-Museum of Natural History B.C Ⓢ

The Great Lawn
Obelisk
The Metropolitan Museum of Art

Delacorte Theater

Swedish Cottage
Shakespeare Garden ③
Belvedere Lake

TRANSVERSE ROAD
79TH ST

American Museum of Natural History

FIFTH AVENUE

NY Historical Society

The Gill
Alice in Wonderland Statue

CENTRAL PARK WEST

Central Park Lake
The Ramble
Loeb Boathouse ④
⑥ Hans Christian Andersen Statue

San Remo Apartments

The Dakota

72 St B.C Ⓢ

② Majestic Apartments

72ND ST

Cherry Hill
TRANSVERSE ROAD

⑤

Summer Stage
The Frick Collection

Bandshell
East Green

CENTRAL PARK WEST

WEST DRIVE

Mineral Springs

Sheep Meadow

THE MALL

Hotel des Artistes

Tavern on the Green

Central Park

EAST DRIVE

Balto Statue

FIFTH AVENUE

Temple Emanu-El

65TH ST
TRANSVERSE ROAD
Tisch Children's Zoo

Friedsam Memorial Carousel
Heckscher Ballfields

①
⑦

Century Apartments

⑨

Bird Sanctuary
Duck Pond

Time Warner Center
59 St-Columbus Circle 1.A.B.C.D Ⓢ
COLUMBUS CIRCLE
CENTRAL PARK SOUTH (OLMSTED WAY)

5 Av-59 St N.Q.R Ⓢ
Plaza Hotel
Grand Army Plaza

TOP 3 CENTRAL PARK BIKE RENTALS

Bike and Roll
451 Columbus Av, at W 82nd St; www.bikeandroll.com

Master Bike Shop
265 W 72nd St; www.masterbikeshop.com

Bike Rental Central Park
1391 Sixth Ave; and 9 W 60th St; bikerentalcentralpark.com

⑤
Bethesda Fountain and Terrace
Between the lake and the Mall, this is the architectural heart of the park. The fountain was dedicated in 1873 and the statue, *Angel of the Waters*, marked the opening of the Croton Aqueduct system in 1842, bringing the city its first supply of pure water; its name refers to a biblical account of a healing angel at the pool of Bethesda in Jerusalem.

⑥
Conservatory Water
Better known as the Model Boat Pond, this is where model yacht races occur every weekend and birdwatchers gather here in spring to see the city's famous red-tailed hawk, Pale Male, nest on the roof of 927 Fifth Avenue. At the north end of the lake, a sculpture of Alice in Wonderland is popular with kids. It was commissioned by George T. Delacorte, who is immortalized as the Mad Hatter. Delightful free story hours take place at H. C. Andersen's statue.

Did You Know?
The opening credits of sitcom *Friends* were filmed in L.A., not in a Central Park fountain.

⑦
Central Park Zoo
🕐 Apr–Oct: 10am–5pm Mon–Fri (to 5:30pm Sat, Sun & state hols); Nov–Mar: 10am–4:30pm daily

This zoo has won plaudits for its creative and humane use of small space. More than 150 species are represented.

⑧
Conservatory Garden
🕐 8am–dusk

The Vanderbilt Gate on Fifth Avenue gives entry to three gardens, each with a landscape style; the Central Garden recreates an Italian style, the South Garden is English, and the North Garden is French.

⑨
Wollman Rink
🕐 Oct–Mar

The Wollman Rink has offered the city's most atmospheric ice-skating since 1949. The location is perfect, providing thrilling views of the park and the skyscrapers along Central Park South. The rink transforms into Victorian Gardens, a small amusement park (Jun–Sep).

⑩
Charles A. Dana Discovery Center & Harlem Meer
This center has exhibits on the park's ecology and overlooks Harlem Meer, where catch-and-release fishing is allowed (fishing poles are loaned out).

EAT

Tavern on the Green
The park's most famous restaurant serves modern seasonal cuisine to well-heeled locals and visitors.
📍 Central Park West and 67th St 🌐 tavernonthe green.com
$$⑤

Loeb Boathouse Restaurant
Set by the Lake, Loeb Boathouse was funded by philanthropist Carl M. Loeb. The restaurant is a popular wedding venue.
📍 East 72nd St and Park Drive North 🕐 Dec–Mar 🌐 thecentralpark boathouse.com
$$⑤

→ Snow-covered statue in Central Park's Conservatory Garden

AMERICAN MUSEUM OF NATURAL HISTORY

📍 M8 🏛 Central Park West at 79th St 🚇 81 St (B, C)
🚌 M7, M10, M11, M79, M104 🕙 10am–5:45pm daily
🌐 amnh.org

Fossils, taxidermy, and skeletons galore – this encyclopedic collection of curiosities comprises one of the world's largest natural history museums, and houses the Rose Center for Earth and Space. Kids in particular will love exploring the museum's hoard of specimens, and getting their hands on the interactive exhibits.

Since the original building opened in 1877, the complex has grown to cover a whopping four city blocks and four floors, jam-packed with more than 30 million specimens and artifacts. The most popular areas are the Dinosaur Exhibit, housing the world's largest dinosaur collection, and the Milstein Hall of Ocean Life, which shows the drama of the undersea world. The Rose Center for Earth and Space includes the Hayden Planetarium, while the Hall of Gems and Minerals houses a stunning array of crystals. This barely scratches the surface – there's reptiles, amphibians, insects, African mammals, and much more.

↑ A parade of African elephants

← An enormous blue whale replica based on a 1925 South American female

→ A young star-gazer

ROSE CENTER

When viewed from the street at night, the Rose Center is breathtaking, and the exhibits inside prove that, as Carl Sagan said, "We are starstuff." Housed within an 87-ft (27-m) sphere, the center contains the technologically advanced Hayden Planetarium; the Cosmic Pathway, a 350-ft (107-m) spiral ramp with a timeline chronicling 13 billion years of evolution; and the Big Bang Theater, where the origins of the universe are explained.

INSECTS AND MYRIAPODS   SEGMENTED WORMS   MOL

MOLLUSKS

The museum *(inset)*, home ↑
to the Hall of Biodiversity
and all its curiosities

EXPERIENCE MORE

Lincoln Center Theaters

M9 ** 10 Lincoln Center Plaza (Columbus Av) **66 St (1) **lincolncenter.org

The Lincoln Center is anchored by a series of spectacular performance venues, beginning with the Metropolitan Opera House. Designed by Wallace K. Harrison, it opened in 1966. Five great arched windows offer views of the opulent lobby and two murals by Marc Chagall. Inside there are curved white marble stairs, red carpeting, and exquisite starburst crystal chandeliers that are raised to the ceiling just before each performance.

Across the main plaza lies the David H. Koch Theater, by architects Philip Johnson and John Burgee, inaugurated in 1964. Gargantuan white marble sculptures by Elie Nadelman dominate the

vast four-story lobby. Because of its rhinestone lights and chandeliers both inside and out, some describe the theater as "a little jewel box."

When David Geffen Hall opened in 1962 as the Philharmonic Hall, critics initially complained about the acoustics, but structural modifications have rendered the hall an acoustic gem,

comparing favorably with other great classical concert halls around the world.

Three more intimate theaters make up the Lincoln Center theater complex, where eclectic and often experimental drama is presented. The theaters are the 1,000-seat Vivian Beaumont, the 280-seat Mitzi E. Newhouse, and

LEGENDARY COMPANIES OF THE LINCOLN CENTER

The thing that makes the Lincoln Center truly special is the caliber of its resident companies. The world-famous Metropolitan Opera Company is currently led by Yannick Nézet-Séguin. The American Ballet Theatre's most famous principal dancer is Misty Copeland. The New York City Ballet, at the David H. Koch Theater, performs Balanchine's *Nutcracker* every November and December. David Geffen Hall is home to the New York Philharmonic and the popular "Mostly Mozart" series. Alice Tully Hall hosts the Chamber Music Society.

The Lincoln Center, the world's most prestigious performing arts complex

building projects in New York City's history.

Multi-use skyscrapers have attracted national and international businesses. Global media company Time Warner has its headquarters in an 80-story skyscraper. The 2.8 million sq ft (260,000 sq m) building provides a retail, entertainment, and restaurant facility, with stores such as Hugo Boss, Williams-Sonoma, and Whole Foods Market; dining at Per Se and Masa; and a Mandarin Oriental hotel.

The Time Warner Center is also home to Jazz at the Lincoln Center. The three venues here – the Appel Room, the Rose Theater, and Dizzy's Club Coca-Cola – together with a jazz hall of fame and education center, comprise the world's first performing-arts facility dedicated to jazz.

Other notable buildings on Columbus Circle include Hearst House, designed by British architect Lord Norman Foster, Trump International Hotel, the Maine Monument, and the eye-catching Museum of Arts and Design (*p182*), formerly the American Craft Museum.

the 112-seat Claire Tow. Works by some of New York's best modern playwrights have featured at the Beaumont. The size of the Newhouse suits Off-Broadway-style plays, while the Clare Tow features work written by emerging playwrights, directors, and designers.

4
Columbus Circle

🔲 M9 🚇 59 St-Columbus Circle (A, B, C, D, 1)
🌐 jazz.org

Presiding over this urban plaza at the corner of Central Park is a marble statue of explorer Christopher Columbus, perched atop a tall granite column in the center of a fountain and plantings. The statue is one of the few remaining original features in this circle, which has become one of the largest

5 🏠
Nicholas Roerich Museum

🔲 L5 🏠 319 West 107th St
🚇 Cathedral Parkway-110 St (1) 🕐 Noon–4pm Tue–Fri, 2–5pm Sat–Sun
🌐 roerich.org

The often overlooked Nicholas Roerich Museum occupies a handsome brownstone near Riverside Park. It contains a small and quirky collection of around 150 original paintings by Nicholas Roerich (1874–1947), a Russian-born

artist who lived in India from the 1920s. Much of his work focuses on nature scenes of the Himalayas, influenced by Buddhist mysticism.

Born in St. Petersburg, his early art was promoted in Europe by Sergei Diaghilev. His association with New York began on an extended visit in 1920; he founded the Agni Yoga Society and Master Institute of United Arts in the city.

6

The Dakota

M9 **1 West 72nd St** **72 St (1, 2, 3)** **To the public**

The name and style reflect the fact that this apartment building was truly "way out West" when Henry J. Hardenbergh, the architect responsible for the Plaza Hotel, designed it in 1880–84. It was New York's first luxury apartment house and was originally surrounded by squatters' shacks and wandering farm animals. Commissioned by Edward S. Clark, heir to the Singer

---

HIDDEN GEM
The Boat Basin

Tucked away off Riverside Park, the 79th Street Boat Basin is a surprisingly tranquil hideaway on the Hudson River. The small marina features the relaxed Boat Basin Café, open from lunch to late evening (Apr-Oct).

---

sewing machine fortune, it is one of the city's most prestigious addresses.

The Dakota's 65 luxurious apartments have had many famous owners, including Judy Garland, Lauren Bacall, Leonard Bernstein, and Boris Karloff, whose ghost is said to haunt the place. The setting for the movie *Rosemary's Baby*, it was also where the tragic murder of John Lennon took place. His widow, Yoko Ono, still lives here.

7

New York Historical Society

M8 **170 Central Park West** **81 St (B, C)** **Galleries: 10am-6pm Tue-Sat (to 8pm Fri), 11am-5pm Sun; Library: 9am-3pm Tue-Fri, 10am-4:45pm Sat (varies by season)** **nyhistory.org**

Founded in 1804, this society houses a distinguished research library and the city's oldest museum. Its collections include historical material relating to slavery and the Civil War, an outstanding collection of 18th-century newspapers, all 435 watercolors of Audubon's *Birds of America*, and the world's largest collection of Tiffany lamps and glasswork. There are also fine displays of American furniture and silver.

> **Riverside Drive is one of New York City's most attractive streets; broad, and with lovely shaded views of the Hudson River, this is a much desired street.**

8

Children's Museum of Manhattan

L7 **212 West 83rd St** **79 St or 86 St (1), 81 St (B, C)** **10am-5pm daily (to 7pm Sat)** **cmom.org**

This particularly imaginative museum is based on the premise that children learn best through play. The exhibit called "Eat, Sleep, Play" links food, the digestive system, and healthy living, while in "Block Party" children can build castles, towns, and bridges out of wooden blocks. Kids also delight in the exhibits on cartoon favorites Curious George and Dora the Explorer and her adventurous cousin Diego, where they learn about travel and cultures around the world.

On weekends and holidays the 150-seat theater hosts performers, from puppeteers to storytellers. There's also a gallery for free events, like "Pajama Day," as well as lively, theme-based museum tours.

←

Exclusive and expensive, The Dakota apartment building

9 〰 🖼 🖥 🛍
American Folk Art Museum

📍M9 ⬜2 Lincoln Sq
🚇66 St (1) 🕐11:30am–
7pm Tue–Thu & Sat, noon–
7:30pm Fri, noon–6pm Sun
🌐folkartmuseum.org

The home for the appreciation and study of American folk art is conveniently located opposite the Lincoln Center complex. Founded in 1961, the museum holds 7,000 artworks dating from the 18th century to the present day.

With colorful quilts, impressive portraits, and major works by self-taught, contemporary artists, the selection is remarkable. Especially worth seeking out are Henry Darger's water-colors, and the incredible urban commentaries of Ralph Fasinella. Exhibitions usually revolve, but the permanent collection is always on display.

↑ Locals enjoying the Upper West Side's leafy Riverside Park

↑ An array of tempting baked goods at Zabar's Café

10
Riverside Drive and Park

📍L5 🚇79 St or 86 St (1), 96 St (1, 2, 3)

Riverside Drive is one of New York City's most attractive streets; broad, and with lovely shaded views of the Hudson River, this is a much desired street. It is still lined with the opulent original town houses, in addition to some more modern apartment buildings. At numbers 40–46, 74–77, 81–89, and 105–107 Riverside Drive are houses designed in the late 19th century by local architect Clarence F. True. The curved gables, bays, and arched windows seem to mirror the curves of the road and the flow of the river.

The bizarrely named Cliff Dwellers' Apartments at 243 (between 96th and 97th streets) is a 1914 building with a frieze featuring early Arizona cliff-dwellers, complete with masks, buffalo skulls, and rattlesnakes.

Riverside Park, stretching for 4 miles (2.5 km) along the Hudson River, was designed by Frederick Law Olmsted, who also laid out Central Park (p238), and is one of only eight official "scenic land-marks" in the city.

(p238)

EAT

Absolute Bagels
Some of the freshest, chewiest bagels in the city.

📍L5 ⬜2788 Broadway
📞(212) 932-2052

💲💲💲

Barney Greengrass
Operating since 1908, the "Sturgeon King" serves up excellent lox, pastrami, salmon, and - of course - sturgeon.

📍M7 ⬜541 Amsterdam Av 🕐Dinner, Mon
🌐barneygreen grass.com

💲💲💲

Jacob's Pickles
Southern fare like pancakes and fried chicken, plus tangy pickles await at this Upper West Side classic.

📍M7 ⬜509 Amsterdam Av 🌐jacobspickles.com

💲💲💲

Zabar's Café
Takeout heaven for smoked fish, pickles, and bagels-and-lox sandwiches since 1934.

📍L8 ⬜2245 Broadway
🌐zabars.com

💲💲💲

A SHORT WALK
LINCOLN CENTER

Distance 0.6 mile (1 km) **Nearest subway** 59 St, 72 St
Time 15 minutes

Lincoln Center was conceived when both the Metropolitan
Opera House and the New York Philharmonic required homes,
and a large tract on Manhattan's west side was in dire need of
revitalization. The notion of a single complex where different
performing arts could exist side by side seems natural today,
but in the 1950s it was considered both daring and risky.
Today, Lincoln Center has proved itself by drawing audiences
of five million each year. Proximity to its halls prompts
both performers and arts lovers to live nearby.

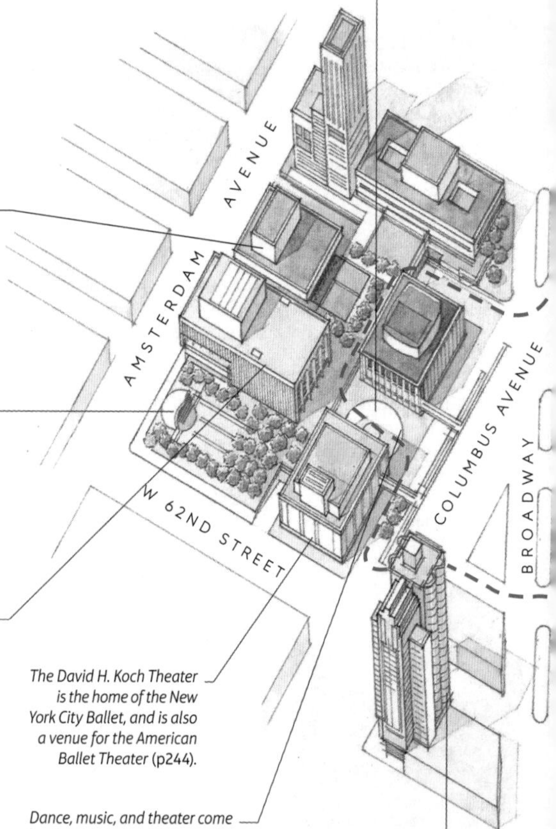

*Composer Leonard
Bernstein, who based
West Side Story in
this neighborhood,
was later instrumental
in setting up the large
music complex that
we see here today.*

*The Vivian Beaumont and
the Mitzi E. Newhouse
theaters, part of Lincoln
Center, are both housed in
this building (p244).*

*The Guggenheim
Bandshell in
Damrosch Park is the
site of free concerts.*

*Lincoln Center's focus is the
Metropolitan Opera House.
The cafe at the top of the
lobby offers wonderful plaza
views (p244).*

*The David H. Koch Theater
is the home of the New
York City Ballet, and is also
a venue for the American
Ballet Theater (p244).*

*Dance, music, and theater come
together in the fine Lincoln Center
for the Performing Arts. It is also a great
place to sit around the fountain
and people-watch.*

*The College Board Building
is an Art Deco delight
that now houses condos
and the administrative
offices of the College
Board, developers of the
college entrance exam.*

AMSTERDAM AVENUE

W 62ND STREET

COLUMBUS AVENUE

BROADWAY

Fountains outside the Metropolitan Opera House, Lincoln Center

Head to the American Folk Art Museum for amazing quilt exhibits (p247).

Artists Isadora Duncan, Noël Coward, and Norman Rockwell once lived at Hotel des Artistes.

James Dean once lived in a one-room apartment on the top floor at 19 West 68th Street.

W 67TH STREET

FINISH

Did You Know?

The stage of the Metropolitan Opera House is the size of a football field.

W 65TH STREET

An ABC-TV sound stage for soap operas is housed in this castle-like building, formerly an armory.

55 Central Park West is an Art Deco apartment building and featured in the film Ghostbusters as the home of Dana Barrett, played by Sigourney Weaver.

CENTRAL PARK WEST

The Society for Ethical Culture was one of the city's first Art Nouveau buildings. It also houses a school.

START

The twin towers of the Century Building are just one of four iconic twin-towered apartment buildings on Central Park West.

Central Park West is home to many celebrities, who like the privacy of its highly exclusive apartments.

0 meters 100
0 yards 100

N

A street scene in Harlem

HARLEM AND MORNINGSIDE HEIGHTS

Harlem has been at the heart of African-American culture since the 1920s, when poets, activists, and jazz musicians came together during the Harlem Renaissance. Today, the neighborhood is home to fabulous West African eateries, Sunday gospel choirs, a vibrant local jazz scene, and some of the prettiest blocks in the city. Morningside Heights, near the Hudson River, is home to Columbia University and two of the city's finest churches. Hamilton Heights is farther uptown – primarily a residential area, it also contains a Federal-style historic mansion and the City College of New York.

HARLEM AND MORNINGSIDE HEIGHTS

Must Sees

1. Cathedral of St. John Divine
2. Schomburg Center

Experience More

3. Hamilton Grange National Memorial
4. Riverside Church
5. General Grant National Memorial
6. Marcus Garvey Park
7. Langston Hughes House
8. Striver's Row (St. Nicholas District)
9. Studio Museum 127
10. Mount Morris Historic District
11. Museo del Barrio
12. National Jazz Museum in Harlem
13. Apollo Theater
14. Graffiti Wall of Fame
15. City College of New York
16. Columbia University

Eat

1. Patsy's Pizzeria
2. Rao's
3. Red Rooster
4. Sylvia's Restaurant
5. Amy Ruth's

Stay

6. Harlem Flophouse
7. Mount Morris House
8. San Fermín Apartments

UPPER EAST SIDE
p214

1 Ⓜ️ 💻

CATHEDRAL OF ST. JOHN THE DIVINE

📍M4 🏛️1047 Amsterdam Av at West 112th St 🚇Cathedral Pkwy-110 St (1)
🚌M4, M11, M60, M104 🕐7:30am-6pm daily 🌐stjohndivine.org

This Gothic cathedral is truly one of a kind. It will be the largest cathedral in the world when it is completed – over 100 years since construction first began – and hosts music, theater, and avante-garde art under its semi-finished roof.

Started in 1892, and still only two-thirds finished, the Cathedral of St. John the Divine will be the world's largest cathedral, surpassing St. Peter's Basilica in Vatican City. The interior is over 600 ft (183 m) long and 146 ft (45 m) wide. It was originally designed in Romanesque style by Heins & LaFarge; Ralph Adams Cram took over the project in 1911, devising a Gothic nave and west front. Medieval construction methods, such as stone-on-stone supporting buttresses, continue to be used to complete the cathedral. The cathedral plays an important role in the community, with various social and cultural events taking place here.

↓ The Cathedral of St. John the Divine

↑ Portal by stonemason Joe Kincannon, showing an apocalyptic New York City

The rose window symbolizes the many facets of the Christian Church.

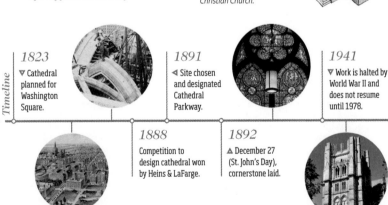

Timeline

1823
▽ Cathedral planned for Washington Square.

1888
Competition to design cathedral won by Heins & LaFarge.

1891
◁ Site chosen and designated Cathedral Parkway.

1892
△ December 27 (St. John's Day), cornerstone laid.

1941
▽ Work is halted by World War II and does not resume until 1978.

Each of the choir's columns is 55 ft (17 m) tall and made of polished gray granite.

Rising to a height of over 100 ft (30 m), the piers of the nave are topped by graceful stone arches.

THE FINISHED DESIGN

The north and south transepts, the crossing tower, and the west towers of the cathedral have yet to be finished. When the money to fund their construction is raised, the proposed design will still take at least another 50 years to complete.

The Bishop's Chair is a copy from the Henry VII chapel in Westminster Abbey, in London.

The pulpit

The bay altar windows are devoted to human endeavor. The sports window shows feats of skill and strength.

↑ The beautiful nave – a calm, reflective space for worshipers

1982

▽ Daredevil aerialist Philippe Petit crosses a high wire between the cathedral and a building on Amsterdam Av.

1978–89

Third phase of building. Stonemasons' Yard opened, and south tower heightened.

2001

Major fire destroys interior and roof of north transept.

2008

Reopens after seven-year closure for renovations.

2017

▽ Cathedral and grounds designated a New York City Landmark.

2

SCHOMBURG CENTER

N2 515 Malcolm X Blvd, at West 135th St 135 St (2, 3) 10am-8pm Tue & Wed, 10am-6pm Thu-Sat nypl.org/locations/schomburg

The largest research center dedicated to black and African culture in the United States, the pioneering Schomburg Center is one of Harlem's premier cultural attractions.

The Home of African-American History

Housed in a sleek contemporary complex, the Schomburg Center is part of the New York Public Library family, and a key research hub. The center, formally called the Schomburg Center for Research in Black Culture, opened in 1991. Its immense collection was assembled by Arturo Schomburg (1874–1938), a black man of Puerto Rican descent. As a child, Schomburg was told by a teacher that there was no such thing as "black history," which inspired him to prove the teacher wrong by documenting African-American history and its heroes. The Carnegie Foundation bought the collection in 1926 and donated it to the NYPL; Schomburg, who lived in Harlem, was made curator in 1932. Today the Schomburg Center holds some ten million items, from film and music recordings to African, Caribbean, and African-American

literature, and hosts superb temporary exhibitions covering a range of themes based around the African-American experience. The center also houses a number of stunning murals by Aaron Douglas, a key artist in the Harlem Renaissance. Douglas stayed in Harlem en route from Kansas City to Paris and was convinced to stay for longer.

Guided tours are a great way to learn more about the history of the Schomburg Center and its brilliant collection. Tours are available from 10am to 3pm, Monday through Friday, and must be booked at least 30 days in advance. Visit the website for more information and to reserve a place on a tour.

Murals by Aaron Douglas
↓ include *From Slavery Through Reconstruction*

INSIDER TIP
Aaron Douglas Murals

From the Latimer/Edison Gallery you can glimpse the main reading room below, and admire the four haunting murals painted by Harlem Renaissance artist Aaron Douglas in 1934. These abstract artworks portray subjects from African-American history and experience.

1 The exterior of the Schomburg Center for Research in Black Culture.

2 The recent *Black Power!* exhibition tracked the ten-year movement that followed the Civil Rights Movement. Ignited by the assassination of activist Malcolm X in 1965, Black Power demanded immediate, physical action in response to white supremacy.

3 Visitors study documents in display cases at Harlem's Schomburg Center.

LANGSTON HUGHES

Seminal poet Langston Hughes was born in Missouri, in 1902. He moved to Harlem in 1929, where he became a key voice in the Harlem Renaissance, writing poetry, plays, and short stories up to his death in 1967. His ashes are interred here, beneath the terrazzo and "cosmogram" in the atrium beyond the main library entrance. This is inscribed with lines from his signature poem *The Negro Speaks of Rivers*: "My soul has grown deep like the rivers."

EXPERIENCE MORE

↑ The "family room" in Alexander Hamilton's home, The Grange

Hamilton Grange National Memorial

📍 M1 🅰 St. Nicholas Park, 414 West 141st St 🚇 137 St-City College (1) 🕐 9am-5pm Wed-Sun 🌐 nps.gov/hagr

The subject of the highly successful Broadway musical, and the face on the $10 bill, Alexander Hamilton was one of the architects of the federal government system, First Secretary of the treasury, and founder of the National Bank. Completed in 1802, this was his country home. Hamilton lived here for the last two years of his life, prior to being killed in a duel with political rival Aaron Burr in 1804.

In 1889, St. Luke's Episcopal Church acquired the site, and the building was moved four blocks west. A second move in 2008 brought it to its current site in St. Nicholas Park.

Riverside Church

📍 L3 🅰 490 Riverside Dr at 122nd St 🚇 116 St-Columbia University (1) 🕐 7am-10pm daily 🌐 trcnyc.org

A 21-story steel frame with a Gothic exterior, the church design was inspired by the cathedral at Chartres, France. It was lavishly funded by John D. Rockefeller Jr., in 1930. The Laura Spelman Rockefeller Memorial Carillon (in honor of Rockefeller's mother) is the largest in the world, with 74 bells. The 20-ton Bourdon, or hour bell, is the largest and heaviest tuned carillon bell ever cast. The organ, with its 22,000 pipes, is among the largest in the world.

At the rear of the second gallery is a figure by Jacob Epstein, *Christ in Majesty*, cast in plaster and covered in gold leaf. Another Epstein statue, *Madonna and Child*, stands in the court next to the cloister. The panels of the chancel screen honor eight men and women whose lives have exemplified the teachings of Christ. They range from Socrates and Michelangelo to Florence Nightingale and Booker T. Washington.

For quiet reflection, enter the small, secluded Christ Chapel, patterned after an 11th-century Romanesque

↑ Glowing stained glass backs the cross on the altar in Riverside Church

church in France. The church is particularly welcoming during the Christmas season, as the public is invited to a host of festive activities. The church also offers guided tours at 12:15pm on Sundays.

General Grant National Memorial

📍 L3 🅰 West 122nd St and Riverside Dr 🚇 116 St-Columbia University (1) 🚌 M5 🕐 9am-5pm Wed-Sun 🌐 nps.gov/gegr

This grandiose monument honors America's 18th president, Ulysses S. Grant, the commanding general of the Union forces in the Civil War. The mausoleum contains the coffins of General Grant and his wife, Julia, in accordance with the president's last wish that they be buried together. After Grant's death in 1885, more than 90,000 Americans contributed $600,000 to build the sepulcher, which was inspired by Mausoleus's tomb at Halicarnassus (now Bodrum), one of the Seven Wonders of the Ancient World.

The tomb was dedicated on what would have been Grant's 75th birthday, April 27, 1897. The parade of 50,000 people, along with a flotilla of ten American and five European warships, took more than seven hours to pass in review.

The interior was inspired by Napoleon's tomb at Les

HARLEM GOSPEL AT ABYSSINIAN CHURCH

New York's oldest black church became famous through its charismatic pastor Adam Clayton Powell Jr. (1908-72), a congressman and civil-rights leader who made it the most powerful black church in America. The 1923 Gothic building is known for the uplifting gospel music of its Sunday services; arrive by 11am at the entrance, at the southeast corner of West 138th Street and Powell Boulevard.

←
The imposing Grant's Tomb, and its spectacular domed ceiling (inset)

Invalides in Paris. Each sarcophagus weighs 8.5 tons. Two exhibit rooms feature displays on Grant's personal life and his presidential and military career. Surrounding the north and east sides of the building are 17 sinuously curved mosaic benches that seem totally out of keeping with the formal architecture of the tomb. They were designed in the early 1970s by the Chilean-born Brooklyn artist Pedro Silva and were built by 1,200 local volunteers, who worked under his supervision. The benches were inspired by the work of Spanish architect Antoni Gaudí in Barcelona. The mosaics depict subjects ranging from the Inuit to New York taxis to Donald Duck.

A short walk to the north of Grant's Tomb is another, much simpler but equally poignant monument. An unadorned urn on a pedestal marks the resting place of a young child who fell from the riverbank and drowned. His grieving father placed a marker that simply reads: "Erected to the memory of an amiable child, St. Claire Pollock, died 15 July 1797 in his fifth year of his age."

6
Marcus Garvey Park

N3 120th–124th streets **S** 125 St (2, 3, 4, 5, 6) **W** nycgovparks.org

This hilly, rocky, two-block square of green is the site of New York's last fire watchtower, an open cast-iron structure built in 1857, with spiral stairs leading up to the 47-ft- (14-m-) high observation deck. The bell below the deck was used to sound the alarm. The tower was temporarily dismantled in 2015 for reconstruction, and the $5.7 million project, which included work on the surrounding plaza, was completed in late 2019.

Previously known as Mount Morris Park, it was renamed in 1973 in honor of Marcus Garvey. He came to Harlem from Jamaica in 1916 and founded the Universal Negro Improvement Association, which promoted self help, racial pride, and a back-to-Africa movement.

7
Langston Hughes House

N3 20 East 127th St **S** 125 St (4, 5, 6) Noon–5pm Tue, Thu, Sat **W** itoo arts.com

Celebrated African-American poet Langston Hughes (p257) lived at this house in Harlem from 1948 until his death in 1967. It was here he penned classics such as Montage of a Dream Deferred. His aging 1869 brownstone was left virtually derelict for years, but was leased by the local I, Too, Arts Collective in 2016. The Collective has since opened parts of it to the public, in conjunction with running their poetry salons and creative conversations series. Hughes' typewriter and piano are displayed in the parlor, and the second and third floors may be open in future.

Overlooking colorful streets and an intersection in Harlem

8 Striver's Row (St. Nicholas District)

◉ M1 ◔ 202-250 West 138th & West 139th streets Ⓢ 135 St (2, 3)

The two blocks here were built in 1891, when Harlem was being promoted as a neighborhood for New York's gentry. Officially designated the St. Nicholas Historic District, they are still among the city's most distinctive examples of row town houses. McKim, Mead & White were responsible for the northernmost row of solid brick Renaissance palaces, while the Georgian buildings by Price and Luce are of buff brick with white stone trim. James Brown Lord's buildings feature outstanding red-brick facades and brownstone bases. In the early 20th century, this came to be the desirable residence for ambitious professionals within Harlem's burgeoning black community – hence the "Striver's" nickname.

A row of attractive town houses in Mount Morris Historic District ↑

9 Studio Museum 127

◉ M3 ◔ 429 West 127th St Ⓢ 125 St (2, 3) ◔ Noon-6pm Thu-Sun ⓦ studiomuseum.org

The Studio Museum in Harlem was founded in 1967 with the mission of becoming the world's premier center for the collection and exhibition of the art and artifacts of African Americans. The current premises at 144 West 125th St will be closed until at least 2021, when an entirely new building, designed by Adjaye Associates (led by Ghanaian-British architect David Adjaye), should be complete.

In the meantime, Studio Museum 127 will act as a temporary programming space, with changing exhibitions featuring major black artists. The museum's permanent collection represents more than 400 artists and over 2,600 works of art, including paintings, drawings, sculptures, photographs, and mixed-media installations. The photographic archives alone comprise one of the most complete records in existence of Harlem in its heyday. The museum's InHarlem program also sponsors art around the neighborhood.

10 Mount Morris Historic District

◉ N3 ◔ West 119th-West 124th streets Ⓢ 125 St (2, 3)

Despite many of the buildings being in need of renovation, it is still clear that the late-19th-century town houses near Marcus Garvey Park were once grand, favored by German Jews moving up in the world from the Lower East Side. After a long period of neglect, redevelopment is underway.

A few impressive churches, such as St. Martin's Episcopal Church, remain and interesting juxtapositions of faiths can be seen: the columned Mount Olivet Baptist Church, at 201 Malcolm X Boulevard, was once Temple Israel, one of the most imposing synagogues in the city; and at the Ethiopian Hebrew Congregation, 1 West 123rd

---

LIVE JAZZ IN HARLEM

Jazz remains a fundamental part of Harlem's appeal. Classic joints such as Showman's and Minton's Playhouse are still going strong, while sax man Bill Saxton still plays Fridays and Saturdays at Bill's Place. Although no relation to the famous original, the Cotton Club (www.cottonclub-newyork.com) offers good swing, blues, jazz, and a Sunday Gospel brunch.

HARLEM SWING STREET
JAZZ SINGER
BILLIE HOLIDAY
DISCOVERED HERE
IN 1933

BILL'S PLACE SPEAKEASY
DR. THEDA PALMER
& BILL SAXTON
2004

> Duke Ellington, Thelonious Monk, Charlie Parker, Count Basie, John Coltrane, and Billie Holiday all got their start in Harlem clubs and speakeasies.

Street, housed in a former mansion, the choir sings in Hebrew on Saturdays.

Museo del Barrio

⦿ N5 **⌂** 1230 Fifth Av
Ⓢ 103 St (6) **⏰** 11am–6pm
Wed–Sat, noon–5pm Sun
Ⓦ elmuseo.org

Founded in 1969, this was North America's first museum devoted to Latin American art, specializing in the culture of Puerto Rico. At the far end of Museum Mile, the museum aims to bridge the gap between the lofty Upper East Side and Spanish Harlem. Exhibitions show contemporary painting and sculpture, folk art, and historical artifacts. About 240 wooden Santos (carved figures of saints) and a reconstructed *bodega*, or Latino convenience store, are highlights. Exhibits change, but Santos are often on display. The Pre-Columbian collection

contains rare artifacts from the Caribbean. A store sells eye-catching items by artists from all over Latin America.

National Jazz Museum in Harlem

⦿ N2 **⌂** 58 West 129th St
Ⓢ 125 St (2, 3) **⏰** 11am–5pm
Thu–Mon **Ⓦ** jazzmuseumin
harlem.org

This tiny museum honors Harlem's important role in the history of jazz. Duke Ellington, Thelonious Monk, Charlie Parker, Count Basie, John Coltrane, and Billie Holiday all got their start in Harlem clubs and speakeasies. The small gallery contains rare jazz memorabilia, including Duke Ellington's white 1920s piano, and a scarf he bought for his wife, as well as Ralph Ellison's collection of jazz recordings. The museum also arranges jazz-related programs, classes, and live events.

EAT

Patsy's Pizzeria
This rare remnant of Italian Harlem is where the pizza slice concept was invented. Cash only.

⦿ Q4 **⌂** 2287 First Av
Ⓦ thepatsyspizza.com

$$\textcircled{\$}\textcircled{\$}\textcircled{\$}$$

Rao's
This authentic Italian restaurant is in high demand, with only ten tables (nine standing only). Cash only.

⦿ Q4 **⌂** 455 East 114th St **⏰** Lunch **Ⓦ** raos
restaurants.com

$$\textcircled{\$}\textcircled{\$}\textcircled{\$}$$

Red Rooster
Southern-style comfort food includes steak with fried green tomatoes, roast pork loin, and fiery jerk chicken.

⦿ N3 **⌂** 310 Malcolm X Blvd **Ⓦ** redrooster
harlem.com

$$\textcircled{\$}\textcircled{\$}\textcircled{\$}$$

Sylvia's Restaurant
The best soul food – from fried chicken with waffles to BBQ ribs and candied yams. The peach cobbler is divine.

⦿ N3 **⌂** 328 Malcolm X Blvd **Ⓦ** sylvias
restaurant.com

$$\textcircled{\$}\textcircled{\$}\textcircled{\$}$$

Amy Ruth's
Soul food at its most comforting. The waffle breakfasts and desserts are equally enticing.

⦿ N4 **⌂** 113 West 116th St **Ⓦ** amyruths.com

$$\textcircled{\$}\textcircled{\$}\textcircled{\$}$$

← The Apollo Theater, a long-established Harlem venue

1980s, the Apollo once again features top entertainers and hosts amateur nights.

---

⑬ Ⓜ 🏛
Apollo Theater

📍 M3 🏠 253 West 125th St
🚇 125 St (A, B, C, D)
🕐 For performances only
🌐 apollotheater.org

Opened in 1913 as a whites-only opera house, the Apollo's great fame came when entrepreneur Frank Schiffman took over in 1934 and opened it to all. It became Harlem's best-known showcase, with artists such as Bessie Smith, Billie Holiday, Duke Ellington, and Dinah Washington.

Wednesday Amateur Nights (begun in 1935), with winners determined by audience applause, were famous, and there was a long waiting list for performers. These amateur nights helped launch the careers of Sarah Vaughan, Pearl Bailey, James Brown, and Gladys Knight. The Apollo was *the* place during the swing band era; following World War II, a new generation of musicians, such as Charlie "Bird" Parker, Dizzy Gillespie, Thelonious Monk, and Aretha Franklin, continued the tradition. Refurbished in the

---

⑭
Graffiti Wall of Fame

📍 P5 🏠 Park Av and East 106th St 🚇 103rd St (6)

Founded in 1980 by street artist Ray Rodríguez, the Graffiti Wall of Fame honors the street art that exploded in the 1970s. The inner side of the concrete wall is actually located in the Junior High School 13 Jackie Robinson playground, so the gates are sometimes locked (ask at the school along 106th Street for a closer look). The wall features art from many of the city's best-known graffiti writers, including Dez, Crash, Flight, Delta, Tats Cru, and Skeme.

---

⑮
City College of New York

📍 M2 🏠 Main entrance at West 138th St and Convent Av 🚇 137 St-City College (1)
🌐 ccny.cuny.edu

High on a hill adjoining Hamilton Heights, the original Gothic quadrangle of this

→ Students relaxing on the lawns of Columbia University's Morningside Heights campus

---

> #### HARLEM RENAISSANCE
> The Harlem Renaissance of the 1920s was inspirational for generations of African-American musicians, writers, and performers. Jazz musicians such as Duke Ellington, Count Basie, and Cab Calloway electrified the Cotton Club, Savoy Ballroom, Apollo Theater, and Smalls Paradise. But the Harlem Renaissance wasn't just about music. It was also marked by a rich body of literature produced by Langston Hughes, Jean Toomer, and Zora Neale Hurston, among many others. Hughes declared the movement over in 1931 after the death of noted African-American socialite and patron A'Lelia Walker.

college, built between 1903 and 1907, is very impressive. The material used for the buildings is Manhattan schist, a stone that had been excavated in building the IRT subway. Later, contemporary buildings were added to the school, which enrolls nearly 15,000 students.

Once free to all residents of New York, City College still offers low tuition rates. Most of the students are from minority groups, and many of them are the first in their families to attend college.

---

16 Ⓜ ▣ ▣

Columbia University

📍L4 🏛West 116th St and Broadway 🚇116 St-Columbia University (1) ℹ Visitors Center: 213 Low Library, 535 West 116th St 🕐9am–5pm Mon-Fri 🌐columbia.edu

Columbia is noted for its law, medicine, and journalism schools and its distinguished faculty and alumni, past and present, include over 50 Nobel laureates. Famous alumni include J. D. Salinger, James Cagney, and Joan Rivers. Across the street is the affiliated Barnard College. Columbia's Morningside Heights campus is the third location of one of America's oldest universities. Visitors can join free tours of the Morningside Heights campus; ask at the visitors center for information.

Founded in 1754 as King's College, it was first located close to where the World Trade

Center stood. In 1814, when a move uptown was proposed, the university approached the authorities for funding but was instead given a plot of land valued at $75,000 on which to build a new home. The university never built on the land itself, but leased it out and spent the years from 1857 to 1897 in buildings nearby. It finally sold the plot in 1985 to the leaseholders, Rockefeller Center Inc., for $400 million.

The present campus was begun in 1897 on the site of the Bloomingdale Insane Asylum. Architect Charles McKim placed the university on a terrace, serenely above street level. Its spacious lawns and plazas still create a sense of contrast in the busy city.

Opened in 2017 about one mile (1.6 km) north of the original Morningside Heights campus, the stylish new **Manhattanville campus** is a showcase for celebrated architect Renzo Piano. His nine-story glass-and-steel Jerome L. Greene Science Center is the largest building ever constructed for Columbia University. It serves as a hub for the neuroscience researchers of the Mortimer B. Zuckerman

Mind Brain Behavior Institute. Piano also designed the eight-story metal panel Lenfest Center for the Arts, containing the Wallach Art Gallery and performance spaces for theater, music, and dance. Piano's University Forum acts as a gateway to the campus and as a multipurpose venue. All the new buildings are glass-enclosed and open to view at street level. The Nash Building, originally built as an automobile showroom, now contains the campus historical interpretive exhibit.

Manhattanville campus
📍L2 🏛West 125th St to 133rd St, between Broadway and 12th Av 🚇125 St (1)

A SHORT WALK
COLUMBIA UNIVERSITY

Distance 1.25 mile (2 km) **Nearest subway**
116 St-Columbia University **Time** 25 minutes

Columbia University's Morningside Heights campus should not be underestimated as a place of interest. After admiring the architecture, linger awhile on Columbia's central quadrangle in front of the Low Library, where you will see the future leaders of America mingling between classes. Across from the campus on both Broadway and Amsterdam Avenue are the coffee houses and bars where students engage in lengthy philosophical arguments, debate the topics of the day, or simply unwind.

116 St-Columbia University subway (line 1)

START

The School of Journalism is one of Columbia's many McKim, Mead & White buildings. Founded in 1912 by publisher Joseph Pulitzer, it is the home of the Pulitzer Prize, awarded for the best in letters and music.

Alma Mater was sculpted by Daniel Chester French in 1903 and survived a bomb blast in the 1968 student demonstrations.

With its imposing facade and high dome, the Low Library dominates the main quadrangle. McKim, Mead & White designed it in 1895–7.

Butler Library is Columbia's main library.

Columbia University's first buildings were designed by McKim, Mead & White and built around a central quadrangle (p265).

BROADWAY

114TH ST

AMSTERDAM AVENUE

← Graduation day at Columbia University's Morningside Heights Campus

The Sherman Fairchild
Center was built in 1977 to
house the university's life
sciences departments.

Designed by the architects
Howells & Stokes in 1907,
St. Paul's Chapel is known for its
fine woodwork and magnificent
vaulted interior. It is full of light
and has fine acoustics.

0 meters   100   N
0 yards   100   ↑

FINISH

Student demonstrations put Columbia University
in the news in 1968. The demonstrations were
sparked by the university's plan to build a
gymnasium in nearby Morningside Park. The
protests forced the university to build elsewhere.

W 116TH ST

W 115TH ST

→
Facade of the
Église de
Notre Dame

MORNINGSIDE DRIVE

W 113TH ST

The Église de Notre Dame was built for a
French-speaking congregation. Behind the
altar is a replica of the grotto at Lourdes,
France – the gift of a woman who believed
her son was healed there.

If the Neo-Gothic Cathedral of
St. John the Divine is ever finished,
it will be the largest in the world.
Although one-third of the structure
has not yet been built, it can hold
10,000 parishioners (p254).

Did You Know?

Columbia University's
second campus,
Manhattanville,
opened in 2017.

Nostalgic amusement park, Coney Island

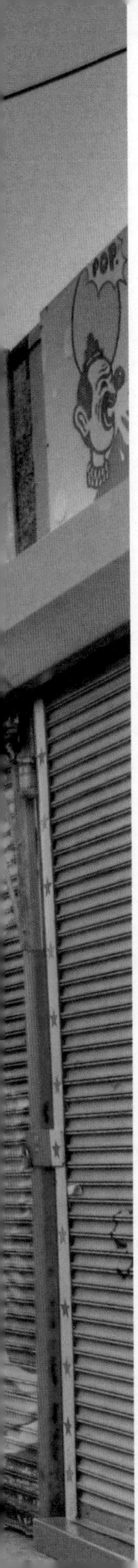

BROOKLYN

Brooklyn became a New York borough in 1898, and for decades after served primarily as a residential and industrial neighborhood. Three times bigger than Manhattan, it has changed dramatically since the start of the 21st century. Districts such as Fort Greene, Williamsburg, Bushwick, and Cobble Hill are now among the most fashionable in the city, popular for their bars, flea markets, and hipster culture. Brooklyn offers a multitude of experiences. Its brownstone town houses and tree-lined streets give way to encyclopedic museums, inventive restaurants, and innovative cultural hubs.

BROOKLYN

Must Sees

1. Brooklyn Bridge
2. Brooklyn Museum

Experience More

3. Fulton Ferry District
4. Dumbo
5. New York Transit Museum
6. Red Hook
7. Fort Greene
8. Williamsburg and Greenpoint
9. Brooklyn Bridge Park
10. Brooklyn Navy Yard
11. Brooklyn Children's Museum
12. Grand Army Plaza
13. Park Slope Historic District
14. Prospect Park
15. Brooklyn Botanic Garden
16. Green-Wood Cemetery
17. Coney Island

Eat

1. The River Café
2. Dough
3. Junior's
4. Peter Luger Steak House
5. Smorgasburg
6. Steve's Authentic Key Lime Pies

Drink

7. Black Flamingo
8. Fresh Kills Bar
9. House of Yes
10. Pete's Candy Store
11. Westlight

Shop

12. Beacon's Closet
13. Brooklyn Flea

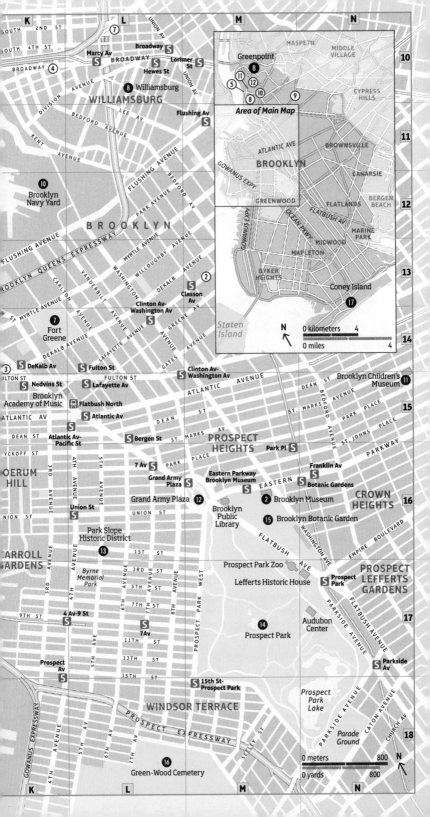

271 ft

The height of the
bridge's Gothic arches
(83 m).

❶

BROOKLYN BRIDGE

📍G13 🚇Chambers St (J, Z), Brooklyn Bridge-City Hall (4, 5, 6) on Manhattan side; High St (A, C) on Brooklyn side 🚌M9, M15, M22, M103

The Brooklyn Bridge is one of New York City's oldest icons. Connecting the boroughs of Manhattan and Brooklyn, it is a vital commuter link, an architectural treasure, and a potent symbol of the American Dream.

Completed in 1883, the Brooklyn Bridge was the largest suspension bridge in the world for 20 years, and the first to be made of steel. Engineer John A. Roebling conceived of a bridge spanning the East River while ice-bound on a ferry to Brooklyn, which was then a separate city. The bridge took 16 years to build, required 600 workers, and claimed over 20 lives, including Roebling's. Most died of caisson disease (known as "the bends") after coming up from the underwater excavation chambers.

The bridge used new and revolutionary building techniques, from making the cable wires to sinking the supports. When finished, the bridge linked the boroughs of Manhattan and Brooklyn, signaling the birth of one great metropolis. New Yorkers themselves were in awe of the Brooklyn Bridge upon completion. Aside from providing new commuter links, the bridge offered a dramatic addition to the landscape long before skyscrapers punctuated the skyline.

↑ Brooklyn Bridge,
with Manhattan's
skyline beyond

Timeline

1872

Roebling's son
takes over con-
struction, but is
partly paralyzed
by "the bends." His
wife oversees the
bridge's completion.

1883

Panic breaks out on
Memorial Day after
a woman trips; of
the 20,000 on the
bridge, 12 are
crushed to death.

1869

△ Engineer
Roebling crushes
his foot between
an incoming ferry
and the ferry slip.
He dies three
weeks later.

1885

◁ Robert Odlum
is the first to
jump off the
bridge, on a bet.
He later dies from
internal bleeding.

1983

△ The bridge's
centennial is
celebrated with
a spectacular
fireworks display.

Crossing the Bridge

The Brooklyn Bridge remains an object of awe and beauty as much as a convenient commuter link between the boroughs – as many Brooklyn cyclists use the bridge to go to work as pedestrians and cars today. Strolling across this landmark has become something of a rite of passage for visitors, and the views from the middle are undeniably spectacular. From here the densely packed skyscrapers of the Financial District seem to soar straight out of the water, while to the north the Empire State Building towers above Midtown. Today you can access the bridge's wooden walkway,

> **Strolling across this landmark has become something of a rite of passage for visitors, and the views from the middle are undeniably spectacular.**

PICTURE PERFECT
Brooklyn Bridge

You can't visit the Big Apple without getting that perfect photo of the Brooklyn Bridge. You'll get the best close-ups of the bridge from the Fulton Ferry District (on the Brooklyn side); for full-length shots, walk up South Street north of the bridge (on the Manhattan side).

which is shared with cyclists, from Centre Street in Manhattan. From here, you can meander all the way to Downtown Brooklyn, or exit at the first set of stairs for Brooklyn Heights (p284) and the Fulton Ferry District (p278). The first section of the bridge does tend to get very crowded, especially in summer – go early if you can, or consider crossing the bridge from Brooklyn to Manhattan instead, which provides spectacular skyline views.

Capturing the spectacular scenery from the Brooklyn Bridge ↓

Pedestrians and cyclists crossing the bridge ↑

EAT

The River Café
Linger at this idyllic spot after crossing from Manhattan. Set charmingly by the water, on the Brooklyn side, this Michelin-star restaurant offers exceptional food and spectacular bridge views.

📍 G13 🏠 1 Water St
🌐 rivercafe.com

$$$

Did You Know?

Elephants marched across the bridge, as a demonstration of its safety, in 1884.

2 🏛️ 🏍️ 🖥️ 🏛️

BROOKLYN MUSEUM

📍M16 🏛️200 Eastern Pkwy 🚇Eastern Pkwy-Brooklyn Museum (2, 3)
🚌B41, B45, B67, B69 🕐11am–6pm Wed–Sun (to 10pm Thu), 11am–11pm
1st Sat of each month (except Sep) 🌐brooklynmuseum.org

This cultural institution houses an encyclopedic collection of some one million objects, including an outstanding assemblage of Native American art, exquisite pieces of ancient Egyptian and Islamic art, and important American and European paintings.

When it opened in 1897, the Brooklyn Museum building, designed to be the largest cultural edifice in the world, was the greatest achievement of New York architects McKim, Mead & White. Today its five floors of galleries, covering 560,000 sq ft (50,025 sq m), house a collection to rival that of the Met. The Connecting Cultures exhibition can be found on the first floor; Arts of Asia and the Islamic World on the second; Egyptian, Classical, and European painting and sculpture on the third; the decorative arts on the fourth; and American art on the fifth. Among its treasures is a sacred ibis coffin, probably recovered from the animal cemetery of Tuna el-Gebel in Middle Egypt; works by great artists like Monet; and a 19th-century deerskin worn by a chief of the Blackfoot tribe. Judy Chicago's *The Dinner Party* installation can be found in the Elizabeth A. Sackler Center for Feminist Art.

←
Downtown, depicted in Francis Guy's *A Winter Scene in Brooklyn* (1820)

↑ John Singer Sargent's *An Out-of-Doors Study* (1889) showing artist Paul Helleu

THE DINNER PARTY

An icon of feminist art, *The Dinner Party* pays homage to women in history. The giant installation comprises a ceremonial banquet, with place settings representing 39 women, starting with a mythological Greek goddess and ending with Georgia O'Keeffe, who symbolizes female artists. Another 999 names line the floor.

↑ Brooklyn Museum and some of its one million artifacts *(inset)*

EXPERIENCE MORE

③
Fulton Ferry District

⑨H13 ⑤High St (A, C)

This small historic district at the foot of the Brooklyn Bridge was once the busiest section of the East River, thanks to Robert Fulton's steamboat ferries. Among the landmarked 19th-century buildings is the Eagle Warehouse, built in 1893 in Romanesque Revival style for the *Brooklyn Eagle* newspaper, which was edited for a while by poet Walt Whitman. Today, it is occupied by expensive apartments.

The old pier area still receives New York Water Taxis from Manhattan, and there are popular classical music concerts at Bargemusic. The original Grimaldi's pizza recipe can be enjoyed at Juliana's Pizza (not to be confused with Grimaldi's restaurant, on the same street), while the Ample Hills Creamery offers freshly made ice creams in numerous delectable flavors.

④
Dumbo

⑨H13 ⑤York St (F), High St (A, C)

Dumbo – "Down Under the Manhattan Bridge Overpass" – is a ritzy area of converted brick factories between the Manhattan and Brooklyn bridges. The spacious lofts were colonized by artists in the 1970s, and since the 1990s the neighborhood has been transformed by art galleries, hip restaurants, luxury condominiums, and bars.

The redeveloped waterfront park offers an unmissable view of Manhattan, and St. Ann's Warehouse, an arts institution, occupies an old warehouse on the park's edge. Another Brooklyn Flea is based here on Sundays (Apr-Oct).

_____

⑤
New York Transit Museum

⑨J15 ⒶBoerum Pl and Schermerhorn St ⑤Borough Hall (2, 3, 4, 5), Jay St-MetroTech (A, C, F, R) ⏰10am-4pm Tue-Fri, 11am-5pm Sat & Sun ⓦnytransitmuseum.org

---

BARGEMUSIC

Chamber music on a river barge? It might seem an odd concept, but the acoustics at Bargemusic are first class. Concerts featuring performers from around the world are held five days a week on the converted coffee barge, moored just under the Brooklyn Bridge, at 1 Water St. Purchase tickets online (bargemusic.org) or call (800) 838-3006. Concerts run for 1 hour to 1 hour and 30 minutes.

←

Amazing views of
Manhattan from Empire
Fulton Ferry Lawn

Charting the evolution of the
city's public transit system,
this museum appropriately
occupies the former Court
Street shuttle station.

Exhibits include models,
photographs, and maps, as
well as aged turnstiles and
a few interactive displays of
fuel technologies. Visitors can
explore various models of
restored subway trains and
tram carts on the old station
platforms. There's also a small
exhibition space and store in
Grand Central Terminal (p188)
in Manhattan.

⑥
Red Hook

**⚲G17 🅂Smith St-9th St
(F, G)**

Settled by the Dutch in 1636,
Red Hook ("Roode Hoek") got
its name from the color of the
soil and the *hoek* (corner)
shape of the land where the
New York and Gowanus bays
meet. It became one of the
busiest and toughest dock-
lands in the US, inspiring the
1954 film *On the Waterfront*
and Arthur Miller's play *A View
from the Bridge* (1955).

↑ A converted town
house in Brooklyn's
Fort Greene

Today, Red Hook's water-
front is a surprising blend of
brick warehouses, cycle paths,
cobblestoned blocks and
stores, and its laid-back vibe
makes it unlike any other part
of the city. A few independent
stores and places to eat dot
Van Brunt Street, the area's
busiest strip. The Red Hook
Ball Fields host soccer tournaments, and Latino food stands
on summer weekends.

⑦
Fort Greene

**⚲K14 🅂Atlantic Av (B, D,
N, Q, R, 2, 3, 4, 5), Fulton St
(G) ⓦbam.org**

Home to Saturday's Brooklyn
Flea, Fort Greene is full of
beautiful Italianate and East-
lake town houses built in the
mid-19th century. At its heart
is Fort Greene Park, designed
by Frederick Law Olmsted and
Calvert Vaux in 1867, crowned
by the Prison Ship Martyrs'
Monument (1908), commem-
orating the estimated 11,500
Americans who died in British
floating prison camps during
the Revolutionary War.

Fort Greene is home to the
Brooklyn Academy of Music
(BAM), at 30 Lafayette Av, a
leading cultural venue where
outstanding performances
often lean toward the avant-
garde. BAM's main building,
the 1908 Howard Gilman
Opera House, is a Beaux Arts
gem, designed by Herts &
Tallant. The nearby 1904
Harvey Theater stages most
of BAM's plays.

⑧
Williamsburg and
Greenpoint

**⚲L10 & M10 🅂Bedford
Av (L) for Williamsburg,
Greenpoint Av or Nassau
Av (G) for Greenpoint**

One of the city's trendiest
neighborhoods, Williamsburg
occupies much of northeast

Brooklyn, its main strip at
Bedford Avenue crowded with
boutiques, record stores, bars,
coffee shops, and restaurants.
Big on nightlife, this area is a
noted indie rock venue.

Culinary attractions include
the Brooklyn Brewery (p32),
Mast Brothers chocolate
factory (tours available) and
Smorgasburg, an outdoor
food market that runs April
through October (p282).

Greenpoint is a traditional
Polish stronghold with an artsy
crowd. The Russian Orthodox
Cathedral of the Transfiguration sits at North 12th Street
on Driggs Avenue, a Byzantine
Revival landmark with five
patinated-copper onion domes
that loom above McCarren
Park's trees. The park forms
an unofficial boundary
between the two neighbor-
hoods and contains a historic
(1936) swimming pool and the
renowned McCarren Hotel.

9

Brooklyn Bridge Park

📍 G13 🚇 From Manhattan Bridge to Atlantic Av 🚇 High St (A, C), York St (F), Clark St (2, 3) 🌐 brooklyn bridgepark.org

A series of playgrounds, sports amenities, stellar viewpoints, and reclaimed docks stretch along the rejuvenated waterfront from Dumbo to Brooklyn Heights. The section of the park just east of the Brooklyn Bridge features the traditional Jane's Carousel, a spacious open lawn (p278), and giant steps for picnicking.

On the other side of the bridge, Pier One offers free kayaking on summer weekends, while Pier Two features shuffleboard courts and a roller rink. Pier Five has sports fields and a picnic area, while Pier Six is brilliant for kids, with a popular water park, climbing area, and a giant slide.

10

Brooklyn Navy Yard

📍 K12 🚇 From Manhattan Bridge to Williamsburg Bridge ℹ️ BLDG 92, 63 Flushing Av 🚇 High St (A, C), York St (F) 🌐 brooklyn navyyard.org

Transformed in recent years from a near-derelict site, the Brooklyn Navy Yard now has over 300 businesses, from Brooklyn Grange Farms to Steiner Studios (where *Boardwalk Empire* and *Girls* were filmed). Get oriented at the Brooklyn Navy Yard Center at BLDG 92, which charts the history of the site, and includes models of well-known ships built here, such as the USS *Ohio*.

↑ Looking out over Brooklyn Navy Yard, a frequent film set

Other highlights include Kings County Distillery, making craft bourbon.

11

Brooklyn Children's Museum

📍 N15 🚇 145 Brooklyn Av 🚇 Kingston Av (3), Kingston-Throop Av (C) 🕐 10am–5pm Tue–Fri (to 6pm Thu), 10am–7pm Sat-Sun 🌐 brooklynkids.org

Founded in 1899, the Brooklyn Children's Museum was the first to be designed especially for children. Since then, it has been a model, inspiration, and consultant for the development of more than 250 museums for children across the country and all over the world. Housed in a hi-tech underground building dating from 1976, it is one of the most imaginative children's museums anywhere. In 2008, a "green" renovation by Uruguayan architect Rafael Viñoly added solar panels and other energy-saving devices, and expanded the museum space.

Galleries contain hands-on exhibitions that focus on the environment, science, and local neighborhood life – which highlights various multicultural districts around Brooklyn. The "Totally Tots" area is dedicated to children under the age of five, with a "Water Wonders" play quarter. The live animals on display downstairs will especially thrill the little ones. There are also play stores and restaurants where children can buy, sell, and even make (fake) pizza. Special events and classes, such as Zumba for kids, workshops, and art projects, take place daily.

→ The sun setting over Manhattan, as seen from Brooklyn

12
Grand Army Plaza

📍 M16 🏛 Plaza St at Flatbush Av 🚇 Grand Army Plaza (2, 3)

Frederick Law Olmsted and Calvert Vaux laid out this grand oval in 1870 as an imposing gateway to Prospect Park (p282). The Eastern Parkway, the world's first parkway, also begins here.

The Soldiers' and Sailors' Arch and its sculptures were added in 1892 as a grand tribute to the Union Army. Designed by John H. Duncan, the arch is reminiscent of Imperial Roman monuments, with its intricate carving and detail. Stanford White modified the arch between 1894 and 1901 to accommodate the bronze sculptures by Philip Martiny and Frederick MacMonnies, along with the columns. The bust of John F. Kennedy here is, somewhat surprisingly, the only official New York City monument to the 35th president of the United States. The arch itself is occasionally open for special exhibitions.

13
Park Slope Historic District

📍 L16 🏛 From Prospect Park West below Flatbush Av, to 8th/7th/5th Avs 🚇 Grand Army Plaza (2, 3), 7 Av (F)

This wonderful enclave of beautiful Victorian town houses on the edge of Prospect Park dates from the 1880s, when it served upper-middle-class professionals who could commute into Manhattan after the Brooklyn Bridge opened in 1883. The shady streets are lined with houses in every architectural style popular in the late 19th century, some with the towers, turrets, and curlicues so representative of the era. Particularly fine examples are in Romanesque Revival style, with rounded entry arches.

The Montauk Club at 25 Eighth Avenue combines the style of Venice's Ca' d'Oro palazzo with the friezes and gargoyles of the Montauks, for whom this popular 19th-century private social club was named.

DRINK

Black Flamingo
Latin and 1970s theme bar with dance floor.

📍 L10 🏛 168 Borinquen Pl, Williamsburg 🕐 Mon 🌐 blackflamingo nyc.com

Fresh Kills Bar
Best of Williamsburg's hand-crafted cocktails.

📍 M10 🏛 161 Grand St 🌐 freshkillsbar.com

House of Yes
Lavish dance parties plus cabaret.

📍 M10 🏛 2 Wyckoff Av, Williamsburg 🕐 Sun-Tue 🌐 houseofyes.org

Pete's Candy Store
Friendly local pub, with free live music.

📍 M10 🏛 111 North 12th St, Williamsburg 🕐 Tue 🌐 petes candystore.com

Westlight
Soak up sensational city views.

📍 M10 🏛 111 North 12th St, Williamsburg 🌐 westlightnyc.com

EAT

Dough

Fabulous, enormous doughnuts, including a delicious hibiscus option.

M13 **448 Lafayette Av**, Bedford-Stuyvesant **doughbrooklyn.com**

⑤⑤⑤

Junior's

Venerable Brooklyn diner most famous for classic NY cheesecake.

K14 **386 Flatbush Av Extension, at DeKalb Av** **juniorscheesecake.com**

⑤⑤⑤

Peter Luger Steak House

Heavenly porterhouse (the only cut served) since 1887. Cash only.

K10 **178 Broadway** **peterluger.com**

⑤⑤⑤

Smorgasburg

America's largest open-air food market has over 100 tempting stands on Saturdays and Sundays in Prospect Park (Apr–Oct).

M10 **East River State Park, 90 Kent Av & Prospect Park, Breeze Hill** **Mon–Fri, Sun, mid-Nov–Apr** **smorgasburg.com**

⑤⑤⑤

Steve's Authentic Key Lime Pies

Some of the tastiest key lime pies in the Northeast.

G17 **Pier 40, 185 Van Dyke St** **keylime.com/jh**

⑤⑤⑤

14

Prospect Park

M17 **S Grand Army Plaza (2, 3), Prospect Park (B, Q)** **prospectpark.org**

Olmsted and Vaux considered this park, which opened in 1867, better than their earlier Central Park (*p238*). The Long Meadow, a sweep of broad lawns and grand vistas, is the longest unbroken swath of green space in New York.

Olmsted's belief was that "a feeling of relief is experienced by entering them" (the parks) "on escaping from the cramped, confining, and controlling circumstances of the streets of the town." That vision is still as true today as it was a century and a half ago.

Notable features include Stanford White's colonnaded Croquet Shelter, and the pools and weeping willows of the Vale of Cashmere. The Music Grove bandstand hosts summer concerts.

A favorite feature of the park is the Camperdown Elm, an old and twisted tree planted in 1872, which has inspired many poems and paintings. Ranger-led tours are the best way to see the park and its wide variety of landscapes, from Classical gardens with statues to rocky glens with running brooks.

15

Brooklyn Botanic Garden

M16 **900 Washington Av** **S Prospect Park (B, Q), Eastern Pkwy (2, 3)** **Tue–Sun; times vary, check website for details** **bbg.org**

Though not vast, this garden has many delights. Designed by the Olmsted brothers in 1910, it features an Elizabethan-style "knot" garden and one of North America's largest collections of roses.

The central showpiece is a Japanese hill-and-pond garden, with a teahouse and Shinto shrine. In late April and early May the promenade is aglow with delicate Japanese cherry blossoms, celebrated in an annual festival of Japanese culture. April is also the time to vist the Magnolia Plaza, where some 80 trees display their beautiful, creamy blossoms against a backdrop of daffodils on Boulder Hill.

The Fragrance Garden has raised beds of heavily scented

Visitors seeking
traditional beachside ↑
fun on Coney Island

> In the mid-19th century, Brooklyn poet
> Walt Whitman composed many of his
> works on Coney Island, which was at that
> time purely untamed Atlantic coastline.

and textured plants all labeled in Braille. The conservatory has a large bonsai collection and some rare rain forest trees.

16

Green-Wood Cemetery

📍 L18 🏠 500 25th St at
Fifth Av 🚇 25 St (R)
🕐 Apr-Sep: 7am-7pm;
Oct-Mar: 7am-5pm
🌐 green-wood.com

This 478-acre (193-ha) cemetery was founded in 1838, and today it is almost a city park, both sprawling and beautiful. Several famous citizens are interred here, including the street artist Jean-Michel Basquiat (1960–88), abolitionist Henry Ward

←

Stunning blossom in
the Japanese Garden,
Brooklyn Botanic Garden

Beecher (1813–87), composer Leonard Bernstein (1918–90), and glass artist Louis Comfort Tiffany (1848–1933). The whole Steinway family of the piano-making dynasty also lie at rest in a 119-room mausoleum.

17

Coney Island

📍 N13 🚇 Stillwell Av (D, F, N, Q), W 8 St (F, Q) 🌐 coney island.com

New Yorkers have been visiting Brooklyn's Coney Island for seaside fun – at the cost of a single journey – since 1867. Crowds continue to flock to this peninsular neighborhood to revel in its kitsch amuse-ment parks, plummeting rollercoasters, and candy floss stands, away from the hubbub of Manhattan.

In the mid-19th century, Brooklyn poet Walt Whitman composed many of his works on Coney Island, which was at

that time purely untamed Atlantic coastline. By the 1920s, Coney Island was billing itself as the "World's Largest Playground," home to three huge fairgrounds. The subway arrived in 1920, and the 1921 boardwalk ensured Coney Island's popularity throughout the Great Depression.

Coney Island has been modernized, much to the chagrin of local residents, who feared that its character would be lost. However, the boardwalk still yields lovely ocean views, and the modern Luna Park features a number of spine-tingling rides, including the Cyclone roller-coaster, which at roughly 90 years old has been designated an official city landmark. The more faint-hearted might prefer the Wonder Wheel, which also has an official landmark status and offers beautiful views of the city. Opening times vary – check the park's website for detailed opening times and price lists.

Further attractions on Coney Island include the New York Aquarium, home to over 350 species. There's also the Coney Island Museum, which has memorabilia, souvenirs, and relics of old rides from the amusement park. The Mermaid Parade in June *(see p54)* is a major annual event.

A SHORT WALK
BROOKLYN HEIGHTS

Distance 1 mile (1.5 km) **Nearest subway** Clark St
Time 20 minutes

Facing Lower Manhattan across the East River, Brooklyn Heights is one of New York's most elegant and historic neighborhoods. The city's wealthy elites built brownstone town houses here in the 1820s, when the Heights became the city's first commuter suburb. The completion of the Brooklyn Bridge in 1883 intensified development. Today, Brooklyn Heights is an affluent neighborhood, and the perfect place to admire Manhattan's famous skyline.

Brooklyn Bridge Park/Dumbo Ferry Terminal

START

Bargemusic, moored just under the Brooklyn Bridge, is a renovated coffee barge dating from the late 19th century, and holds nightly chamber music performances (p278).

Ample Hills Creamery is based in an early 20th-century fireboat house on the Fulton Ferry Pier, and serves exotic flavors of ice cream.

FURMAN ST

COLUMBIA HEIGHTS

↑ Ample Hills Creamery in a striking fireboat house

BROOKLYN QUEENS EXPY

WILLOW

COLUMBIA HEIGHTS

70 Willow Street is said to be where Truman Capote wrote Breakfast at Tiffany's.

COLUMBIA HEIGHTS

Brooklyn Heights Promenade is a pedestrian path providing sensational views of the Statue of Liberty, Lower Manhattan's skyscrapers, and the Brooklyn Bridge.

CLARK ST

0 meters	75
0 yards	75

N ↑

FINISH ●

Just below the Brooklyn Bridge, Fulton Ferry District is a historic wharf area named after Robert Fulton, the steamboat king. It features iconic landmarks such as the Eagle Warehouse with its large, glass clock-window (p278).

Juliana's Pizza is the original location of Patsy Grimaldi's famous coal-oven pizzas, not to be confused with the newer Grimaldi's next door.

Locator Map
For more detail see p270

BROOKLYN BRIDGE

VERIT ST

OLD FULTON ST

DOUGHTY ST

VINE ST

VINE ST

POPLAR ST

MIDDAGH ST

CRANBERY ST

ORANGE ST

Did You Know?

Brooklyn Heights, or "America's first suburb," was one of the first areas outside of Manhattan to be settled.

24 Middagh St is the area's oldest house, erected in 1824. Other examples of old buildings can be found along Middagh and Willow.

Plymouth Church was the base of pastor Henry Ward Beecher, abolitionist and campaigner for women's rights. It was also a stop on the Underground Railroad, where slaves were hidden on their way to freedom.

Clark St subway
(lines A,C)
Ⓜ

↑ Fulton Ferry District, a wharf area with spectacular views across the river

Yankee Stadium, the Bronx

BEYOND
THE CENTER

Though officially part of New York City, Upper Manhattan and the outer boroughs (the Bronx, Queens, and Staten Island) are quite different in feel. Largely residential, and without the world-famous sights that are typically associated with New York, these calmer areas are still well worth exploring for their numerous attractions. Here you'll discover the country's biggest zoo, idyllic botanical gardens, ground-breaking museums, iconic sports arenas, and a restaurant scene representing almost every ethnicity.

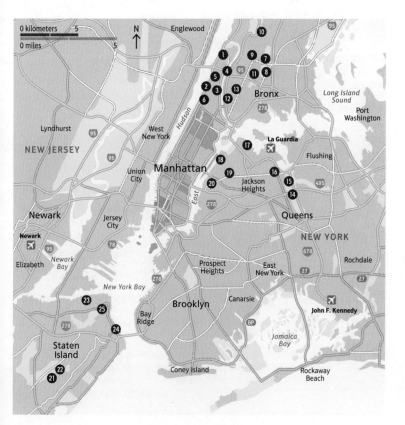

GETTING TO KNOW
BEYOND THE CENTER

Leave the hubbub of downtown Manhattan behind you and experience the city beond the center. Explore Upper Manhattan and, to the north, the Bronx, which is the only borough on the mainland. Across the East River lies multicultural Queens, while suburban Staten Island sits in the harbor.

PAGE 290

UPPER MANHATTAN

Once a Dutch settlement, now a residential area with little of the bustle of Downtown, Upper Manhattan is perfect for discovering lesser-known sights. Here you'll find museums, idyllic green spaces, and beautiful houses.

Best for
History, medieval art, escaping the crowds

Home to
The Cloisters Museum, Fort Washington Park

Experience
The peaceful gardens of the Cloisters Museum

PAGE 294

THE BRONX

This once prosperous suburb became a byword for urban decay in the mid-20th century, but the Bronx is slowly making a comeback. There are large pockets of beauty waiting to be found in this borough, comprising historic mansions, tranquil parks, an outstanding botanic garden and zoo, and the famous Yankee Stadium.

Best for
Baseball, green spaces

Home to
New York Botanical Garden, Bronx Zoo, Yankee Stadium

Experience
The thrill of a baseball game at Yankee Stadium

PAGE 300

QUEENS

Queens, the city's largest borough, has a trove of cultural attractions – from piano showrooms and sculpture parks to a museum dedicated to the art of filmmaking, and Louis Armstrong's house. It's a real melting pot of cultures, and there's a huge array of ethnic restaurants here, with the aromas of Greek, Thai, and Indian food lingering in its streets. Queens is also one of the epicenters of New York's craft beer renaissance, and most breweries operate tasting or "tap" rooms.

Best for
Mulitcultural New York, diverse cuisines, craft beer, unique museums

Home to
Queens Museum, Museum of the Moving Image, Steinway & Sons, Louis Armstrong House Museum

Experience
Seasonal pours at one of Queens' craft breweries

PAGE 302

STATEN ISLAND

Its famous ferry ride aside, Staten Island and its attractions are not well known to New Yorkers in general, but it would be a mistake to dismiss the "forgotten borough" so readily. Visitors who venture beyond the ferry terminal will be pleasantly surprised to find hills, lakes, and greenery, with expanses of open space, amazing harbor views, and well-preserved early American buildings. One of the biggest surprises here is a cache of Tibetan art that is hidden away in a replica of a Buddhist temple.

Best for
A different view of Manhattan, Sri Lankan food, Tibetan art

Home to
Historic Richmond Town, Jacques Marchais Museum of Tibetan Art, Little Sri Lanka

Experience
Life in the 19th century at Historic Richmond Town

→

① ⊘ Ⓜ ▣ ⑪

THE CLOISTERS MUSEUM

🅐 Fort Tryon Park 🅢 190 St (A) 🚌 M4 🕐 10am–5:15pm daily (Nov–Feb: to 4:45pm) 🚫 Thanksgiving 🌐 metmuseum.org/visit/met-cloisters

Crowning a hilltop in Upper Manhattan, this extraordinary museum transports visitors to a European monastery thanks to its authentic, medieval-style building, reconstructed cloisters, and rich art collection.

Despite appearances, the Met's museum of medieval art resides in a building constructed in the early 20th century. Sculptor George Grey Barnard founded the museum in 1914 before John D. Rockefeller Jr. funded the Metropolitan Museum of Art's 1925 purchase of the collection. Rockefeller also donated the site at Fort Tryon Park for the museum's construction. Designed by modern architect Charles Cullens, who was responsible for Riverside Church (p258), the stunning building reflects the content of its collection, incorporating medieval cloisters, chapels, and halls from Europe that were then rebuilt here. The cloisters, for example, are named Cuxa, Saint-Guilhem, Bonnefont, and Trie, after their French origins. The museum is organized roughly in chronological order, starting with the Romanesque period (AD 1,000) and moving to the Gothic (1150–1520). Sculptures, stained glass, and paintings are on the lower floor and the Unicorn Tapestries are on the upper floor. There are also gardens to enjoy.

UNICORN TAPESTRIES

This set of seven beautiful tapestries (also known as "The Hunt of the Unicorn"), woven in Flanders around 1500, depicts the quest for, capture, sacrifice, and ultimate resurrection of the mythical unicorn. Its incredible detailing and mysterious symbolism - critics still argue about its meaning - make it one of the greatest medieval artworks. The tapestries have been interpreted both as complicated metaphors for Christ and a celebration of matrimony.

←

Monastic in appearance, Upper Manhattan's Cloisters Museum

←

Visitors enjoy the Benedictine Cuxa cloister gardens, surrounded by marble columns

1934

The year construction of this unique museum began.

↑ The beautiful sanctuary at the Cloisters Museum

EXPERIENCE MORE

❷ Ⓜ 🏛
Hispanic Society

🏠 Broadway at 155th St
🚇 155 St (C), 157 St (1)
🔒 For renovations
🌐 hispanicsociety.org

The Hispanic Society of America owns one of the greatest collection of Hispanic art outside of Spain. The extensive collections include Spanish sculpture, decorative arts, prints, and photographs, with changing exhibits throughout the year. The main gallery, in Spanish Renaissance style, holds Goya's famous *Duchess of Alba*. The adjacent Bancaja Gallery contains Joaquín Sorolla y Bastida's *Vision of Spain*, commissioned in 1911. Its 14 large murals depict people and life in Spain. The balcony above offers some of the best works: paintings by El Greco, such as *Holy Family*, and portraits by Velázquez.

The Hispanic Society is based in Audubon Terrace, a complex of Classical Revival buildings in Washington Heights, completed in 1908 by Charles Pratt Huntington. Funded by the architect's cousin, civic benefactor Archer Huntington, the entrance plaza contains statues by Archer's wife, Anna Hyatt Huntingdon. The majority of the complex is occupied by Boricua College, and the society is the only museum here.

---

❸ ♿ Ⓜ 🏛
Morris-Jumel Mansion

🏠 65 Jumel Terrace at West 160th St and Edgecombe Ave 🚇 163 St-Amsterdam Av (C) 🕐 10am-4pm Tue-Fri, 10am-5pm Sat & Sun
🌐 morrisjumel.org

This is one of New York's few pre-Revolutionary buildings and it has a long and, at times,

↑ The beautifully restored exterior of Morris-Jumel Mansion

scandalous history. Now a museum with nine restored period rooms, it was built in 1765 for Roger Morris. In 1810 it was bought and updated by Stephen Jumel, a merchant of French-Caribbean descent, and his wife Eliza. The museum exhibits include many original Jumel pieces. Tours take place at noon on Saturday and 2pm on Sunday.

The couple furnished the house with souvenirs of their many visits to France. Her boudoir has a "dolphin" chair, reputedly bought from Napoleon. Eliza's social climbing and love affairs scandalized New York society. Rumors said she let her husband bleed to death in 1832 so she could inherit his fortune. She later married Aaron Burr, aged 77, and divorced him three years later on the day he died.

The exterior of the Palladian-style, wood-sided Georgian house, with a Classical portico and octagonal wing, has been restored.

❹
George Washington Bridge and Fort Washington Park

🚇 175 St (A), 181 St (1)
🌐 panynj.gov

French architect Le Corbusier called this "the only seat of grace in the disordered city." While not as famous a landmark as its Brooklyn equivalent, this bridge by engineer Othmar Ammann and his architect Cass Gilbert has its own individual character and history. Plans for a bridge linking Manhattan to New Jersey had been in the pipeline for more than 60 years before the Port of New York Authority raised the necessary $59 million to fund the project. It was Ammann who suggested a road bridge rather than a more expensive rail link. Work began in 1927, and the bridge was opened in 1931. Today it is a vital link for commuter traffic between Manhattan and New Jersey's Fort Lee, and is in constant use, carrying over 53 million vehicles per year.

Gilbert planned to clad the bridge's two towers with masonry but funds did not permit it, leaving an elegant skeletal structure 600 ft (183 m) high and 4,760 ft (1,451 m) long. The lower deck was added in 1962.

Below the eastern tower, in Fort Washington Park, is a lighthouse that dates from 1889 and was saved from demolition in 1951 by public pressure. Many thousands of young New Yorkers and children all around the world have loved the bedtime story *The Little Red Lighthouse and the Great Gray Bridge* (1942), and wrote letters to save the lighthouse. Author Hildegarde Hoyt Swift wove the tale around her two favorite New York landmarks.

The Little Red Lighthouse Festival is held here every September and includes a special guest reading of the famous book.

⑤ Ⓜ 🏛
Shabazz Center

🏠 3940 Broadway, at West 165th Street ☎ (212) 568-1341 Ⓢ 168 St (A, C, 1) 🕐 11am–5pm Tue; Wed–Fri 11am–6pm

In Washington Heights, the Shabazz Center, or, to quote its full name, the Malcolm X and Dr Betty Shabazz Memorial and Educational

Center, commemorates the life of the influential African-American Muslim minister and political activist Malcolm X. The center holds events and film screenings honoring the work of Malcolm X, while the first floor contains touch-screen panels that highlight key phases of his life via interviews and videos.

The center occupies what's left of the Audubon Ballroom, the scene of Malcolm X's assassination in 1965. It is now part of the Columbia-Presbyterian Hospital.

Born Malcolm Little in Nebraska, in 1925, Malcolm X spent much of his later life in New York as a committed follower of Elijah Muhammad's Nation of Islam. He was a key inspiration for the Black Power movement.

⑥
Ralph Ellison Memorial

🏠 West 150th St and Riverside Dr Ⓢ 145 St (1)

African-American author Ralph Ellison is commemorated by this small but poignant memorial. The bronze structure, with a cut-out male figure, was created by Elizabeth Catlett and dedicated in 2003. The four surrounding stone markers are engraved with Ellison quotes, notably the opening lines of *Invisible Man* (1952): "I am invisible, understand, simply because people refuse to see me."

Born in the segregated Deep South in 1913, Ralph Ellison moved to Harlem in 1936, living nearby at 730 Riverside Drive.

→ George Washington Bridge, linking New York with New Jersey

7 🚲 Ⓜ 🖥 🛍

NEW YORK BOTANICAL GARDEN

📍 Kazimiroff Blvd, Bronx River Parkway (Exit 7W) Ⓢ Bedford Pk Blvd (4, B, D) 🚌 Bx26 🕐 10am–6pm Tue–Sun (to 5pm mid-Jan–Feb) 🌐 nybg.org

One of the oldest and largest botanical gardens in the world, this lush park provides a nature escape in the heart of the bustling Bronx.

The New York Botanical Garden offers 250 acres (100 ha) of dazzling beauty and hands-on enjoyment. From the nation's most glorious Victorian glasshouse to the Everett Children's Adventure Garden, this green space is alive with things to discover. Perhaps most importantly, the New York Botanical Garden has 50 gardens and plant collections, and 50 acres (20 ha) of uncut woodland in the Thain Family Forest. This is some of the most important woodland in the city; it follows the same trails used by the Lenape tribe and is home to trees that date back to the American Revolution. A great way to see the garden is by joining the tram tour. This 20-minute narrated ride includes nine stops, so visitors can hop on and off.

1 The Enid A. Haupt Conservatory is a stunning Victorian-style glasshouse, and consists of eleven interconnecting glass galleries. These house "A World of Plants," which comprises rain forests, deserts, aquatic plans, and seasonal exhibitions.

2 The Peggy Rockefeller Rose contains over 2,700 rose bushes, and is best visited in early summer when the roses are in bloom. Named by David Rockefeller for his horticulturalist wife, the garden was laid out in 1988.

3 Blossoming trees in the Japanese Garden.

Did You Know?
—
The grounds are free to enter all day Wednesday and 10am-noon Saturday.

↑ Fall colors and falling leaves in the Thain Family Forest

8 ⊗ ⊗ ⊡ ⊡

BRONX ZOO

🏠 2300 Southern Blvd, Bronx 🚇 E Tremont Av (2, 5) 🚌 Bx9, Bx12, Bx19, Bx22, Bx39, BxM11, Q44 🕐 10am–5pm Mon–Fri, 10am–5:30pm Sat & Sun (Nov–Mar: 10am–4.30pm daily) 🌐 bronxzoo.com

America's biggest urban wildlife park is right here in the Bronx. Popular with little and big kids alike, the zoo's residents include bears, bison, baboons, and everything in between.

A Day at the Zoo

Opened in 1899, the Bronx Zoo is home to more than 4,000 animals of 500 species, which live in realistic representations of their natural habitats. The zoo is a leader in the perpetuation of endangered species, such as the Indian rhinoceros and the snow leopard.

Its 265 acres (107 ha) of woods, streams, and parklands accommodate, in season, a children's zoo, the Butterfly Garden, and the Wild Asia Monorail; other attractions include World of Reptiles, a one-of-a-kind bug carousel, and a 4D theater experience. Tours take place at 10:15 and 11:45am, and last an hour.

The attractive Wildlife Conservation Society building, Bronx Zoo ↓

INSIDER TIP
Children's Zoo

If the little ones need to let off steam, head to the Children's Zoo, which can be found near the Zoo Center and Madagascar! exhibit. Here, kids can monkey around by crawling through prairie dog tunnels, trying on turtle shells, and even petting and feeding the animals. Check the website for opening times.

↑ Magnificent Amur tigers are on view all year at Tiger Mountain

↑ Visitors look for residents at the tropical rain forest JungleWorld

THE CONGO GORILLA FOREST

This award-winning replica of a central African rain forest is home to the largest population of Western Lowland gorillas in the US, as well as a family of pygmy marmosets, the world's smallest monkeys.

← Edgar Allan Poe's charming, snow-topped cottage in the Bronx

9

Poe Cottage

⌂ 2640 Grand Concourse
Ⓢ Kingsbridge Rd (D, 4)
🕘 10am-3pm Thu & Fri, 10am-4pm Sat, 1-5pm Sun
Ⓦ bronxhistorical society.org

Built as a modest laborer's dwelling around 1812, this white-clapboard house, set incongruously today in the midst of working-class Latino housing blocks, was Edgar Allan Poe's rural home from 1846 to 1849. The charming house originally stood on farmland a short distance away on East Kingsbridge Road, but it was moved here (at the northern tip of the specially created Poe Park) in 1913.

Although Poe was already relatively successful as the writer of *The Raven*, he was dogged by financial problems in the mid-1800s. He moved here with his wife, Virginia, and her mother, Maria, in search of fresh rural air. Sadly, soon after they arrived at the cottage, Virginia died of tuberculosis, aged just 24. Heartbroken, Poe managed to write a few revered works while in mourning, including the moving poem *Annabel Lee*, which was written in memory of his wife. Maria outlived them both, and moved out of the cottage shortly after Poe's mysterious death in Baltimore two years later.

Today, the restored cottage contains several rooms set up to look as they did during Poe's time. There is also a small gallery of artwork from the 1840s within the vicinity.

The elegant Poe Park Visitor Center stands separate from Poe Cottage itself, at 2650 Grand Concourse. Designed by the Japanese architect Toshiko Mori, the educational facility features rotating exhibitions of art. Open Tuesday through Saturday, its sharply angled roof was inspired by a raven's outstretched wings, in honor of the writer's most famous literary work.

10

Woodlawn Cemetery

⌂ Webster Av and East 233rd St Ⓢ Woodlawn (4)
🕘 8:30am-4:30pm daily
Ⓦ thewoodlawn cemetery.org

Established in 1863, Woodlawn Cemetery is the burial place of many a wealthy and

distinguished New Yorker. Memorials and tombstones are set on beautiful grounds. F. W. Woolworth and many members of his family are interred in a mausoleum only a little less ornate than the building that carries the family name (*p87*). The pink marble vault of meat magnate Herman Armour is oddly reminiscent of a ham.

Other New Yorkers who are buried here include Mayor Fiorello La Guardia; Rowland Hussey Macy, the founder of the great Macy's department store; author Herman Melville; and jazz legend Duke Ellington.

11

Belmont and Arthur Avenue

Ⓢ Fordham Rd (B, D, S), then 🚌 Bx12 Ⓦ arthuravenue bronx.com

Within walking distance of the botanical garden and zoo, Belmont is home to one of New York's largest Italian-American communities. This is a more authentic and much larger alternative to Little Italy in Manhattan, and its main thoroughfare, Arthur Avenue, is lined with Italian bakeries, pizzerias, and restaurants.

The Arthur Avenue Retail Market includes pastry shops, butchers, pasta-makers, places selling Italian sausages, fish stands, and coffee shops. Every September, the neighborhood celebrates Ferragosto, a traditional harvest festival, with dancing, food stalls, live performances, and a cheese-carving contest.

← Hero sandwiches, among treats in store along Arthur Avenue

12 ⊛ Ⓜ

Yankee Stadium

📍 East 161st St at River Av, Highbridge 🚇 161 St (B, D, 4) 🕐 10am–12:40pm daily (except game days) 🌐 mlb.com/yankees

This was first home of the New York Yankees baseball team in 1923. Among Yankee heroes are two of the greatest players of all time: Babe Ruth and Joe DiMaggio (also famous for marrying actress Marilyn Monroe in 1954). In 1921, left-hander Babe Ruth hit the stadium's first home run – against the Boston Red Sox, his former team. The stadium was completed two years later, and became known as "the house that Ruth built."

One of the largest annual gatherings has been that of the Jehovah's Witnesses, and in 1950, 123,707 attended on one day. In 1965, Pope Paul VI celebrated Mass before more than 80,000 people – the first visit to North America by a pope; in 1979, John Paul II also visited the stadium.

In 2009, the Yankees moved to a stadium constructed parallel to the old site. This remains one of the most expensive venues built on US soil, estimated at around $1.5 billion, and honors aspects of the 1923 stadium, such as the granite and limestone facade.

The Yankees remain one of the top teams in the American League. Multiple Yankee Clubhouse stores in New York sell tickets for tours and games.

---

13 Ⓜ ⊡

The Bronx Museum of the Arts

📍 1040 Grand Concourse 🚇 167 St (B, D) 🕐 11am–6pm Wed, Thu, Sat & Sun, 11am–8pm Fri 🌐 bronxmuseum.org

Founded in 1971, the museum showcases contemporary works by Asian, Latino, and African-American artists, with over 1,000 items in the permanent collection. It also hosts readings and performances.

Among artists represented are Romare Bearden (1911–88), a multimedia artist known for his depictions of everyday African-American life; Bronx-born Whitfield Lovell (b. 1959), renowned for his African-American figures in pencil and charcoal; Cuban installation and performance artist Tania Bruguera (b. 1968); lauded photographer Seydou Keïta (1921–2001) from Mali; Brazilian visual artist Hélio Oiticica (1937–80); contemporary African-American artist Kara Walker (b. 1969); and the Chinese artist Xu Bing (b. 1955).

Since 1982, the museum has been housed in a former synagogue, donated by the City of New York. In 2006, the museum, with a striking new jagged steel-and-glass "accordion" facade, was reopened after an expansion completed by Miami-based company Arquitectonica.

BIRTHPLACE OF HIP HOP TOUR

This is the home of hip hop. The Bronx scene emerged in the mid-1970s with pioneers such as DJ Kool Herc. (Run-DMC formed in Queens in 1981 and Fab Five Freddy hailed from Brooklyn). Hush Hip Hop Tours *(www.hushtours.com)* runs the "Birthplace of Hip Hop Tour" through Harlem and the Bronx, hosted by Grand Master Caz, Rahiem, and Ralph McDaniels.

International icon, Yankee Stadium in the Bronx

14

Flushing Meadows-Corona Park

🚇 Mets-Willets Point (7)

The site of New York's two World's Fairs offers expansive waterside picnic grounds and a multitude of attractions. The 41,000-seat Citi Field stadium is home to the New York Mets baseball team, and is a popular rock concert venue. Flushing Meadows is also home to the National Tennis Center, where the US Open is played. The courts are available the rest of the year.

The Unisphere, symbol of the 1964 fair, still dominates the remains of the fairground. The giant hollow ball of green steel, 12 stories high and weighing 350 tons, is at the center of a circular fountain, and is always busy with casual photographers and families.

15

Queens Museum

🏛 New York City Building, Flushing Meadows-Corona Park 🚇 111 St (7) 🕐 11am-5pm Wed-Sun 🌐 queensmuseum.org

Next to the Unisphere, the museum occupies the only

remaining building from the 1939 World's Fair, designed as the New York City Pavilion. There are temporary exhibitions and three long-term installations. The Neustadt Collection of Tiffany Glass has pieces by Louis Comfort Tiffany, whose design studios were in Corona in the 1890s. "From Watersheds to Faucets: The Marvel of the NYC Water Supply System" features a large wood-and-plaster relief map, created for the 1939 World's Fair. Other World's Fair artifacts are also on display.

The other major attraction is the Panorama of the City of New York, from the 1964 World's Fair. At 9,300 sq ft (864 sq m), it is the world's largest architectural model, with 895,000 buildings carved out of wood, plus harbors, rivers, and bridges.

16

Louis Armstrong House Museum

🏛 34-56 107th St 🚇 103 St-Corona Plaza 🕐 10am-5pm Tue-Fri, noon-5pm Sat & Sun 🌐 louisarmstronghouse.org

Legendary trumpeter Louis Armstrong (1901–71) lived here from 1943 until his death in

1971, and is buried in nearby Flushing Cemetery. The jazz artist's home is preserved just as he and his fourth wife, singer Lucille Wilson, left it. Audio recordings reveal everyday goings-on, casual conversations with friends and relatives, and impromptu trumpet practice sessions. Guided tours, which take place hourly until 4pm, provide context. Concerts are held in the garden.

The visitors center across the street displays more of Armstrong's personal archives.

17

Steinway & Sons

🏛 1 Steinway Place, 19th Av 🚇 Ditmars Boulevard (N, W) 🌐 steinway.com

Heinrich Steinweg (1797–1871) emigrated from Germany in 1850, anglicized his name to Henry Steinway, and founded Steinway & Sons in 1853.

Recognized for producing the finest pianos, and winning prizes at international trade fairs, the company grew rapidly and about 1,250 grand pianos a year are built here. Among the most complex objects still made by hand, the pianos, made of maple, walnut, pear, or spruce wood, are assembled from over 12,000 parts, a process that takes a year. Visitors can join a tour at 9:30am to noon on Tuesdays (Sep–Jun) and Thursdays (Jan–Mar). Reservations essential.

18

Noguchi Museum and Socrates Sculpture Park

🏛 9-01 33rd Rd 🚇 Broadway (N, W), then 🚌 Q104 🕐 Noguchi Museum: 10am-5pm Wed-Fri, 11am-6pm Sat & Sun 🌐 noguchi.org

Devoted to Japanese-American abstract sculptor Isamu Noguchi (1904–88), this museum and garden provides

CRAFT BREWERIES

Thirsty? Head for Queens and its craft breweries. Long Island City is home to Rockaway Brewing (English ales and stouts; www.rockawaybrewco.com) and tiny Transmitter Brewing (farmhouse ales; www.transmitterbrew.com). SingleCut Beersmiths in Astoria (www.singlecut.com) is a lager specialist, while out in Ridgewood, Finback Brewery (www.finbackbrewery.com) offers seasonal pours.

↑ Queens Museum offers free tours, in English and Spanish, on Sundays.

an artistic space for visitors to experience his creative vision. Probably best remembered for his work with the Herman Miller company in 1947, when he created the iconic Noguchi table, Noguchi also designed the *Red Cube* outside the Marine Midland Building in Lower Manhattan.

Nearby, on Vernon Boulevard, Socrates Sculpture Park was created in 1986, when Abstract Expressionist sculptor Mark di Suvero converted an old landfill into an outdoor studio. Several artists have used the space to exhibit their work. The park is open from 9am until sunset daily, and tours take place at 2pm, Wedneday through Sunday.

19

Museum of the Moving Image and Kaufman Astoria Studio

⌂36-01 35th Av at 36th St, Astoria 🚇36 St (N, W), Steinway St (R) ⏲10:30am–5pm Wed–Thu, 10:30am–8pm Fri, 10:30am–6pm Sat & Sun 🌐movingimage.us

In New York's filmmaking heyday, Rudolph Valentino, W. C. Fields, the Marx Brothers, and Gloria Swanson all made movies in the Astoria Studio,

which was opened in 1920 by Paramount Pictures. When the movies went west, the army made training films here from 1941 to 1971.

In 1977, the Astoria Motion Picture and Television Foundation was created to preserve the studios. *The Wiz*, a musical starring Michael Jackson and Diana Ross, was made here, helping to pay for restoration. Today, the studios house the largest moviemaking facilities on the East Coast.

One of the studio buildings houses the Museum of the Moving Image, with displays of memorabilia, from Ben Hur's chariot to *Star Trek* costumes. Its main gallery draws from the permanent collection of over 130,000 movie artifacts. State-of-the-art amenities include a 254-seat theater, a video-screening amphitheater, and an educational screening room, with screenings taking place on Friday through Sunday. Tours take place at 2pm on Satuday and Sunday.

---

20 ⊗ ▭

MoMA PS1, Queens

⌂22-25 Jackson Av at 46th Av, Long Island City 🚇23 St-Court Sq (E, F, M), 45 Rd-Courthouse Sq (7), Court Sq (G), 21 St-Van Alst (G) 🚌B61, Q67 ⏲Noon–6pm Thu–Mon 🌐momaps1.org

In a former elementary school, PS1 was founded in 1971 under a scheme to transform abandoned city buildings into exhibition, performance, and studio spaces. It is affiliated with the Museum of Modern Art *(p202)* and is one of the oldest art organizations in the US devoted solely to contemporary art. Exhibitions are hosted alongside permanent works and many interactive pieces. On Saturdays in summer, the outdoor courtyard hosts a daytime dance party, with live performers.

EAT

Empanadas Café
Tasty Latin American meat pies (try the beef and cheese).

⌂56-27 Van Doren St, Corona 🌐empanadas cafe.com

$⑤⑤

Jackson Diner
The best-known Indian restaurant in Jackson Heights, with outstanding curries.

⌂37-47 74th St, Jackson Heights 🌐jacksondiner.com

$⑤⑤

Adda
A contemporary "Indian canteen" offering authentic tandoor grill dishes, curries, and biryanis.

⌂1-31 Thomson Av, Long Island 🕒Sun 🌐addanyc.com

$⑤⑤

SriPraPhai
Truly authentic Thai food, light years ahead of anything over the river in Manhattan. Cash only.

⌂64-13 39th Av, Woodside 🌐sripra phai.com

$⑤⑤

Taverna Kyclades
Friendly and popular Greek taverna specializing in seafood.

⌂33-07 Ditmars Blvd, Astoria 🌐taverna kyclades.com

$⑤⑤

21 🖼️🎭🍴🛍️

Historic Richmond Town

📍 **441 Clarke Av** 🚌 **S74 from ferry** 🕐 **1–5pm Wed–Sun** 🌐 **historicrichmondtown.org**

There are 29 buildings here, around 14 of which are open to the public, in New York's only restored village and living history museum. The village was first named Cocclestown, after the local shellfish, but this was soon corrupted to "Cuckoldstown," much to the annoyance of the residents. By the end of the Revolutionary War, the name Richmondtown had been adopted.

The community was the county seat until Staten Island was made part of the city in 1898, and has been preserved as an example of an early New York settlement.

The Voorlezer's House, built in Dutch style around 1695, is the oldest elementary school in the country. The Stephens General Store, which opened in 1837, doubled as the local post office – it has been well restored, right down to the contents of the shelves. The complex, on 100 acres (40 ha), includes wagon sheds, an 1837 courthouse, houses, several stores, and a tavern. There are also seasonal

↑ Historic Richmond Town recalling Staten Island's past

workshops where traditional crafts are demonstrated. St. Andrew's Church (1708) and its graveyard are just across the Mill Pond stream. The Historical Society Museum, in the County Clerk's and Surrogate's Office, has a delightful toy room.

---

22 🖼️🎭🛍️

Jacques Marchais Museum of Tibetan Art

📍 **338 Lighthouse Av** 🚌 **S74 from ferry** 🕐 **1–5pm Wed–Sun** 🌐 **tibetanmuseum.org**

On a tranquil hilltop is one of the largest privately owned collections of Tibetan art of the 15th to the 20th centuries outside Tibet, completed in 1947 by Mrs Jacques Marchais, a dealer in Asian art. The main building is a replica of a mountain monastery, with an authentic altar in three tiers, crowded with gold, silver, and bronze figures. The second building is a library.

Stone sculptures in the peaceful garden include life-size Buddhas. The Dalai Lama paid his first visit here in 1991 and praised the collection.

23 💬

The Snug Harbor Cultural Center and Botanical Garden

📍 **1000 Richmond Terrace** 🚌 **S40 from ferry to Snug Harbor Gate** 🕐 **Grounds: dawn–dusk daily** 🌐 **snug-harbor.org**

Founded as an affluent retirement community for "aged, decrepit, and worn-out sailors" in 1801, this became a complex of museums, galleries, gardens, and art centers in 1975. With an 83-acre (34-ha) leafy campus, the center has 28 buildings, which range from grand Greek Revival-style halls to sophisticated Italianate structures. The oldest is the beautiful restored Main Hall (Building C), which functions as the Visitor Center. The adjacent Newhouse Center for Contemporary Art showcases the work of local artists, and is open Thursday to Sunday, March through November.

Other buildings here house attractions such as the award-winning Staten Island Children's Museum (open Tuesday to Friday), and the Noble Maritime Collection, which features prints and paintings created by the nautical painter John Noble (1913–83); visitors can view his houseboat studio as well. The Staten Island Museum, which relocated to this complex in 2016, has a major exhibition on Staten Island history, spanning three centuries.

Most of the Snug Harbor grounds belong to the charming Botanical Garden. Attractions here include an exhibit designed to attract butterflies, a charming antique rose garden, other themed areas, and various events throughout the year. The tranquil Chinese Scholar's Garden, with its goldfish ponds, pagoda-roofed halls, and bamboo groves, was built in 1999 by artists from Suzhou, China.

> The tranquil Chinese Scholar's Garden, with its goldfish ponds, pagoda-roofed halls, and bamboo groves, was built in 1999 by artists from Suzhou, China.

EAT

Denino's Pizzeria & Tavern

Staten Island's favorite pizzeria since 1937. It still slings pizzas with a slightly thicker, chewier crust than most brick-oven spots in New York. Try the signature clam pie or garbage pie (sausage, meatballs, pepperoni, mushrooms, onions). Cash only.

🏠 **524 Port Richmond Av**
🌐 **deninossi.com**

$$$

Ralph's Famous Italian Ices

In business since 1928, this spot is handily just across from Denino's Pizzeria – an ideal dessert stop off. The specialty of this small takeout is Italian "water ices," made with fruit or other flavorings.

🏠 **501 Port Richmond Av**
🕐 **Summer: 11am–11.30pm daily**
🌐 **ralphsices.com**

$$$

Alice Austen House

🏠 **2 Hylan Blvd**
🚌 **S 51 from ferry to Hylan Blvd** 🕐 **House: 1–5pm Tue–Fri, 11am–5pm Sat & Sun; Grounds: to dusk daily**
🌐 **aliceausten.org**

This small, charming cottage, built around 1690, has the delightful name of Clear Comfort. It was the home of the prolific photographer Alice Austen, who was born in 1866 and who lived in this house for most of her life. Her photography documented life on Staten Island, across the water in Manhattan, on trips to other parts of the country, and on her travels to Europe. She lost all her money in the stock market crash of 1929, and her poverty forced her into a public poorhouse in 1950, at the age of 84.

One year later, Austen's photographic talent was finally recognized by *Life* magazine. The publication printed an article about her, which earned her enough money to enter a nursing home. When she died in 1952, she left 3,500 photographic negatives dating from 1880 to 1930.

Her house was rescued and restored, and the Friends of Alice Austen House mount exhibitions of her best work.

Little Sri Lanka

🏠 **2 Hylan Blvd** 📞 **(718) 816-4506** 🚌 **S 51 from ferry to Hylan Blvd** 🕐 **Business hours vary**

New York's Little Sri Lanka is centered along Victory Boulevard (at Cebra Avenue), in the Tompkinsville neighborhood of Staten Island, a 20-minute stroll from the ferry terminal. It's one of the largest Sri Lankan communities outside of Sri Lanka itself. Cheap hoppers (a type of pancake) and curries are available at New Asha (322 Victory Boulevard), while Lanka Grocery at 353 Victory Boulevard is piled high with a range of Ceylon teas, chutneys, spices, candy, and other delicacies.

→
Alice Austen House, also called Clear Comfort

NEED TO KNOW

BEFORE
YOU GO

Forward planning is essential to any successful trip. Be prepared for all eventualities by considering the following points before you travel.

AT A GLANCE

CURRENCY
US Dollar (USD)

AVERAGE DAILY SPEND

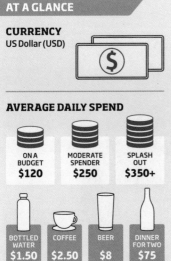

ON A BUDGET	MODERATE SPENDER	SPLASH OUT
$120	$250	$350+

BOTTLED WATER	COFFEE	BEER	DINNER FOR TWO
$1.50	$2.50	$8	$75

CLIMATE

The longest days occur Jun–Aug. Nov–Feb sees the shortest daylight hours.

Temperatures average 84°F (29°C) in summer, and fall below freezing in winter.

The heaviest rainfall is in March and August; showers occur all year round.

ELECTRICITY SUPPLY

The standard US electric current is 110 volts and 60 Hz. Power sockets are type A and B, fitting plugs with two flat pins.

Passports and Visas

Canadian visitors just require a valid passport to enter the US. Citizens of Australia, New Zealand, and the EU do not need a visa, but must apply to enter in advance via the Electronic System for Travel Authorization (**ESTA**) and have a valid passport.

Visitors from all other regions will require a tourist visa and passport to enter, and will be photographed and have their fingerprints checked. Be sure to allow plenty of time for the US border agency's thorough passport and visa checks at the airport.

A return airline ticket is required to enter the country. Entry regulations may change, so always check well in advance of travel with the **US Department of State** for the most up-to-date visa and travel information.
ESTA
W esta.cbp.dhs.gov/esta
US Department of State
W travel.state.gov

Travel Safety Advice

Visitors can get up-to-date travel safety information from the US Department of State, the UK Foreign and Commonwealth Office, and the Australian Department of Foreign Affairs and Trade.
Australia
W smartraveller.gov.au
UK
W gov.uk/foreign-travel-advice

Customs Information

All travelers need to complete a **Customs and Border Protection Agency** form when crossing the US border. Passengers may carry $100 in gifts; 1 liter of alcohol as beer, wine, or liquor (if aged 21 years or older); and one carton of cigarettes, 50 cigars (not Cuban) or two kilograms (4.4 lbs) of smoking tobacco into the US without incurring tax.
Customs and Border Protection Agency
W cbp.gov/travel

Insurance

Emergency medical insurance is highly recommended for international travelers to the US, as costs for medical and dental care can be high. Travel insurance for cancellations, delays, theft, and loss of belongings is recommended. Car rental agencies offer vehicle and liability insurance; check your policy before traveling.

Vaccinations

No inoculations are required for visiting the United States.

Booking Accommodation

With over 130,000 hotel rooms available, New York offers something for everyone. The city's top hotels are among the most expensive in the US, but there are also many budget and mid-priced hotels, family-run B&Bs, and hostels.

Hotels are busiest during the week, when business travelers are in the city, so most of them offer budget weekend packages. Hotel rooms are subject to a total 14.75% tax, plus a $3.50 room fee per night.

Money

Most establishments accept major credit, debit, and prepaid currency cards. Contactless payments are becoming increasingly common, with plans underway to introduce a contactless payment system on the subway and some bus routes by 2020.

Cash is still required on New York buses and by some smaller businesses and street vendors. ATMs are available at nearly every bank and street corner.

Travelers with Specific Needs

New York City law requires that all facilities built after 1987 provide entrances and accessible restroom facilities for the disabled. All city buses now have steps that can be lowered to allow wheelchair access, and most street corners also have curb cuts for wheelchairs.

The **Mayor's Office for People with Disabilities** is the liaison between New York City government and the disability community. It offers a range of support services and provides information on accessibility in the city.

The **Theater Development Fund** offers the superb Theater Access Project, which aims to increase access to theater for those who are hearing- and visually-impaired, as well as for those with other disabilities. The **Lighthouse Guild** offers tips on exploring New York for the visually impaired.

Lighthouse Guild
w lighthouseguild.org
Mayor's Office for People with Disabilities
w nyc.gov/site/mopd/index.page
Theater Development Fund
w tdf.org

Language

New York City is a cosmopolitan city in which you will hear multiple languages spoken. Many tour companies cater for those with limited English by offering foreign language headsets and guided tours in a range of languages.

Closures

Mondays and Tuesdays Some museums close on Monday, Tuesday, or both, though the majority are open daily.
Sundays All banks close and many smaller businesses close for the day.
Federal and State Holidays Museums, attractions, post offices, banks and many businesses close, especially for major holidays. It is best to check with individual venues for specific closures ahead of your visit.

FEDERAL HOLIDAYS 2020	
1 Jan	New Year's Day
20 Jan	Martin Luther King, Jr. Day
17 Feb	President's Day
25 May	Memorial Day
4 Jul	Independence Day
7 Sept	Labor Day
26 Nov	Thanksgiving Day
25 Dec	Christmas Day

GETTING
AROUND

Whether exploring New York City by foot or public transportation, here is all you'll need to know to navigate the city like a pro.

AT A GLANCE

PUBLIC TRANSPORT COSTS
The following tickets are valid on bus and subway services operated by MTA.

ONE-WAY TICKET

$3

1 transfer permitted within 2 hours of first use

PAY-PER-RIDE METROCARD

$2.75

1 transfer permitted within 2 hours of first use

METROCARD 7-DAY PASS

$33

Unlimited travel on bus and subway services

SPEED LIMIT

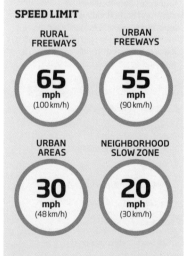

RURAL FREEWAYS	URBAN FREEWAYS
65 mph (100 km/h)	**55** mph (90 km/h)

URBAN AREAS	NEIGHBORHOOD SLOW ZONE
30 mph (48 km/h)	**20** mph (30 km/h)

Arriving by Air

Three major airports serve New York City. The two main international airports in the New York City area are John F. Kennedy International (JFK) and Newark Liberty International (EWR) in New Jersey. Both also handle domestic flights. The third major airport is LaGuardia (LGA), which mostly handles domestic flights. All three airports offer connecting flights to most US cities.

Be sure to allow plenty of extra time at the airport, both on arrival and departure, as there are often long lines for passport control and thorough security checks.

For a list of transportation options, approximate journey times, and travel costs for transport between each of New York City's airports and Midtown Manhattan, see the table opposite.

Train Travel

Amtrak, the US passenger rail service, Long Island Rail Road (**LIRR**), and New Jersey Transit (**NJT**) commuter trains all pull in to Penn Station, situated on Seventh and Eighth avenues and 31st and 34th streets, beneath Madison Square Garden. Amtrak has its own designated area in Penn Station for ticket sales, and separate waiting rooms for coach and high-speed passengers.

Metro-North regional trains use Grand Central Terminal (often referred to as Grand Central Station), located at 42nd Street and Park Avenue in Midtown Manhattan.

Tickets can be bought on the day of travel, or ahead of your trip online or over the phone. Pre-paid tickets can be collected at ticket windows or automated kiosks at the station. If you collect tickets at the window, photo ID will be requested. Ensure you get the cheapest fares by booking in advance.

You can buy tickets for multiple journeys with Amtrak's USA Rail Pass, which allows eight journeys over a 15-day period for $459; children pay half-fare.

The most popular train service from New York is Amtrak's Northeast Corridor

GETTING TO AND FROM THE AIRPORT

Airport	Transport to Midtown	Journey Time	Price
John F. Kennedy	AirTrain JFK + LIRR	1 hr 30 mins	from $13
	NYC Airporter	1 hr 45mins-2 hrs	$19
	SuperShuttle	1-2 hrs	from $22
	Taxi	1 hr-1 hr 45 mins	from $52
Newark Liberty	AirTrain Newark + NJ Transit	40 mins	$13
	Newark Airport Express	45 mins-1 hr	$18
	SuperShuttle	1-2 hrs	from $21
	Taxi	45 mins-1 hr	$70-95
La Guardia	LaGuardia Link + subway	50 mins	$2.75
	NYC Express Bus	1 hr 30 mins	$16
	SuperShuttle	1-2 hrs	from $20
	Taxi	1hr-1 hr 30 mins	$30-$40

route between Boston, New York, Philadelphia, and Washington, DC. Most of the trains on this route have unreserved seating, but Amtrak's high-speed **Acela Express** trains offer an hourly service with reserved first- and business-class seating plus electrical outlets for laptops.

Amtrak also offer a Northeast Corridor sleeper service, which is often preferable to flying as it avoids traveling long distances to and from the airport. Included in the service is a private cabin and restroom, a complimentary meal onboard, and private lounge access.

Acela Express
W amtrak.com/acela-express-train
Amtrak
W amtrak.com
LIRR
W mta.info/lirr
Metro-North
W mta.info/mnr
NJT
W njtransit.com

Long-Distance Bus Travel

Intercity buses are a great and economical way to get to New York City, or to travel farther afield around the state with the city as your starting point.

Coach and intercity buses from all over the US, as well as New York City commuter lines, arrive at the **Port Authority Bus Terminal** (PABT), which is the central hub for interstate buses in New York City.

Taxis can be found on the Eighth Avenue side of the terminal; the A, C and E subway stops are located on the lower floors in the terminal; and a one-block-long tunnel leads to Times Square station along with other subway connections.

Buses from the Port Authority connect with all three airports, and the terminal also serves many busy commuter bus lines to New Jersey. With over 6,000 buses arriving and departing daily, the atmosphere can be hectic at rush hour.

Greyhound offer low-cost routes between New York and Philadelphia (2 hours), Washington, DC (4 hours), Boston (4.5 hours), Toronto (11.5 hours), and Montreal (8.5 hours), among many other cities. Discount long-distance bus services, such as **Megabus** and **Bolt Bus**, depart and arrive at 34th Street between 11th and 12th avenues.

Bolt Bus
W boltbus.com
Greyhound
W greyhound.com
Megabus
W megabus.com
Port Authority Bus Terminal
W panynj.gov/bus-terminals/port-authority-bus-terminal.html

Public Transportation

New York City's extensive bus and subway transportation system is operated by the Metropolitan Transportation Authority (**MTA**). Timetables, ticket information, transport maps, and a useful route planner can be found on the MTA website. Subway maps are also available for free at any station fare booth.

MTA
ⓦ mta.info

Planning Your Journey

Buses and subways are busiest during the rush hours: 7–9:30am and 4:30–6pm, Monday to Friday. Throughout these periods, it may be much faster and easier to face the crowds on foot than attempt any journey by bus, taxi, or subway. At other times of day and during certain holiday periods, the traffic is often much lighter, and you should reach your destination more quickly. Note that public transportation runs a reduced service during major holidays.

Tickets

MetroCards and SingleRide tickets are valid on buses and the subway. Cards may be purchased for any number of individual rides. One free transfer ride is allowed between the subway and bus (and vice versa), or between two different bus lines. This must be used within 2 hours of first use.

A single trip costs $3 with a SingleRide paper ticket and a SingleRide MetroCard, or $2.75 with a Pay-Per-Ride MetroCard, no matter how far you travel. If you are making several trips, buy a weekly unlimited ticket for $33 and the cost per journey will work out to be less.

MetroCards and tickets are sold at newsstands, drugstores, and all subway stations. They can be purchased for amounts from $5.50 to $80. Seven-day ($33) or 30-day ($127) unlimited-ride options are also available.

The MTA charges a $1 "new card fee" for the purchase of a new MetroCard. By refilling and reusing your current MetroCard, you will avoid this additional fee.

Subway

The subway is the fastest way to get around, with over 470 stations across all five boroughs, and routes that fan out to the farthest reaches of New York City. The subway runs 24 hours a day, though late-night service patterns change.

Generally, the 1, 2, 3, 4, 5, 6, A, B, C, D, Q trains cover the main parts of the city, running north–south, originating in Upper Manhattan or the Bronx and, with the exception of the 1 and 6, all continue east to Brooklyn. The L train runs east–west across Manhattan along 14th Street to Brooklyn. The 7 train runs along 42nd Street

to Queens. The E, F, M, N, R, and W originate in Queens and make a few stops in the city before continuing into Brooklyn (except for the E which terminates in Lower Manhattan).

Bus

Most buses run every 3–5 minutes during the morning and evening rush hours, and every 7–15 minutes from noon to 4:30pm and from 7 to 10pm. Bad traffic or adverse weather conditions can cause delays. A reduced service operates on weekends and holidays.

Certain buses on the busiest crosstown routes require you to enter the MetroCard into the kiosks at the bus stop to get a receipt for your journey. Inspectors do check occasionally, and riders without a receipt are fined.

Many lines run 24 hours, but be sure to check the schedule posted at your stop. After 10pm, many buses run every 20 minutes or so. From midnight to 6am, expect to wait 30–60 minutes for a bus.

Bus Tours

One of the most popular ways to see the sights is aboard a hop-on-hop-off bus tour. Get off wherever you like, stay as long as you want, and catch another bus when you are ready.

Gray Line is the best-known company offering these tours aboard double-decker buses. Routes include a Downtown loop, Uptown loop, Brooklyn loop, as well as night and holiday lights tours (not hop-on-hop-off). Buy a 48- or 72-hour pass, and you can see a great deal of New York this way.

Gray Line
ⓦ grayline.com

Taxis

Manhattan's iconic yellow taxis can be hailed anywhere and can be found waiting outside most hotels and stations. The light atop the cab goes on when it is available. All cabs accept cash and should also accept credit cards. For any taxi complaints, you can call 311.

The green Boro taxis operate in areas of New York not commonly served by yellow cabs – north of West 110th Street and East 96th Street in Manhattan, the Bronx, Queens (excluding the airports), Brooklyn, and Staten Island. They can drop you off anywhere in the city, but cannot pick up passengers in Manhattan below 96th and 110th Streets.

All taxis are metered and can issue printed receipts. The meter starts ticking at $3. The fare increases 50 cents after each additional fifth of a mile or every 60 seconds of waiting time. There is an additional 50-cent charge from 8pm to 6am, and an extra $1 charge 4–8pm on week- days. Tolls are extra and are added to the fare. The base fare for an Uber is $2.55, with an additional $1.75 per mile. Lyft and Gett offer similar rates.

Driving

Busy traffic, lack of parking, and expensive rental cars make driving in New York a frustrating experience. To get around stress-free, opt for public transport outside of rush hour.

Car Rental
Rental car companies are located at airports, major stations, and other locations in the city.

Most companies will only rent cars to drivers 25 years and older in the US (Budget allows over 21s, but at a much higher rate). A valid driving license and clean record are essential. All agencies require a major credit card. Damage and liability insurance is recommended just in case something unexpected should happen. It is advisable always to return the car with a full tank of gas; otherwise you will be required to pay the inflated fuel prices charged by the rental agencies.

Be sure to check for any pre-existing damage to the car and note this on your contract before you leave the rental lot.

Parking
If you do decide to drive in the city, check with your hotel to see if they offer parking; this will usually add at least $25 per night to your bill.

Otherwise, there are parking meters across the city, where you can park for up to 12 hours, starting at $3.50 per hour (meters do not have to be paid on Sundays), and you will have to return every 1 or 2 hours to top up. If not, a parking fine will set you back $65.

New York also has numerous parking lots, but these can be expensive, starting from an average of $50 per day.

Rules of the Road
All drivers are legally required to carry a valid driver's license and must be able to produce registration and insurance documents. Most foreign licenses are valid, but if your license is not in English, or does not have a photo ID, apply for an International Driving Permit (IDP)

Traffic drives on the right-hand side of the road, and the speed limit is usually 30 mph (48 km/h) in Midtown unless otherwise stated.

Seat belts are compulsory in front seats and are suggested in the back. Children under three years old must ride in a child seat in back. It is also compulsory to wear seat belts in cabs at all times.

Most streets are one-way, and there are traffic lights at almost every corner. Unlike the rest of New York State, you can never turn right on a red light unless there is a sign indicating otherwise. If a school bus stops to let passengers off, all traffic from both sides must stop and wait for the bus to drive off.

A limit of 0.08 per cent blood alcohol is strictly enforced at all times. For drivers under the age of 21 there is a zero tolerance policy for drink-driving. Driving while intoxicated (DWI) is a punishable offense that incurs heavy fines or even a jail sentence. It is advisable to avoid drinking altogether if you do plan to drive.

In the event of an accident or breakdown, drivers of rental cars should contact their car rental company first. Members of the American Automobile Association (**AAA**) can have their vehicle towed to the nearest service station to be fixed. For simple problems like a flat tire or a dead battery, the AAA will fix it or and install a new battery on site for a fee.
AAA
🆆 aaa.com

Walking and Biking

New York City is always busy, so streets have pedestrian walk lights at most intersections; some also have audio cues. Exploring by foot is a great way to experience the city, but central attractions are quite spread out, so pack a pair of comfortable shoes if you plan to walk.

It takes courage to cycle alongside busy traffic in Midtown. Bike trails along the East River and Central Park are more pleasant.

Bike Rent NYC offer daily bike rentals and guided tours in the city. One-day, three-day, or monthly subscriptions are available.

Citibike has 12,000 bicycles at 750 stations all over the city; reserve at a particular address through the app *(p313)* or use a credit card at the pick-up location.

There is no law requiring cyclists to wear a helmet, but it is highly recommended.
Bike Rent NYC
🆆 bikerent.nyc
Citibike
🆆 citibikenyc.com

Boats and Ferries

New York Waterway ferries connect New Jersey and Manhattan. You can buy tickets online or at the ferry terminals. **NYC Ferry** connects Manhattan, Brooklyn, Queens and the Bronx.

The 24-hour Staten Island Ferry is free and offers spectacular views of Lower Manhattan and the Statue of Liberty.
New York Waterway
🆆 nywaterway.com
NYC Ferry
🆆 ferry.nyc

PRACTICAL
INFORMATION

A little local know-how goes a long way in New York City. Here you will find all the essential advice and information you will need during your stay.

AT A GLANCE

EMERGENCY NUMBER

GENERAL EMERGENCY

911

TIME ZONE
EST/EDT
Eastern Daylight Time (EDT) runs mid-Mar–early Nov 2020
PST +3
GMT -5
AEDT +14

TAP WATER
Unless otherwise stated, tap water is safe to drink.

TIPPING

Waiter	15–20%
Bartender	$1 per drink
Hotel Porter	$2 per bag
Housekeeping	10% of room bill
Cab Driver	10–15%

Personal Security

New York is a large, cosmopolitan city. Petty crime does exist, so always be alert to your surroundings, and be wary of pickpockets on public transportation and in crowded areas.

If you have anything stolen, report the crime within 24 hours to the nearest police station and take ID with you. Get a copy of the crime report in order to claim on your insurance. Contact your embassy if you have your passport stolen, or in the event of a serious crime or accident.

Health

It is possible to visit a doctor or dentist in New York without being registered, but you will be asked to pay in advance. Keep receipts to make a claim on your insurance later.

There are plenty of walk-in medical clinics and emergency rooms, as well as 24-hour pharmacies. **Mount Sinai** offers convenient walk-in or by-appointment services for adults and children at locations around the city, from the West Village to Midtown. Another option is **NYC Health + Hospitals**.

Hospital emergency treatment is available 24 hours a day. If you are able, call the number on your insurance policy first, and check which hospitals your insurance company deals with. For immediate treatment in an emergency, call an ambulance.

Payment of hospital and other medical expenses is the patient's responsibility. As such it is important to arrange comprehensive medical insurance before traveling (p307).
Mount Sinai
W mountsinai.org
NYC Health + Hospitals
W nychealthandhospitals.org

Smoking, Alcohol, and Drugs

The legal minimum age for drinking alcohol in the USA is 21, and you will need photo ID as proof of age in order to purchase alcohol and be allowed into bars. It is illegal to drink alcohol in public parks or to carry an open container of alcohol in your car, and penalties for driving under the influence of alcohol are severe (p311).

Smoking is prohibited in all public buildings, bars, restaurants, and stores. Cigarettes can be purchased by those over 18 years old; proof of age will be required.

Possession of narcotics is prohibited and could result in a prison sentence.

ID

It is not compulsory to carry ID at all times in New York City. If you are asked by police to show your ID, a photocopy of your passport photo page (and visa if applicable) should suffice. You may be asked to present the original document within 12 or 24 hours.

Local Customs

There is a knack to navigating New York City's busy streets. Always walk on the right side of the sidewalk and stairwells. If you want to take a picture or consult a map while walking, don't just stop, move to the side first. Avoid walking three or four abreast. The locals will be quick to tell you if you are doing something wrong.

Visiting Churches, Cathedrals, and Synagogues

Dress respectfully: cover your torso and upper arms. Ensure shorts and skirts cover your knees.

Cell Phones and Wi-Fi

Free Wi-Fi hotspots are widely available throughout the city, including in some MetroRail stations. Cafés and restaurants will usually let you use their Wi-Fi if you make a purchase.

Cell phone service in New York City is generally excellent. If you are coming from overseas and want to guarantee that your cell phone will work, make sure you have a quad-band phone.

In order to use your phone abroad you may need to activate the "roaming" facility, which is notoriously expensive. If you are planning on using your phone for Wi-Fi only, ensure that data roaming is turned off. Other options include buying a prepaid cell phone in the US or a SIM chip for a US carrier.

Post

Stamps can be bought from post offices, drugstores, and newsstands. On-street mailboxes are usually blue, or red, white, and blue. Mail is not collected on Sundays.

The city's post offices are generally open from 9pm to 5pm Monday to Friday, until 9pm on Saturdays, and 7pm on Sundays.

Taxes and Tipping

A sales tax of around 9 per cent is added to most items, including meals. Waiters generally receive 15–20 per cent of the bill, including tax. A quick way to calculate restaurant tips is simply to double the tax, which adds up to about 18%.

Discount Cards

New York City offers a number of visitor passes and discount cards for exhibitions, events, museum entry, and even transportation. These are available online and from participating tourist offices. The cards are not free, so consider carefully how many of the offers you are likely to take advantage of before purchasing.

City Pass
W citypass.com
New York Explorer Pass
W smartdestinations.com
The New York Pass
W newyorkpass.com

WEBSITES AND APPS

Citibike
Find bike docking stations near you and receive real-time updates on bike and dock availability using this app.

NYC & Co.
Check out New York City's official tourist information website at nycgo.com.

NYC Ferry
This app provides route maps, schedules, and transport links for New York's ferry services. The app also allows users to buy paperless tickets and present their phone as proof of purchase.

INDEX

Page numbers in bold refer to main entries

ACKNOWLEDGMENTS

DK Travel would like to thank the following people whose help and assistance contributed to the preparation of this book

Cartographic Data ERA-Maptec Ltd (Dublin) adapted with permission from original survey and mapping by Shobunsha (Japan)

PICTURE CREDITS

The publisher would like to thank the following for their kind permission to reproduce their photographs:

Key: a-above; b-below/bottom; c-centre; f-far; l-left; r-right; t-top

123RF.com: jovannig 19cb, 160–1.

4Corners: Arcangelo Piai 21t, 198–9; Maurizio Rellini 21bl, 214–5.

500px: Nina Sauer 22cb, 250–1; Tim Snell 144–5.

Alamy Stock Photo: Tomas Abad 204–5br; age fotostock / Jose Peral 210bl, / Paul Hakimata 297br; Arcaid Images / Exterior view of Whitney Museum of American Art; New York City by Renzo Piano Building Workshop architects 39cl; Batchelder 176cra; Susan Candelario 20cb, 184–5cl; Paul Chauncey 297cr; Robert K. Chin – Storefronts 43cl ; Citizen of the Planet / Peter Bennett 40cra; Dinodia Photos 70bl; Randy Duchaine 28crb, 43br, 226tc, 226cl, 276br, 280tc, 302tl, / Cooper Hewitt Smithsonian Design Museum / Mathias Bengtsson Studio, *Slice Chair* (1999), 224bl, / Francisco Goya *The Black Duchess* 46cra; E.J.Westmacott 73bc; Entertainment Pictures 61bl; Everett Collection Inc / Schomburg Center for Research in Black Culture / Aaron Douglas © Heirs of Aaron Douglas / DACS, London / VAGA, NY 2018 *From Slavery Through Reconstruction* (1934) 256–7bl; Alexander Farmer 40b; Stephen Foster 42–3b; Chuck Franklin 276–7; Elly Godfroy 242bl; Tim Graham 73clb; Grangér Historical Picture Archive 57bc, 57br, 69clb, 129bl, 273bc; Richard Green 222t, 283t; Jeff Greenberg 38tl; David Grossman 279bl; Hemis / Bertrand Rieger 8–9b, / Philippe Renault 242cb, / Whitney Museum of American Art / © Estate of Tom Wesselmann / DACS, London / VAGA, NY 2018 *Still Life Number 36* (1964) 129clb, / Sylvain Sonnet 177; Paul Hennessy 171bc; Ovidiu Hrubaru 294bl; John Kellerman 164–5t; Raimund Koch-View 118bl; Douglas Lander 262bc; Luis Leamus 262–3t; Robert Lehmann 264tl; Richard Levine 100br, 210tc, 300bl; Keith Levit 183bl; Felix Lipov 48–9b, 255br, 290cl; Terese Loeb Kreuzer 230bl, 258tl; Look Die Bildagentur der Fotografen GmbH / Daniel Schoenen 278t; mauritius images GmbH 168tl; Patti McConville 77crb, 147br, 154crb, 193br, 246bl, 296–7b; Ellen McKnight 33cla, 243c; Moviestore collection Ltd 61crb; Alfonso Vicente / MoMA, Museum of Modern Art, New York City / Pablo Picasso © Succession Picasso / DACS, London 2018 *Les Demoiselles d'Avignon, The Young Ladies of Avignon* (1907) 202crb; National Geographic Creative / Gerd Ludwig 69crb; NiKreative 232tr; NPS Photo 69bc; Mark O'Flaherty / © Maxfield Parrish Family, LLC / DACS, London / VAGA, NY 2018 / *The Old King Cole mural* 52–3t; Sean Pavone 53cla; The Photo Works 194–5tc; Stefano Politi Markovina 146–7t; Realy Easy Star / Giuseppe Masci 228–9; Sergi Reboredo 294clb; Frances M. Roberts 298bc; Ed Rooney 79t, 113cr, 176clb; RosalreneBetancourt 13 33br; RosalreneBetancourt 14 225tr; Francois Roux 42tl, 280–1b, 293br; Philip Scalia 143tc, 282br, 298tl; Science History Images 56br; Alex Segre 247bl; Lee Snider 254br; Tetra Images 74–5; P Tomlins 202–3t; travelstock44.de / Juergen Held 212b; Elizabeth Wake 31br; Anthony Wallbank 13br; WENN 54clb; Edd Westmacott / Guggenheim Museum / Frank Lloyd Wright © ARS, NY and DACS, London 2018 *The Spiral Rotunda* (1942) 218–9t; Colin D. Young 288cl.

AWL Images: Jordan Banks 17bl, 114–5; Alan Copson 6–7; Michele Falzone 22tl, 98–9, 234–5; Franck Guiziou 289tc.

Bridgeman Images: Museum of Modern Art, New York / Henri J.F. Rousseau, *The Dream* (1910) oil on canvas 205tc.

Bua Bar: Rich Wade 18bl, 138–9.

Death & Co.: Eric Medsker 53crb.

Dorling Kindersley: Edvard Huember 233bl; Michael Moran 88bl, 267crb.

Dreamstime.com: Adeliepenguin 134–5t; Agaliza 244–5t; Mira Agron 182bl; Aiisha / Per Krohg © DACS, London 2018 *United Nations Security Council hall mural* 191bl; Alexpro9500 12–3b; Allard1 275tl; Andersastphoto 75cra; Leonid Andronov 36tr; Paul Bielicky 164br; Bigapplestock 158bl, 182tr; Cpenler 87br; Demerzel21 78tc, 87tc, 101br, 130tl, 258cb, 259tc; Ganeshkumar Durai 54cl; Esusek 26cl; F11photo 255tr; Alexandre Fagundes De Fagundes 169crb; Frwooar 211t; Giovanni Gagliardi 36tl; Leo Bruce Hempell 284cl; Christian Horz 137b; Wangkun Jia 259cla; Kmiragaya 84–5t, 220–1t; Lavendertime 17t, 102–3; Leungphoto-graphy 44tr; Littleny 169tl, 294cr; Steve Lovegrove 192tr; Meinzahn 180–1t, 190tr; Palinchak / Fernand Leger © ADAGP, Paris and DACS, London 2018 *United Nations General Assembly Hall murals* 191t; Sean Pavone 57cla, 81br, 208–9tl, 239crb, 242–3t, 292tr; David Pereiras Villagrá 101t; Louise Rivard 45cl; Eq Roy 247t; Gergely Szucs 23bl, 286l; Simon Thomas 80tl; Tupungato 221bl; *Fearless Girl* by Kristen Visbal/ Statue Commissioned By SSGA / Michaelfitzsimmons 84bc; Gaspard Walter 46–7t; Jannis Werner 197cra; Witgorski 47crb; Yang Zhang 266bl; Zhukovsky 30tl.

Eataly: 155; Virginia Rollison 154clb; Evan Sung 154bl.

Getty Images: AFP / Kena Betancur 55cl, / Torsten Blackwood 24bl, / Timothy A Clary 40–1t, / Don Emmert 40tl, / Oliver Lang 219cla; Archive Photos 60t; Jon Arnold 34b, 221cb; Bettmann 254clb; Bruce

Bi 188–9; Bloomberg 26cr, 31t, 54cra, 59bl; Andrew Burton 31cl; Buyenlarge 49cla; CBS Photo Archive 51br; Julie Dermansky 59tr; James Devaney 297tr; Dia Dipasupil 54crb; Keith Draycott 28clb; Alija 166bl, 239cla; Elsa 44b; EyeEm / Ricardo Ramirez 89br; Fine Art 57tl; FPG 57tr; Victor Fraile Rodriguez 39t; Noam Galai 13t, 50–1t; Robert Giroux 58–9t; Steven Greaves 46bc; Heritage Images 49crb, / Brooklyn Museum 276bl; Gary Hershorn 55br; John Kobal Foundation 165tr; Stacy Kay 303br; Keystone-France 69tr; Library of Congress 95tr; Lonely Planet 47cl; Brad Mangin 299b; Maremagnum 34–5t, 212bl; Gonzalo Marroquin 51cla; MCNY / Gottscho-Schleisner 77cla; Mondadori Portfolio 204clb; John Moore 95ca; Hal Morey 188cl; Francis G. Mayer / Brooklyn Museum 276cl; National Archives 165crb; New York Daily News / James Keivom 59cra; New York Daily News Archive 58crb, 58bc, 167bl, 254cb, 255bc; The New York Historical Society 56tc, 167clb; Johnny Nunez 50b; Pacific Press 54cr; Andria Patino 241bl; Sean Pavone 46tl; Bob Peterson 58cr; Steve Kelley aka mudpig 273crb; Photolibrary / Toshi Sasaki 119t; Kyle Reid 23t, 268–9cl; Jason Carter Rinaldi 167br; Douglas Sacha 96cl; Mark Sagliocco 97; Steve Schapiro 60br; Merten Snijders 24clb; Sunset Boulevard 60crb, 60bl; Claire Takacs 26br; Mario Tama 43tr, 96cb; Tetra Images 68; Tony Shi Photography 156bl, 304–5b; Universal History Archive 70ca, 273clb; Jack Vartoogian 12t; Roger Viollet 254bl; Slaven Vlasic 54cla, 55tr; The Washington Post 13cr; Westend61 188cra; Barry Winiker 206cl.

Governors Island: Kreg Holt 77cra.

iStockphoto.com: 400tmax 73cra, 120tr; ablokhin 24tc; AlbertPego 289bl; AlexPro9500 218clb; Alija 166bl, 239cla; andykazie 55tl; andyparker72 221br; BirgerNiss 75tl; Boogich 26t, 166–7t, 239cra; Matt Burchell 10clb; c3nsored 28cr; chang 170cr; deberarr 132–3; dell640 238–9b; diegograndi 134cl; Eloi_Omella 192bl, 240tr; espiegle 11t; ferrantraite 38–9b, 41clb; Frogman1484 59br; GCShutter 10–1b; iShootPhotosLLC 48–9t; JayLazarin 157tl; jejim 206cr; johnandersonphoto 32–3t; Juntaski 37t; kasto80 274–5b; littleny 19tl, 150–1; lucagavagna 35cla, 202bl; Lya_Cattel 45br; MaximFesenko 8cla; mbbirdy 62–3b; MBPROJEKT_ Maciej_Bledowski 288cb; Meinzahn 291; mizoula 131bl, 231bl, 265bl; naphtalina 28bl; NicolasMcComber 112cl, 122cl, 272–3t; nuiiko 244br; OlegAlbinsky 227bl; Andrei Orlov 28t; peeterv 4bc, 111b; pidjoe 24crb; PJPhoto69 35bl; robertcicchetti 178cb; RolfSt 285br; S. Greg Panosian 71tr; sangaku 76–7b; santypan 52–3b; SeanPavonePhoto 86t; SergeYatunin 255crb; Snowshill 12bl; tatarac 260–1; tomeng 176br; Torresigner 32–3b; visualspace 72–3t, 131t, 239bc; wdstock 18t, 94–5b, 123br, 124–5, 142bl, 148bl, 149tl, 170tc, 249tl; xavierarnau 20tl, 172–3.

La Bernardin: Daniel Krieger 30br.

The Metropolitan Museum of Art: Water Lilies by Claude Monet (French, Paris 1840–1926 Giverny), 1916–19, Gift of Louise Reinhardt Smith, 1983 39br; Marble statue of an old woman

(A.D. 14–68), Early Imperial, Julio-Claudian, Rogers Fund, 1909 222br; The Last Communion of Saint Jerome (early 1490s) by Botticelli (Alessandro di Mariano Filipepi) (Italian, Florence 1444/45–1510 Florence), Bequest of Benjamin Altman, 1913 223tr; Washington Crossing the Delaware (1851) by Emanuel Leutze (American, Schwäbisch Gmünd 1816–1868 Washington, D.C.) Gift of John Stewart Kennedy, 1897 223bl.

Museum of Chinese in America: 108–9b, 109tl.

Museum at Eldridge Street: 96bl, 96br.

New Museum: Dean Kaufman 106–7; Benoit Pailley 106tc; Scott Rudd 106bl.

New York Botanical Garden: Robert Benson 295.

New York Public Library: 178–9b, 179cra.

Picfair.com: Dan Martland 196bl; Tetra Images 82–3.

The Public Theater / Tammy Shell: Photo of free Shakespeare in the Park 10ca.

Courtesy of Queens Museum: David Sundberg, Esto 301tl.

Rex by Shutterstock: Kobal / Warner Bros TV / Bright / Kauffman / Crane Pro / 61cb.

Robert Harding Picture Library: Wendy Connett 11cr; Richard Cummins 159cr, 206crb; Apocalypse of the Twin Towers by Joe Kincannon, St. John the Divine Cathedral, New York / Godong 254cl; KFS 16cb, 90–1; Tetra Images 16cl, 64–5.

Schomburg Center / NYPL: 257tr, 257cl, 257c.

SPiN: 44cla.

studio ai architects: Ed Caruso 135br.

SuperStock: 3LH 57cr; age fotostock / Jeff Greenberg 11br, / Spencer Grant 290bc, / Richard Levine 44–5t, 55clb, Riccardo Sala / MoMA, Museum of Modern Art, New York / Henri Matisse © Succession H. Matisse / DACS 2018 Dance I (1909) 202–3bl; Album 58tl; Peter Barritt / Solomon R. Guggenheim Museum / Pablo Picasso © Succession Picasso / DACS, London 2018 Woman Ironing (1904) 218bc; Hemis / Patrice Hauser 41c; imageBROKER / Daniel Schoenen 8clb; Stock Connection 55cr, 242cl; Underwood Photo Archives 77tc; World History Archive 56bc.

Tenement Museum: 95tl, 95cla.

Whitney Museum of American Art: © Jasper Johns / DACS, London / VAGA, NY 2018, Three Flags, 1958. Encaustic on canvas, 30 5/8 × 45 1/2 × 4 5/8in. (77.8 × 115.6 × 11.7 cm). purchase, with funds from the Gilman Foundation, Inc., The Lauder Foundation, A. Alfred Taubman, Laura-Lee Whittier Woods, Howard Lipman, and Ed Downe in honor of the Museum's 50th Anniversary 80.32 129cra; George Bellows *Dempsey and Firpo* (1924), Oil on canvas, 51 1/8 × 63 1/4in. (129.9 × 160.7 cm); purchase, with, funds from Gertrude Vanderbilt Whitney 31.95 129crb; Ben Gancsos / Whitney Museum of American Art, 99 Gansevoort Street, New York, N.Y. 10014 by Renzo Piano Building Workshop, architects. Opened May 1, 2015 128–9.

Front flap: Alamy Stock Photo: Hemis cla; **AWL Images:** Jordan Banks cra; Michele Falzone t; **Getty Images:** Alexander Spatari br; **Robert Harding Picture Library:** Wendy Connett cb; **iStockphoto.com:** Matt Burchell bl.

Sheet map cover: iStockphoto.com: dell640.

Cover images:
Front and spine: **iStockphoto.com:** dell640.
Back: **iStockphoto.com:** dell640 b; espiegle tr; GCShutter cl; MaximFesenko c.

For further information see: www.dkimages.com

MIX
Paper from responsible sources
FSC
www.fsc.org   FSC™ C018179

Penguin Random House

Main Contributers
Stephen Keeling, Eleanor Berman
Senior Editor Alison McGill
Senior Designer Laura O'Brien
Project Editor Lucy Richards
Project Art Editors Bess Daly, Tania Gomes, Ben Hinks, Stuti Tiwari Bhatia, Bharti Karakoti, Priyanka Thakur, Vinita Venugopal
Factchecker Todd Obolsky
Editors Danielle Watt, Penny Phenix
Proofreader Kathryn Glendenning
Indexer Helen Peters
Senior Picture Researcher Ellen Root
Picture Research Harriet Whitaker
Illustrators Richard Draper, Robbie Polley, Hamish Simpson
Cartographic Editor James Macdonald
Cartography Ashutosh Ranjan Bharti, Uma Bhattacharya, Zafar ul Islam Khan, Chez Picthall, Kunal Singh
Jacket Designers Maxine Pedliham, Bess Daly
Jacket Picture Research Susie Peachey
Senior DTP Designer Jason Little
DTP Coordinator George Nimmo
Senior Producer Stephanie McConnell
Managing Editor Rachel Fox
Art Director Maxine Pedliham
Publishing Director Georgina Dee
This edition updated by Hansa Babra, Stephen Keeling, Sumita Khatwani, Lucy Sara-Kelly, Christine Stroyan, Lucy Richards, Priyanka Thakur

First edition 1993

Published in the United States by DK Publishing, 1450 Broadway, Suite 801, New York, NY 10018

Published in Great Britain by Dorling Kindersley Limited, 80 Strand, London, WC2R 0RL

Copyright 1993, 2019 © Dorling Kindersley Limited, London

A Penguin Random House Company

19 20 21 10 9 8 7 6 5 4 3 2 1

A CIP catalog record for this book is available from the British Library.

A catalog record for this book is available from the Library of Congress.

ISSN: 1542-1554
ISBN: 978-0-2413-6875-6

Printed and bound in China

www.dk.com